JUN – 7 2010

1-19(30)

The EVERYTHING®
MUSIC COMPOSITION
BOOK

Dear Reader,

The subject of composition is particularly near and dear to me. Indeed, I have spent much of my creative life composing extensive works for various ensembles. The genres I have written for include contemporary classical, blues, jazz, and modern rock. I began writing music when I was a child and my earliest compositions were written for my primary instrument, percussion. They began as simple snare drum pieces, then single-line xylophone etudes.

Later, through my obsession with the jazz pianist Bill Evans, I was exposed to the French composers Debussy and Ravel. Then as an undergraduate music student, I learned about a variety of composers from all eras. I was especially moved by the power and sophistication of Gustav Mahler's symphonies. It is my hope that this book encourages you to listen with an open mind to music that is "new" or "foreign." This is how we grow and learn as students of composition! Ultimately, I hope this book motivates you to embrace the spirit of music, a force that exists in all of us. Unfortunately, this book cannot address everything you need to know about composition. However, it will give you an insider's look at both the mechanics and the inspiration behind this beautiful art form.

With warmest regards,

Eric Alan

Welcome to the EVERYTHING Series!

These handy, accessible books give you all you need to tackle a difficult project, gain a new hobby, comprehend a fascinating topic, prepare for an exam, or even brush up on something you learned back in school but have since forgotten.

You can choose to read an *Everything*® book from cover to cover or just pick out the information you want from our four useful boxes: e-questions, e-facts, e-alerts, and e-ssentials. We give you everything you need to know on the subject, but throw in a lot of fun stuff along the way, too.

We now have more than 400 *Everything*® books in print, spanning such wide-ranging categories as weddings, pregnancy, cooking, music instruction, foreign language, crafts, pets, New Age, and so much more. When you're done reading them all, you can finally say you know *Everything*®!

E-QUESTION
Answers to
common questions

FACTS
Important snippets
of information

ALERTS!
Urgent
warnings

ESSENTIALS
Quick
handy tips

PUBLISHER Karen Cooper

DIRECTOR OF ACQUISITIONS AND INNOVATION Paula Munier

MANAGING EDITOR, EVERYTHING SERIES Lisa Laing

COPY CHIEF Casey Ebert

ACQUISITIONS EDITOR Lisa Laing

SENIOR DEVELOPMENT EDITOR Brett Palana-Shanahan

EDITORIAL ASSISTANT Hillary Thompson

Visit the entire Everything® series at *www.everything.com*

THE
EVERYTHING®
MUSIC
COMPOSITION
BOOK

A step-by-step guide to writing music

Eric Starr

Aadamsmedia
Avon, Massachusetts

Dedicated to my children Iain Wesley and Delia Leigh:
my inspiration—my music.

An Everything® Series Book.
Everything® and everything.com® are registered trademarks of F+W Media, Inc.

Published by Adams Media, a division of F+W Media, Inc.
57 Littlefield Street, Avon, MA 02322 U.S.A.
www.adamsmedia.com

ISBN 10: 1-60550-093-3
ISBN 13: 978-1-60550-093-5

Printed in the United States of America.

J   I   H   G   F   E   D   C   B   A

Library of Congress Cataloging-in-Publication Data
is available from the publisher.

The following figures (and associated musical excerpts) are used with the permission of the author: Figures 9-5 and 10-4, borrowed from *The Windsong of Crazy Horse*; Figures 9-6, 16-9, and 16-10, borrowed from the *Stones of Carnac*; Figure 15-17, *Percy's Bounce*; Figure 15-18, *Blues for Franny*; Figure 18-6, borrowed from *The Philosopher's Stone*.
© Eric Starr

This publication is designed to provide accurate and authoritative information with regard to the subject matter covered. It is sold with the understanding that the publisher is not engaged in rendering legal, accounting, or other professional advice. If legal advice or other expert assistance is required, the services of a competent professional person should be sought.

—From a *Declaration of Principles* jointly adopted by a Committee of the American Bar Association and a Committee of Publishers and Associations

Many of the designations used by manufacturers and sellers to distinguish their products are claimed as trademarks. Where those designations appear in this book and Adams Media was aware of a trademark claim, the designations have been printed with initial capital letters.

This book is available at quantity discounts for bulk purchases.
For information, please call 1-800-289-0963.

Contents

Acknowledgments

Thanks to Marc Schonbrun for the "circle of fifths" diagram, guitar chords, and scales information, Jeffrey Starr for the guitar neck diagram, and David Meyers for figured bass and four-part writing examples. Also, thanks to Charles Freeman for his jazz composer and songs lists, Nelson Starr Jr. for his insights on jazz and electric bass, Rafael Ramirez for his clarification on voice, and Alex Freeman and Nelson Starr Sr. for information about the trumpet and other brass instruments.

Very special thanks to Dr. Craig Bove for reviewing and proofreading the content of this book. His scholarship has been integral to both the creation and the development of this book.

Top Ten Things You Will Learn From This Book

1. Music theory, and music's building blocks, including pitch, equal temperament, intervals, time signatures, scales, chords, motives, cadences, melody, harmony, rhythm, counterpoint, and much more.

2. How to tell a musical story through mood, texture, tension and release.

3. How to read standard notation, figured bass, Roman numerals, chord symbols, and guitar tablature.

4. The variety of musical forms as used in classical and popular genres.

5. The origins and evolution of a variety of musical styles from medieval music to the present day.

6. Rock, jazz, Latin, and other popular styles of music from a compositional perspective.

7. Tips on how to write for many instruments in western music including: strings, voice, brass, woodwinds, percussion, drums, piano, the guitar, and the electric bass. Make sure you have a pencil and staff paper on hand (or score writing software) as you work your way through this book.

8. Dozens of essential composers and their legacies.

9. Tips for orchestrating and arranging music for a variety of ensembles: from string quartets to jazz quartets to the symphony orchestra itself.

10. Where to find additional resources to further your education (Appendix B).

Introduction

▶ Welcome to *The Everything® Music Composition Book*! This book is designed to give you practical and realistic information about a subject that is complicated by gray areas, vagaries, and even contradictions. Many of these complexities derive from the sheer enormity of the subject matter. Composition in western history encompasses musical thought from (at least) the archaic period in ancient Greece to the present. That's over 2,500 years!

This book attempts to pare down this rich and detailed history to its essentials. However, the serious student of composition must view this text strictly as a starting point. On the other hand, if you want to compose just to have fun, you should find enough information here to get you up and running.

If you've ever studied composition, you probably know that educators and authors tend to advocate strict "rules." Truth be told, this book *does* fall into this category on occasion. However, great care has been taken to educate and inform you without stifling your creativity and imagination. After all, the goal is to create music that is unique to you.

Compositional rules are helpful since they are modeled after the works of great composers such as J.S. Bach. Therefore, you shouldn't violate these musical "laws" out of ignorance, laziness, or just plain stubbornness. However, rules ultimately do not tell the story of music as an art form. If the rules were never broken, visionaries like Wolfgang Amadeus Mozart, Frédéric Chopin, John Cage, and Billy Strayhorn would not have existed. Instead, the world would be listening to academic exercises. In the end, composition is more about you and your relationship with sound than any "rule."

Before you begin studying this book, keep in mind that this publication views music, like all art, as subjective. As such, aesthetic judgments about what is "superior" and what is "inferior" are not considerations. For example, this book will not compare composers in an attempt to prove that one is "better" than another.

This book also rejects the derogatory term "serious music" and instead suggests that *all* music is serious and worthy of consideration. Along these same lines, music will not be judged by a hierarchy and you will not hear the terms "low art" or "high art" used to describe any composition or musical style.

This book has three main categories:

1. "How to" Instruction
2. Historical Background
3. Resource guide (Appendices)

Further, the instructional aspects of the book are divided into two parts:

1. General information about composition.
2. General information about specific instruments and voice. Bear in mind: this book seeks only to introduce you to select instruments. See Appendix B for additional resources.

You may move through the chapters in any order you choose since information is not necessarily presented in a strict, cumulative fashion. The only exceptions to this are Chapters 4–8, which deal with the basic elements of music.

Lastly, this book assumes that you play an instrument of some kind. If you don't, your first task is to take one up. Every composer should have a primary instrument for the simple reason that composers who are not musicians generally do not make good composers. As a composer, it's important to be involved with the actual mechanics of making music. (As you will learn later in the book, the central instrument in western music is the piano, so it would be a good idea to study this instrument even if you don't plan to write piano music.)

It's hoped that *The Everything® Music Composition Book* gives you the tools you need to begin composing music. In some ways, composing music is a lot like a treasure hunt. It is the search, and the hopeful acquisition, of something rare and exceptional. Your mission begins now; enjoy the journey.

Chapter 1
Before You Begin

In this opening chapter, you will learn about the fundamental steps needed to begin composing. Before you write even one note, you will first want to determine what it is you wish to compose. Next, you will need to know how to kindle and harness that all-important creative spark. Lastly, you will need to have a realistic outlook on your chances of success. This chapter shows you how to get started. It also gives you some key information on copyright law and self-publishing.

What Do You Want to Write?

Before you sit down to write music, you need to know *what* you want to compose. Unless you've been commissioned to write a specific piece for a particular ensemble, this seemingly easy question can be a real stumbling block.

There are many factors that determine what you write. First, you need to select the instrument(s). What instrument(s) do you wish to write for? And what tool(s) will you use to compose your music? Some people use a piano or keyboard to write music. Others, particularly those who write pop music, choose a guitar. Still others use the built-in sound libraries from their score writing software (usually Sibelius or Finale) to compose.

In rare cases, a composer may sit down with pen and ink, using no pitch reference. The composer who writes without a pitch reference usually has perfect pitch. This means that pitches can be identified without a point of reference. Perfect pitch is a gift that some claim can be taught. More often than not, however, perfect pitch is an innate skill.

Trained musicians have relative pitch, which means that they can *only* determine specific pitches with the help of a point of reference. Timpanists, for example, often carry around an "A" pitchfork. Once they know "A," they count whole and half steps in an ascending or descending order until they find the other pitches they need to tune their drums.

Determining Style

Once you've established what instrument(s) you will use to compose for, think about the style of music you wish to write. To be clear: You do not have to limit yourself to *one* style of music. In fact, most professional composers cull from a myriad of influences. However, if you're a fledgling composer, a narrower scope may help you to create music that is better focused and, most importantly, grounded in musical history. Start on terra firma then shoot for the stars!

Determining genre can be tricky, because most styles are actually substyles, hybrids, or outgrowths of other musical forms. However, you can begin to flesh out what you wish to write by thinking about genre. Most of you will write music that falls under one of the following categories:

- Contemporary Classical (solo pieces, chamber pieces, symphonic works, opera, ballet, etc. This is an open-ended modern genre that allows you great compositional freedom.)
- Period specific "classical" music (solo pieces, chamber pieces, symphonic works, opera, ballet, etc. in the style of x or y. Examples might include a neo-baroque chamber piece or a neo-romantic symphony.)
- Soundtrack Music (This is another wide-open genre; music for soundtracks may run the gamut from "classical" genres to "popular" genres.)

Macro popular genres include:

- Blues
- Jazz (small combo or big band)
- Rock
- Folk or Roots Music
- Country and Western
- Urban (R&B, hip-hop, or rap)
- Latin
- Contemporary Religious Music (Christian rock, gospel, etc.)

Still others may write so-called "world" music. "World" music refers to various ethnic or indigenous styles found around the globe. Usually, these styles are determined by the country or region from which they originate.

Overall, the label you use to determine your style may only partly describe your work since these musical "tags" are essentially pat descriptions. However, labeling your music will help you to zero in on what it is you want to write. Again, by establishing a style you narrow your focus. From there, you can begin to concentrate on the details, particulars, and subtleties of your composition.

Instrumentation, Texture, and Mood

Once you're determined what "style" of music you want to write, the next step is to think about instrumentation, texture, and mood. The best way to settle on instrumentation is to think about music as color. This notion will be further defined in Chapters 9 and 19. For now, think about what instruments sound "bright" or "dark" to you. You might also wish to think about what instrument(s) have the ability to sound *both* "bright" and "dark" or perhaps neutral. As you move through this book, and learn about various instruments, think about what colors you would assign to each one.

E-QUESTION

What if I can't determine the style of music I'm writing?
Don't fret. If you can't determine what style you'd like to write, trust your creative impulses. Try to let your musical ideas flow from you naturally, irrespective of genre. Sometimes the urge to write music comes from a deep, inscrutable place. In this case, allow the music to reveal itself to you; let your intuition guide you.

Next, think about texture. Some instruments produce a sweet and smooth texture. Others are harsh or coarse. For example, the flugelhorn produces a velvety texture. In contrast, a distorted electric guitar is raspy and rough-hewn. It's important to choose textures that best convey your music. This will be further explored in Chapter 9 where you will also learn how layering (monophony, polyphony, etc.) affects texture.

Once you've determined texture, think about what mood each instrument evokes. Long tones on a clarinet, for example, can sound melancholy. Conversely, fast rhythms on a piccolo sound chirpy and sunny. Timpani can produce both ominous and regal effects, and a trumpet with a Harmon mute sounds sultry and sensual. A slide trombone is good at creating silly or humorous tones, and violinists can create a carefree atmosphere by using a bowing technique called "spiccato." The list could go on and on. By defining instrumentation through color, texture, and mood, you will be able to communicate your musical ideas more lucidly.

The Creative Spark

Musical ideas develop gradually inside the mind (or as some would have it—the soul) of the composer. When a musical idea is ready to be born, something miraculous occurs called the creative spark.

But what is the creative spark? It is the union of inspiration, motivation, and knowledge. It is an "ah hah" moment when a composer realizes that an idea is ready to be birthed. No book or teacher can tell you when this moment will occur. Only *you* can determine when an idea is "full term" or ready to see the light of day.

Composition is the tangible result of an inspiration. Music without inspiration is only an organized set of notes. Your job is to transcend these notes. Great composers struggle for purity and perfection in their art because they know that music's job is to transform the listener in some way.

Often, the creative spark comes when a composer doodles at the piano or on a guitar, etc. and suddenly—wham—something strikes him. It may be a colorful chord voicing or a unique melodic fragment. Or perhaps it is the combination of several musical factors. Either way, a light bulb goes off inside the brain of the composer, and suddenly, the basic (perhaps inert) thought of composing is turned into *action*.

But what if you can't find that spark? One thing is true: You can't force it. However, there are ways to get the spark to smolder and glow. First, live in a state of awe. If you observe toddlers at play, you will notice their eyes beaming with excitement and wonder. You may not remember, but you were once like this too! Then you grew up, went to school, got a job, and started looking at the world from a practical point of view. You need to have a practical and realistic outlook regarding your career as a composer. However, when you sit down to compose, you should remember that unbridled, even risky and impulsive, thinking best fuels creativity. The greatest composers—from Mozart to Mussorgsky, Ravel to Reich—challenged conventional ideas about art and music. Their minds wandered past narrow roads of practicality, and instead, embraced abundant fields of possibility.

Gustav Mahler once famously remarked about the stunning vistas of Austria: "Don't bother looking at the view—I have already composed it." There are many ways to hasten your creative spark. One way is to spend time in nature. The natural world has long been a source of inspiration for composers. Mahler, for example, sought inspiration from his alpine home at Wörthersee, Austria. Rainstorms captivated Ludwig Van Beethoven, and Antonio Vivaldi even wrote a set of violin concertos built thematically on the changing seasons called *The Four Seasons*. These examples are but a few.

The bottom line is: if you want to compose meaningful works of art, you must create music that sounds (indeed *is)* inspired. Bucolic surroundings often stoke these creative flames. In addition to *The Four Seasons*, listen to *La Mer* by Claude Debussy and *Pini Di Roma* by Ottorino Respighi. Depicting the sea and pine trees, respectively, these works are paragons of the twentieth century. Lastly, although it may sound counter-intuitive, there is no substitute for listening to music that already engages you in order to kindle that all-important spark. Great composers are also great listeners.

Skills Needed

Seeing a composition through to its logical end requires more than just knowing what you want to write. A creative spark, alone, will also not ensure that your work will be of any quality. The next step is to learn *how* to turn your creative spark into a full-fledged piece of music. Virtually anybody can begin a piece of music but only gifted composers know how to develop their work and conclude it at just the right moment.

The following chapters detail the specific information, skills, and knowledge you must possess in order to begin writing music. But if you're looking for a quick checklist to see what you should concentrate on—or to determine what you do and don't know—see the following page.

In order to begin the process of composing music, you must understand the following:

- **Basic historical information.** While you could contend that you don't need to understand music history in order to write music, a stronger case could be made that great music comes from those who root themselves in the culture of music. (See Chapters 2–3.)
- **Basic theoretical elements and building blocks.** These elements include melody, harmony, rhythm, and counterpoint and they are discussed throughout this text. (See Chapters 4–8.)
- **Texture.** As mentioned earlier, texture is a critical element in music. In a 2008 interview, the celebrated Israeli-American violinist, conductor, and teacher Itzhak Perlman talked about how musical texture is like food texture. He is absolutely right! Indeed, you might hear instrumentalists and singers using phrases such as "creamy," "crunchy," "lumpy," and "crispy" to describe the texture of music. (See Chapter 9.)
- **How to tell a story through music.** This is absolutely vital to creating meaningful music that will stand the test of time. Music without a story has no purpose. (See Chapter 10.)
- **Form.** Form is to music as steel girders are to buildings. Without form, your music will lack direction. Moreover, it will not speak in a powerful way to your audience. (See Chapter 11.)
- **Understand the instrument or instruments you wish to write for.** You don't need to know how to play the instrument(s) you wish to compose for, but you do need to understand its strengths and weaknesses. It's okay to write music that challenges the performer but it must also be playable. (See Chapters 12–14 and 16–19)
- **The ability to read and write standard notation.** Technically, you don't *need* to know how to use notation. Not all composers know how to read music (e.g., Paul McCartney has written orchestral and choral works with the help of an orchestrator). But remember: musical illiteracy is never an asset. (See Chapter 4.)

Music Writing Software

If you want to compose music, buy score writing software. Period. As of this writing, two companies rule the roost. These companies are Sibelius or Finale, respectively. Why use this software? For one, you will save lots of time. No more rewriting whole scores just because of a few revisions. No more fumbling around with liquid cover up. No more writing out individual parts. With score writing software, parts are extracted for you! Simply put, Sibelius and Finale have made it possible for composers to lay out their music with the same kind of legibility and professional appearance as a top-notch publishing house.

Both Finale and Sibelius contain sheet music templates. With a click of the mouse, you can choose a variety of staff papers. For example, you can select a jazz quartet staff, a symphony orchestra staff, a wind quintet staff, or you may create your own. Once you choose your staff, you then select a key and time signature. If you wish, you may also indicate tempo. After this, you input notes either through a keypad on the screen or by using a variety of keyboard shortcuts; you may also use a MIDI hookup to make this process go faster.

FACT

MIDI is an acronym for Musical Instrument Digital Interface. MIDI is a protocol that allows various electronic devices, such as computers and keyboards, to communicate with each other through digital data transmissions. MIDI was introduced in the early 1980s and it remains the industry standard.

Sibelius and Finale also offer excellent sound libraries to play back your music. This helps you to proofread with your *ears* as well as your eyes. There's no telling how far this software will evolve, so get involved with it today. Again, these products will save you hours and hours of time!

Copyrighting Your Music

Copyright law is essentially the same in most countries. For composers, it serves as a protective measure, granting you exclusive rights to your music. By holding copyright, you control the reproduction and distribution of your work. You also authorize its use in public performance. Basically, when you copyright your music you are safeguarding your work. Once you've filled out the correct forms, paid the filing fee, and submitted your score(s) to the copyright office, others cannot use your work without your express permission; this may or may not include royalty fees paid to you.

There are some limits to your control, however, and this can lead to legal disputes. When litigants wrangle over intellectual property rights, the doctrine of "fair use" is often cited. "Fair use" laws make allowances for certain artistic works to be reproduced or utilized under specific conditions. Disputes often boil down to how much of your work has been appropriated and for what use(s).

You cannot copyright an idea, so don't waste your time registering a description of a piece of music you are composing. Send only completed scores or phonographic recordings to the copyright office. In the United States, you may not receive a response letter for many months but your copyright takes effect upon receipt of materials.

The law also allows others to create "derivative" works. This provision is debatable in court, since the distinction between a derivation and a "near reproduction" can be hazy. Lastly, there is a statute of limitations on your copyright. Long after you're dead, your work will become "public domain." In most countries, your copyright is protected for 70 to 120 years after your death.

Publishing Sheet Music

You don't have to publish your work to copyright it. However, publishing your music will allow you to make some money, which is always a good thing. Unfortunately, publishers are mainly interested in works by composers who are known quantities, so if you're just completing your first piece for solo guitar it would be wise to wait until your resume boasts enough legitimate accolades to warrant a publishing deal. Like record companies, publishers are not philanthropists eager to help you become the next Felix Mendelsohn (see Chapter 2).

In addition to offering hard copies of your sheet music, you should provide "downloadable" versions of your scores at slightly reduced prices. When you sell your music as downloads, you have virtually no costs. You will also target younger musicians who generally prefer this form of media.

If you're reading this book, you're likely in the beginning stages of your career. The best advice at this stage is to self-publish your work by setting up an online sheet music store. Using the latest score writing software, you can produce sheet music that rivals any publishing firm, so by all means, take advantage of this exciting technology.

What if I don't know how to build a website?
If you're not computer savvy, you may need to invest in web design. You also may need to hire a Webmaster to run your site. However, with a little time, perseverance, and enthusiasm, *you* can learn this skill through "how-to" books. Yes, you can do it!

What is an online sheet music store? It's basically a website. However, your "store" should do more than list your compositional catalog. It should showcase your talents through testimonials and a well-written biography. Additionally, you should include sheet music samples and audio (MP3) clips. If you have photos or streaming videos of ensembles performing your work, be sure to include those too. You want prospective buyers to think that you're the "hot" new composer that "everybody is playing." This kind of bandwagon appeal has long driven the advertising industry.

After you've built your website, specify your target market and solicit those who you think would be enticed by your work. For starters, your best bet is to capture the attention of college music students. They are always hungry for new repertoire and they perform regularly.

Lastly, don't overprice your music. You're not John Adams or John Corigliano (yet). You must accept that you're a relatively unknown (or totally unknown) composer and can't price your work the same. However, if you develop creative strategies for selling your work, you just might see a major publisher come knocking on *your* door. But at this point, you may not need them.

Chapter 2

History of Composition

Your music should be original. However, it should never exist in a vacuum. Instead, your work should be an extension of the music that has come before. In order to do this, you must understand musical history.

This chapter will take you on a whirlwind tour through each major musical era in western history. You'll be exposed to the key movements and the people who have shaped history. However, this is just a *brief* survey. Any college music library will reveal a rich abundance of books on all of these eras, styles, and composers.

Medieval Music and Its Antecedents

Medieval Music refers to music written from approximately 500 to 1400 A.D. Also known as "early music," medieval music is the first period in European classical music. This doesn't mean, however, that there was no music prior to 500 A.D. On the contrary, the ancient Greeks, influenced by Pythagoras, laid the groundwork for modern harmony through their philosophical musings on a concept they called "the music of the spheres." Ancient Greeks also codified a system of musical scales, which paved the way for contemporary modality. (You will learn about modes and scales in Chapters 5 and 15.) Moreover, Plato and Aristotle often refer to music—principally its effects on the individual and society—in their writings.

In the Early Middle Ages, several forms of monophonic (unison) plainsong arose (see Chapter 9). Plainsong or *cantus planus* is a style of religious singing centered on the liturgies of the Catholic Mass. Early plainsong was always sung *a cappella* or without instruments. Plainsong was also sung in Latin, the official language of the church.

Though music was undoubtedly played during the Roman Republic and Empire periods, little is known about its development and role in society. With the gradual shift toward Christianity and the rise of Byzantine (Eastern Roman) Empire, Europe transitioned into a period known as Late Antiquity, then into the Dark Ages or Early Middle Ages. During the Dark Ages, Roman authority, crippled by the fall of their empire, became increasingly weak and decentralized.

Around 1000, the High Middle Ages (eleventh to thirteenth centuries) brought major developments in art, music, technology, and science. Like the Dark Ages, most of the known music from this period is monastic. Once again, plainsong predominated, especially Gregorian chant. Around 900, Gregorian chant unified the music of the liturgy all over Europe. Its use of neumes (square notation) also foreshadowed modern staff notation.

In the Late Middle Ages (fourteenth to sixteenth centuries), Europe descended into a period of desperation, war, and depopulation. In this period, the Black Death killed 25 to 50 million people in Europe alone. Despite this, several musical advances were made.

For example, in 1322, French composer and theorist Philippe de Vitry authored a musical treatise called *Ars Nova*. This publication sparked many innovations in notation and rhythm. De Vitry's own motets (choral music) also reflected this concept of "new art." Marked by prolific use of *isorhythms* (repeated rhythmic patterns called *talea* as well as pitch patterns called *color*), De Vitry's work influenced Guillaume de Machaut, Europe's most distinguished Late Middle Ages composer. Machaut is remembered in part for his secular music of "courtly love." This includes vocal music of varied poetic forms (ballades, lais, virelais, rondeaux, and others). Machaut's mass setting *Messe de Nostre Dame* (c. 1365) is also a seminal work from the period.

The Renaissance

Historians cite changes in intellectual life occurring around 1400 in Florence as the beginning of a cultural "rebirth" in Europe, the Renaissance. The Medici, one of the most powerful families in Tuscany, spearheaded many of these changes. As patrons of the arts, they created an environment where musical creativity flourished.

In music, the Renaissance produced advanced polyphony. Polyphony is defined by the use of independent melodic lines. Initially, polyphony featured only two autonomous melodic lines but soon composers used several (often four or five) independent lines. While there were experiments with polyphony during the High and Late periods of the Middle Ages, it became more complex and common during the Renaissance. Additionally, the interval of the third became more accepted as a harmonic consonance in polyphonic writing. The "third" is important in defining major and minor chords (see Chapter 6).

During this period, composition of sacred music continued, especially in Italy, the seat of Catholicism. However, the motet, the French chanson, and the madrigal (among other forms) became very popular vehicles for secular composition. In some cases, instruments accompanied these songs.

In the Renaissance, pure instrumental music also began to flourish in formal or courtly settings leading to the development of the chamber ensemble. These small groups were called consorts and they featured such instruments as the viol (early stringed instruments of various sizes), cornettos (early cornet), sackbut (early trombone), shawm (early oboe), kortholt (early bassoon), and the recorder. The lute—a guitar-like instrument—was arguably the most popular instrument from this period.

FACT

A madrigal is a secular, polyphonic song originally written for two, or occasionally three, voices. Developed in Italy, madrigals were often settings of Petrarch's (1304-1374) poetry. "Word painting" was a key feature of madrigals. When a composer uses word painting, music imitates the literal meaning of the text. For example, notes might ascend on the word "rise." Later in Italy and in England, the madrigal expanded to five or sometimes six voices.

Key composers from the Renaissance include William Byrd, Guillaume Dufay, Josquin de Prez, Giovanni Gabrielli, Giovanni Pierluigi da Palestrina, and Claudio Monteverdi. The latter's innovations in counterpoint sparked the transition to the Baroque era.

The Baroque Era

When you think of the baroque era (c. 1600–1750), several composers come to mind: Antonio Vivaldi, George Frideric Handel, Georg Philipp Telemann, and Domenico Scarlatti. However, virtually all music scholars would agree that J.S. Bach stands alone as the most important voice of this era. A prodigious talent, Bach brought depth, nuance, and detail to several musical forms including cantatas, motets, passions and oratorios, toccatas, and fugues. Bach's legacy is immeasurable. Without a doubt, he helped to define our modern sense of harmony and harmonic function.

While polyphony was explored meticulously in the Renaissance, tonal (harmonic) functions didn't fall into place until the baroque era.

FIGURE 2-1: Baroque ornaments

TRACK 1

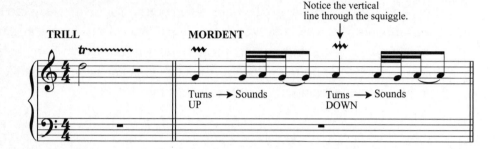

Listen to the CD to hear what these ornaments sound like!

Tonal functions emphasized *cadences*. Cadences "magnetize" the music, if you will, so that notes, now understood as chord progressions, become attracted to a *tonal center* or *key*. Bach and others commonly used authentic, plagal, and deceptive cadences in their music to highlight the key. (You will learn about cadences in Chapter 6.)

Music with a tonal function *always* contains a key. The piece may weave and wind its way through a maze of complex diversions and digressions, but the underlying chords always maintain a connection to one another. Moreover, they ultimately seek to elucidate the key. In nonmusical terms, the key could be called "home base."

If you listen to baroque music, you may hear melodic lines wandering independently (often in contrary motion). However, every note—except for select ornaments, passing tones, and scalar runs—serves to illuminate the harmonic structure of the piece. If you've never studied eighteenth century music, your ear may not be able to discern between ornaments and chord tones (see Chapter 8). But if you know what to listen for, you will learn to differentiate between the two.

Figure 2-1 shows some typical ornaments found in baroque music. Only the appoggiatura has a harmonic function since it creates a *suspension* (see Chapter 6). Notice that the appoggiatura contains two notes that sound like successive quarter notes; the acciaccatura sounds more like successive thirty-second notes. Percussionists call this a *flam*. Note: if you're new to notation, you may want to bone up on "the basics" in Chapter 4 before studying Figure 2-1.

Figured Bass

As harmonic functions developed in the baroque era, a system of shorthand was used to detail chord types, chord inversions, and functionality. This form of "number notation" was called basso continuo, figured bass, or thoroughbass. In this system, a bass note is shown together with subscript numbers detailing the intervals or chord tones to be played above the bass note. When the chords are added to the bass notes, this is called a "realization."

Figure 2-2 shows a figured bass example in the key of F Major. The first measure contains no figured bass integers. When this occurs, you should play a simple root position triad built on the bass note. In this case, the chord would include the notes "F," "A," and "C." If you wanted to be literal, you could write a "5" and "3" underneath this measure, telling the performer to play the intervals located a fifth and third above the root (F). However, this indication would be superfluous in figured bass. The next chord (D minor) contains a "6" under the staff, telling the keyboardist to play a sixth (D) above the bass note (F). The third chord (B♭major) contains a "6" and a "4" under the staff; this tells you to play a fourth (B♭) and sixth (D) above the bass note (F).

The fourth measure contains a seventh chord (C7) on beat three. Accordingly, a "7" is indicated in the figured bass. Here, the seventh scale degree (B♭) resolves down to an "A" on beat one of the next measure. Formal part writing requires that you never leave unresolved or dangling sevenths.

FIGURE 2-2: Figured bass

TRACK 2

The musical analysis of Figure 2-2 may require you to first learn musical concepts detailed later in the book. Be sure to reference Chapters 4–8 if you come across terminology and musical concepts that are foreign to you. It's okay to use this book nonsequentially.

ALERT!

On beat three of the fifth measure, you will see a sharp symbol in the figured bass. This tells you to *sharp* the third above the bass note. The same concept applies to the *natural* symbol seen on beat one of the sixth measure. Again, at the end of measure six (beat four) the B♭(seventh) is resolved in the root chord of beat one (measure seven).

Understanding figured bass is essential if you wish to grasp the musical language of the baroque era. But it is not limited to this. In order to better understand chord functions and inversions (see Chapter 6), you'll need to familiarize yourself with this system. While continuo groups are used only in renaissance and baroque contexts, figured bass has become the universal language employed in all academic settings to analyze a wide variety of musical styles.

Classical Music

In the mainstream media, music written for a symphony orchestra, or the various instruments that make up the orchestra, is generically labeled "classical." There is even the oxymoronic label: "contemporary classical." However, "classical" is also a specific period in European musical history dating from about 1730 to 1820.

First developed in France during the first quarter of the eighteenth century, the *Rococo* movement marked the transition from baroque to classical. In architecture, Rococo moved away from the weighty, often ostentatious, design of the baroque period. Rococo still contained many ornate elements, but the rich complexities of the baroque era were toned down to reflect the elegance and sophistication of the emerging eighteenth century elite. In music, *style gallant* mirrored Rococo's ideals. Style gallant was lighter than baroque and it emphasized soloists (or featured instruments) rather than the harmonically functional polyphony of the baroque era. This was reflected in the work of Bach's son Johann Christian Bach and the Italian composer Felice Giardini, among others.

However, style gallant eventually gave way to full melody-dominated homophony (see Chapter 9), which allowed greater transparency in the harmonic structure. Composers who used homophony began to write melodies that soliloquized over a chord structure. This chordal structure often moved as one, creating buoyant blocks of sound. When a rhythmic texture moves en masse it's called a *homorhythm*.

Haydn, Mozart, and Alberti Bass

In the classical era, the symphony emerged as a popular form of expression. Franz Joseph Haydn was one of several composers to spearhead this new form composing over 100 symphonies and earning the posthumous title, "Father of the Symphony." But just as J.S. Bach best personified the baroque era, Wolfgang Amadeus Mozart epitomized the classical period. Historians and musicians alike hold few composers in such high regard. Mozart was born in Salzburg, Austria. A prodigy, he composed his first pieces of music at age five. His doting father, Leopold, was himself a composer and violinist. He taught his son basic compositional and instrumental skills though his son soon surpassed him. Mozart would go on to compose over 600 pieces in his brief life; he died at age thirty-five. He was an irrefutable master of many genres including chamber works, opera, symphonies, masses, sonatas for violin and piano, concertos, and dances. Despite his genius, however, his career was fraught with great ups and downs as well as financial woes.

FIGURE 2-3: Alberti bass

Alberti bass lines use broken chords or arpeggios.

Like many composers of his day, Mozart composed most of his symphonic movements in *sonata form* (see Chapter 19). He was also known for using a popular bass pattern called *Alberti bass*, named after Domenico Alberti, a singer and harpsichordist from the period. Alberti bass uses broken chords or arpeggios to add a light, bouncy feel to the music. Figure 2-3 shows one example. Notice that the pattern begins with the lowest note of the chord followed by the highest note of the chord. The next note is the middle pitch of the chord. Lastly, the highest pitch of the chord completes the cycle. The simplest rendering of this would be: root – fifth – third – fifth (see measure one) though other variations could be employed. If you don't know the terminology used here, see Chapters 6 and 7.

The Romantic Era

The Romantic Era (1820–1910) represents a period of sweeping musical change. It includes compositions that are marginally removed from formal classicism as well as works that have virtually nothing to do with the structural forms and musical concepts of the eighteenth century. There is a vast difference, for example, between the Germanic music of Franz Schubert and Gustav Mahler. In this sense, these two composers do not belong in the same "period." Rather, Mahler would be best described as *post-romantic* while Schubert is best labeled *early romantic.* Such is the ambiguity of stylistic labels.

As the Romantic Era dawned, Ludwig Van Beethoven emerged as the dominant figure. Although the German-born Beethoven lived most of his life in the so-called "classical" era, his mature music is too mercurial and expansive to be tethered to classical methodologies. In general, Beethoven challenged the compositional mores of the day. This unwittingly ushered in the Romanic Period, which built upon forms developed in the baroque and classical eras.

Beethoven composed symphonies, chamber works, concertos, sonatas, one opera, and other vocal repertoire. In particular, his nine symphonies are marked by complex thematic development. Moreover, his use of modulation (key changes) and strident rhythmic punctuations allowed his music to expand beyond the previously observed boundaries of sonata form. This compositional style is manifested as early as Symphony No. 3 *(Eroica).*

With Symphony No. 9, Beethoven added a choral finale (*Ode to Joy*) in the closing movement. The Ninth transformed the future of the symphonic form, as evidenced by the works of major composers who paid homage to Beethoven's masterpiece. For example, Johannes Brahms' *Symphony No. 1,* Anton Bruckner's *Symphony No. 3*, and Antonin Dvorak's *New World Symphony* all contained elements pulled directly from Beethoven's Ninth.

Romantic composers also emphasized the very large and the very intimate in their music. Orchestral, solo piano, and piano/vocal music represent much of the output of the period. The orchestra expanded in size and instrumental variety to what we now regularly experience in concert settings. Additionally, the solo piano recital became a significant outlet for piano virtuosity. This was best epitomized by Franz Liszt, who revolutionized piano artistry through works he wrote for himself. Lieder (song) also became an important focus for Franz Schubert, Robert Schumann, Hugo Wolf, and Johannes Brahms, resulting in hundreds of songs that typify the genre.

The Romantic Period also saw the rise of patriotic music sometimes referred to as Nationalism. The ardent works of Russia's so-called *Mighty Handful,* for example, best symbolize nationalistic composition. Also referred to as "The Five," these composers (Mily Balakirev, César Cui,

Modest Mussorgsky, Nikolai Rimsky-Korsakov, and Alexander Borodin) sought to create a distinct Russian art form. Oddly enough, however, it was their compatriot, Pyotr Ilyich Tchaikovsky, who wrote the most famous nationalistic piece of the era. Largely influenced by Western European music, his composition *1812 Overture* depicts Russia's victory over Napoleon. It is known for its percussive use of real cannon fire (minus the cannonballs of course).

In the late nineteenth century, another style of music developed in France called *impressionism*. Evolving alongside the artwork of Monet, Renoir, Degas, and Manet, impressionism focused on musical "atmospheres." Additionally, it was often concerned with story telling (program music). You will learn more about program music in Chapters 10 and 19.

Twentieth Century and Beyond

Many labels have been used to describe music of the twentieth and twenty-first centuries. Labels such as neo-romantic, atonality, avant-garde, contemporary classical, minimalist, serial, aleatory, microtonal, new simplicity, postmodern, etc. have been used to describe a wide range of creative output produced over the last hundred years or so.

Arguably the most important composer of the twentieth century is the Russian born Igor Stravinsky. Stravinsky's career contains three periods. His first period is marked by nationalistic works, the second by a preoccupation with classical forms (neo-classicism), and the third by a radical departure into serial music.

Around 1903, *expressionism* developed in Vienna. This style reacted against the ponderous romantic compositions of the nineteenth-century. *The Second Viennese School* was largely responsible for the development of expressionism. They were a group of composers guided by the musical theories of Arnold Schoenberg. During the early part of the century, Schoenberg and his disciples Alban Berg and Anton Webern experimented with atonality, and beginning in 1923, twelve-tone serial music.

Atonal music does not contain a tonal center or key. Nor is it concerned with harmonic function. Its central concern is to produce an equality among all of the pitches in a musical passage, which results in a removal of the musical gravity or magnetism that is caused by traditional keys and scales, thereby creating a different sense of "expression." Serial music, however, attempts to give structure to free atonality. In simple terms, serial music uses fixed "tone rows" or "sets" of notes as the basis for a musical composition. All twelve chromatic pitches are organized in a non-tonal (key/scale) sequence and presented in that order without any repetition until all twelve notes have sounded.

The avant-garde movement, led by John Cage, further questioned traditional definitions of music. Cage has been described as a revolutionary who developed music based on chance or indeterminacy. Using unusual instruments and sometimes non-instruments, or *found instruments,* Cage created a body of work that challenged the very notion of sound itself. One of his pieces, *4'33,"* asks the performer to sit in silence for four minutes and thirty-three seconds. During the piece, the random noises in the performance space become the music. This may seem like a silly idea, but there is also something quite groundbreaking and brilliant about this concept.

During the expressionist and avant-garde movements, western tonality never went away. In fact, American composers Aaron Copland, George Gershwin, Leonard Bernstein, Gian Carlo Menotti, and Samuel Barber kept tonal music alive and well during the twentieth century. Drawing from their Romantic predecessors, and in some cases American folk and jazz music, these composers produced indelible works (symphonies, chamber pieces, operas, musicals, and film scores) that will likely stand the test of time. Among these pieces are Barber's *Adagio for Strings,* Copland's *Fanfare for the Common Man* and *Appalachian Spring,* George Gershwin's *Rhapsody in Blue* and *Porgy and Bess,* Bernstein's *West Side Story,* and Menotti's *Amahl and the Night Visitors.*

Chapter 3

Composition in Popular Music

This chapter highlights composition in popular culture. However, some of these forms have unpopular beginnings or they pass through a popular phase before evolving into art or niche music. Such is the case with jazz, which was initially scoffed at as "devil's music" then became alienating to pop audiences as bebop emerged in the late 1940s. Also, bear in mind that popular music, as a historical and cultural phenomenon, predates the music industry itself—including the practice of *charting*. *Billboard Magazine* first introduced charting with "Chart Line" in 1936.

Defining Popular Music

When you hear the word "pop," you might think of Michael Jackson, the so-called "king of pop." Or perhaps you might think of Britney Spears, Kylie Minoque, Beyonce, or Justin Timberlake. These *are* all pop stars. However, in this book, pop music will have a more expansive definition. Specifically, it will be defined as a historical and cultural phenomenon not *just* a contemporary genre.

Popular music varies from decade to decade and century to century. For example, in the Middle Ages, popular music consisted of secular folk songs, often about love or conquest. In the late nineteenth and early twentieth centuries, the music of Tin Pan Ally—a group of Manhattan songsmiths and publishers—dominated popular music. In the early 1940s, Glenn Miller's music was considered pop. These days, the terms rock, modern R&B, hip-hop, and pop are often discussed interchangeably.

FACT

Scores of popular songs from the eighteenth, nineteenth, and early twentieth centuries are still sung today. For example, "Yankee Doodle Dandy" is a pre–Revolutionary War tune that is widely known even among children. Other songs such as "When Johnny Comes Marching Home" (1863) and "I've Been Working on the Railroad" (1894) remain fixed in the American canon of popular music.

What is pop music? On the surface, pop seems like a musical chameleon that changes over time. Indeed, the repertoire and genres pop represents does change. However, the heart of pop does not. Simply put, pop is music enjoyed, and often created by, "the common man." This definition does not imply that the common man is crude or unsophisticated. In contrast, the common man can be bright, insightful, and even visionary. For example, nineteenth century songwriter Stephen Foster had little musical training but he wrote such unforgettable tunes as "Oh! Susanna" and "Camptown Races."

These days, pop music is intended for commercial sale (and marketing) to the so-called *majority*. In the old days—before the phonograph record and the radio—popular music was disseminated orally. Either way, popular music has always been the opposite of "art" music or "academic" music. (Art and academic music is designed to appeal to a small, specific audience.) If you go back far enough, pop music also contrasts with the official music of the liturgy (see Chapter 2).

Pop music genres have a few basic tenets in common, despite the changes that occur over time:

1. Pop music is always tonal. You will never hear *atonal* pop music (though atonality may be used for brief passages).
2. Pop music usually contains lyrics or spoken word. Some noted exceptions exist. These include select jazz, swing, and rhythm and blues tunes such as Glenn Miller's "In the Mood."
3. Pop music almost always uses *song* form. However, this form has many varieties. There is a big difference, for example, between Renaissance period chanson, German lieder, blues song form, music of the Great American songbook, and modern rock songs. You will learn about song forms in Chapter 11.
4. Pop music contains memorable melodies or catchy vocal "hooks." Pop music captures the ears of the majority because, the listener can sing along if he hears the tune a few times. Pop music is generally welcoming and participatory.
5. Most pop music is written in 4/4 time, which means that there are four pulses or beats in a measure (see Chapter 4). 4/4 is called "common time." This time signature also generally encourages dancing.

One misconception about pop music is that it's "simple." Yes, there are *many* three chord pop tunes. However, this stereotype has scores of exceptions. For example, Latin pop—bossa nova and salsa in particular—contain advanced harmonies and rhythmical structures. Popular music from the Jazz Age (The Roaring Twenties) and swing era (1935–1945) also contains complex harmonies, advanced syncopations, and clever modulations. The same is true of select contemporary pop songwriters. Some of these artists include: Burt Bacharach, Stevie Wonder, Paul McCartney, Joni Mitchell, Donald Fagen, and Sting.

Blues

To understand the blues, you have to go back to slavery and the struggles of Black Americans after the Civil War. In this climate, the blues was born. It comes from unspeakable work conditions on cotton and tobacco plantations and in the timber, turpentine, and levee camps of the Deep South. Ultimately, it is the story of oppression and unyielding racism.

Blues melodies, singing styles, structures, and rhythms can *all* be traced back to the tribal music of West Africa. Griot singing influenced the blues the most. Griot singers are storytellers that typically perform solo. They also accompany themselves on a stringed instrument similar to the acoustic guitar.

The Mississippi Delta is considered the birthplace of the blues since it was here that the blues was first documented around 1900. Blues historians cite Charley Patton as a key figure in the development of the blues. Some even call him the founding father. Clearly, Patton influenced blues legends such as Son House, Robert Johnson, Howlin' Wolf, John Lee Hooker, and a host of others.

In the beginning, the blues was played strictly in the American South. However, W. C. Handy transformed the blues from a back-woods style of music to a new form of popular entertainment that could be bought, sold, and mass marketed. By the 1920s, musicians of all races were performing and recording the blues. The blues could be heard on concert stages and on 78 RPM recordings by record labels such as Victor, Okeh, The American Record Corporation, and Paramount.

From about 1910 to 1940, black musicians from the Delta moved to northern cities such as Detroit and Chicago in search of employment and a better life. This was called the "Great Migration." When Delta musicians arrived in Chicago they began using electric guitars. Soon the legendary Chicago style, epitomized by Muddy Waters and Howlin' Wolf, was born. The Chicago style of blues was a direct precursor to rock-n-roll, especially the music of bands such as The Rolling Stones and Led Zeppelin, who were infatuated with the "Chicago" sound.

Jazz

As early as 1895, jazz was emerging in New Orleans. Early jazz blended the syncopated rhythms of ragtime (itself a form of popular music) with the harmonic elements of the blues and the raw energy of New Orleans marching bands. The most salient feature of jazz was its use of improvisation. The spontaneity of this music and the colorful nature of many of its early practitioners caused black audiences to become captivated by jazz. Before long, jazz was thriving—alongside blues—in brothels and saloons in the South. Soon, white musicians got in on the act, forming their own groups. However, the white status quo wouldn't *fully* embrace jazz as popular music until the swing era (1935–1945).

FACT

Jazz might have remained a regional phenomenon if it weren't for a boom in the recording industry and a migration of New Orleans jazz musicians, including Louis Armstrong, to cities like Chicago and New York City. It was in these urban settings that "hot jazz" truly took shape.

By 1935, swing captivated audiences throughout the world due in large part to the popularity of the radio. During this period, big bands led by Tommy Dorsey, Benny Goodman, Count Basie, Chick Webb, Duke Ellington, and others ruled the airwaves. The first number one hit (1940, *Billboard Magazine*) was Tommy Dorsey's "I'll Never Smile Again" featuring the voice of Frank Sinatra. Sinatra would go on to become one of America's first major pop stars. However, swing's dominion was short-lived. By the mid 1950s, America's youth had fallen in love with a new rough-n-tumble style of music called rock-n-roll.

Country and Western

Country and Western helped to give rise to rock-n-roll. Like all styles of music, country and western (C&W) is a pat term used to describe many different sub-styles of music. Most of these styles are regional. For example, Texas swing and Appalachian mountain music are two distinct genres found in the West and East, respectively. Despite regional distinctions, there is a lot of cross-pollination between country and western's sub-styles, which include honky tonk, Bakersfield sound, Nashville sound, outlaw country, alternative country, and country rock. Other styles such as bluegrass are closely aligned with European folk traditions, especially Anglo-Celtic fiddle music. Country is also influenced by blues and African American gospel music. This stems from the regular interaction between black and white musicians in the American South during the first half of the twentieth century.

FACT

The two biggest pioneers in country music are Jimmie Rodgers, an early folk singer and yodeler, and Hank Williams Sr., a blues influenced honky tonk singer who is known for penning such iconic songs as "Move it On Over," "I Saw the Light," "Lovesick Blues," "Jambalaya (On the Bayou)" and many more.

Key innovators in country and western include cowboy crooners Roy Rogers and Gene Autry, bluegrass virtuosos Bill Monroe and Earl Scruggs, Texas troubadour Ernest Tubb, swing bandleader Bob Wills, guitar legend Chet Atkins, outlaw stylists Johnny Cash, Willie Nelson, and Waylon Jennings, and female vocalists Patsy Cline, Kitty Wells, Loretta Lynn, and Dolly Parton. Moreover, country music churns out major pop stars each decade.

Rock-n-Roll

Shortly after World War II, the swing era was in decline and a new form of music began to take shape. This new style culled from the "race records" of the rural south and the urban blues of Chicago. It also borrowed from country and western styles, and later, from the politically charged folk music of Woody Guthrie and Pete Seeger.

When rock-n-roll emerged in the early 1950s, it forever changed the face of popular music. Rock-n-roll gained in popularity due in large part to the development of the electric guitar, jukeboxes, television and the 45 RPM record.

Key figures such as Alan Freed, Sam Phillips, Jerry Leiber, Mike Stoller and others all took advantage of this technology by drawing white audiences and musicians alike to participate in the birth of a new era.

Rhythm and blues (R&B) is arguably rock's most significant precursor. Rhythm and blues is an "umbrella" term used to describe music made by black artists in the post-war era. Rhythm & blues typically combined elements of blues, jazz, and gospel. However, traditional R&B should not be confused with modern R&B, which is an amalgam of funk, soul, dance, and hip-hop.

Although rock-n-roll's roots were predominantly black, rock's first superstar was Elvis Presley, a white kid from Tupelo, Mississippi. Presley blended gospel and country with a hefty dose of the blues and a spirited drumbeat. The result was an infectious and energetic brand of rock-n-roll called *rockabilly*. Sam Phillips' record label, Sun Records, had a major impact on the rise of this style by signing Presley and assembling what would later be known as the "Million Dollar Quartet" featuring Jerry Lee Lewis, Carl Perkins, Johnny Cash, and Presley.

Early rock-n-roll borrowed from many styles, but it was also inimitable in its own right. For instance, rock was distinctly "attitude" oriented and it rebelled against the conservative mores of the 1950s. Further, rock used heavy backbeats and it relied on amplification to get a larger than life sound. As well, rock's practitioners often engaged in suggestive dancing on stage. Additionally, rock songs avoided the stock AABA song form used by composers of the Great American Songbook tradition.

Rock-n-roll made its crossover to white audiences when Elvis recorded "That's Alright Mama" in 1954, though he wouldn't earn a number one hit until 1956 with "Heartbreak Hotel." As fate would have it, Presley placed his career on hold in 1958 to serve in the army. By the time he received his discharge from the Army Reserve in 1964, the British Invasion was well underway. Rock-n-roll, as he knew it, would never be the same.

Modern Rock

In the 1960s, rock would drop its "roll" and mature into a whole range of sub-styles due to the influence of such icons as Jimi Hendrix, The Who, The Rolling Stones, Bob Dylan, and of course, The Beatles.

In 1964, with the arrival of the Fab Four on American shores, rock music firmly imbedded itself into the collective consciousness of society and it has never left since. Today, The Beatles are seen as a cultural institution. Their music has influenced thousands of artists and, indeed, the very course of popular music. The song "Yesterday," for example, has been covered more than any other song in history. According to the United World Chart, The Beatles have also tallied more number one hits than any other band in history.

However, modern rock was dealt a harsh blow when "urban" music topped it in CD sales in the 1990s. Still, it continues to thrive and have an enormous impact around the globe. It is doubtful that rock will ever cease to be played. Even as the music industry shifts toward dispensable "one hit wonders" and "manufactured" stars, the renegade rock star of the past keeps turning up in the new faces of each generation. In the 1990s, Nirvana and Pearl Jam typified this with *grunge* rock. In the 2000s, The Black Keys, Coldplay, Linkin Park, Seether, The White Stripes, and other veteran artists, such as the Rolling Stones, endeavor to keep the flame alive.

Latin Jazz

Like early blues and country music, Latin American styles vary based on region. Latin music comes from Mexico, Central and South America, and the Caribbean islands. The islands of Cuba, Puerto Rico, The Dominican Republic, Jamaica, and Trinidad and Tobago are particularly important to Latin's development. Latin has a large following in the United States, and cities such as Miami, New York, and Los Angeles teem with Latin American culture and music.

One important Latin style is "Latin jazz." Latin jazz dates back to the early 1900s. For example, the Argentinean tango was used in a section of W.C. Handy's classic tune "St. Louis Blues" (1914). During the 1930s, Duke

Ellington, influenced by valve trombonist, Juan Tizol, wrote the now famous "Caravan." After World War II, the Latin jazz explosion occurred, due in part to Dizzy Gillespie, a bebop trumpeter, who was enchanted by Afro-Cuban music. By the 1950s, Latin big bands led by Tito Puente, Perez Prado, Chico O'Farrill, and Machito sparked many of the trends in dance we now consider commonplace; these include the cha-cha and the mambo. The enchanting Desi Arnaz also helped to expand Latin's appeal through performances by his orchestra on the hit TV show, *I Love Lucy*.

Latin music is rooted in Africa, namely the musical cultures of Nigeria, Angola, and the Congo. Moreover, European folk music, especially Spanish music, influenced early Latin styles. More recently, jazz, rock, and modern R&B have had an enormous impact on Latin's evolution.

In the '60s, the bossa nova emerged in Brazil. Its most important composer, Antonio Carlos Jobim, combined relaxed samba rhythms with cool jazz. He found the perfect blend in tunes such as "Desafinado" and "One Note Samba," which became pop hits in the United States.

In 1963, Joao Gilberto collaborated with Jobim and jazz saxophonist Stan Getz to record an album entitled, *Getz/Gilberto*. The last minute addition of Gilberto's wife, Astrud, on a tune called "The Girl from Ipanema" proved to be quite significant. Because of Astrud's silky voice, "Ipanema" became a megahit in the United States, and eventually, a worldwide classic. Additionally, *Getz/Gilberto* won the 1964 Grammy for "Best Album of the Year" as well as other honors. This album's Grammy success was a major triumph for both jazz and Latin.

Latin Pop

As a genre, "Latin pop" currently enjoys a wide fan base and includes several number one hits. Much of this is due to the success of Latin-rock guitarist Carlos Santana and singers Gloria Estefan, Marc Anthony, Jon Secada,

Ricky Martin, Jennifer Lopez, Selena, Celia Cruz, Julio and Enrique Iglesias, and others.

Latin pop's appeal goes back to the 1930s. The Portuguese-born Brazilian singer, Carmen Miranda, was one of Latin's earliest icons. Her charismatic singing and flamboyant costumes were featured in fourteen Hollywood films (from 1933 to 1953).

Also, the Jamaican-American singer Harry Belafonte popularized the *calypso* with his 1957 single, "The Banana Boat Song," sometimes referred to as *Day-O*.

Today, *meringue* is very popular with Latin music fans, especially young people who go out "clubbing." Like most Latin styles, the meringue goes all the way back to the slave trade. However, its lively feel—marked by thumping quarter notes—has proven infectious in discotheques across the globe.

Lastly, no mention of Latin pop would be complete without a nod to the late Bob Marley. Marley is known for writing such historic songs as "I Shot the Sheriff," "Waiting in Vain," "Is This Love," and the especially moving "Redemption Song." Marley almost single-handedly made *reggae* popular around the globe.

Reggae music was born in Jamaica. However, the etymology of the word "reggae" is in dispute. Some say Toots and the Maytals first used it formally on a 1968 single called "Do the Reggae," but others trace its origins back much further. The music itself is very old. Early versions of reggae date all the way back to a tribe called the *Regga* who lived in West Africa. Bob Marley claimed that the word reggae meant "the king's music" in Spanish.

American and British pop artists have long borrowed from reggae, and by extension, from Bob Marley's music. For example, Paul Simon used a reggae feel for his 1972 hit, "Mother and Child Reunion." Also, Sting used a reggae groove on several songs including "Walking on the Moon," (1979) and "Love is the Seventh Wave" (1985). Further, Bobby McFerrin scored a big hit with his reggae inspired tune, "Don't Worry, Be Happy" in 1988. And Bonnie Raitt used a reggae feel on her 1989 single "Have a Heart." These are but a few examples of reggae's huge crossover and hit making potential.

Chapter 4

The Elements of Music

In this chapter, you will learn about the most fundamental elements of standard notation including the staff, clefs, note types, note relationships, rests, time signatures, and a whole host of other markings used in written music. If you're looking for information on pitch, harmony, and melody, you should skip ahead to the next three chapters. The following pages concentrate exclusively on rhythm, time keeping, dynamics, and tempo.

Using Standard Notation

The ability to read music is very important. You should learn how to read music for the same reasons you learn how to read words. If you're musically literate, your chances of survival in the world of music greatly improve. Musical notation is also an important educational tool. Through notation you will be able to visualize music better, and therefore, be able to conceive of music more clearly. This is not to say that playing or composing by ear is wrong or bad. On the contrary, all musicians need to have a sensitive and discriminating musical ear.

However, as a composer, you will need some tangible format to communicate your musical ideas. Writing music without notation is common in certain pop milieus and you will explore the pluses and minuses of this in Chapter 14. However, you will need to be able to write down your music if you are to compose for orchestral instruments (strings, winds, percussion) and for piano, classical guitar, and operatic voices.

Other forms of notation—tablature, figured bass, lead sheets, etc.—have their place too, but nothing is as universal as standard notation. This is why it's called *standard* notation! That said, if you are rusty on the basics or don't know how to read at all, be sure to study the material found in this chapter. It could make or break your career.

The Staff, Clefs, and Notes

All music can be divided into two parts: sound and silence. Notes represent the sounds a musician makes. Rests indicate silence. Both are written on a staff. A staff is a set of five parallel lines on which a composer writes notes, rests, and other musical symbols. Figure 4-1 shows a blank staff.

The lines and spaces on a staff represent pitch varieties and a clef is used to name each line and space. The most common clefs are treble or G clef and bass or F clef. These clefs are indicated in Figure 4-2.

In Chapter 5, you will learn about the significance of clefs, but first, you must learn about the rhythmical components of a note. Therefore, in the following figures you will see a neutral clef. Neutral clefs are used for nonspecific pitches (usually drums).

FIGURE 4-1: A blank staff

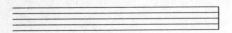

A staff contains five parallel lines.

FIGURE 4-2: Treble and bass clefs

Treble clef or G clef

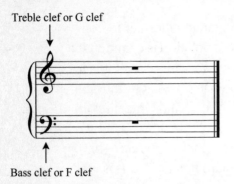

Bass clef or F clef

A note is made up of a *note head* and a *note stem,* except for a whole note, which does not contain a stem. A note head is seen either as an empty circle (whole or half notes) or as a solid dot (all other notes). A note stem is a vertical line that is attached to the note head. Sometimes notes are connected or barred together by a single horizontal line. This is used to indicate eighth notes. Sometimes you will see a double horizontal line. This is used to indicate sixteenth notes. Some single notes have a wavy line that curves down the stem. This is called a *flag.* A single flag is used to signify single eighth notes. A double flag is used to signify single sixteenth notes. All of these note types are shown to you in Figure 4-3.

Notice that individual eighth notes look exactly the same as quarter notes but with a flag attached. The individual sixteenth note also looks like the quarter note but with two flags attached.

FIGURE 4-3: Types of notes

Whole   Half   Quarter   Eighth   Two Eighths   Sixteenth   Two Sixteenths

FIGURE 4-4: Divisional relationship of notes

1:2 Ratio

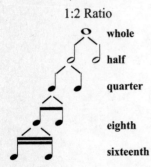

whole

half

quarter

eighth

sixteenth

Standard notation is based on mathematics and it follows the same rules as fractions. Figure 4-4 shows the division of notes.

As you can see, notes divide into two equal parts. A whole note divides into two half notes, a half note divides into two quarter notes, a quarter note divides into two eighth notes, and an eighth note divides into two sixteenth notes. When making these divisions, a 1:2 ratio occurs between whole and half notes, half and quarter notes, quarter and eighth notes, and the eighth and sixteenth notes.

The pie charts in Figures 4-5 through 4-8 show you the divisional relationship of notes.

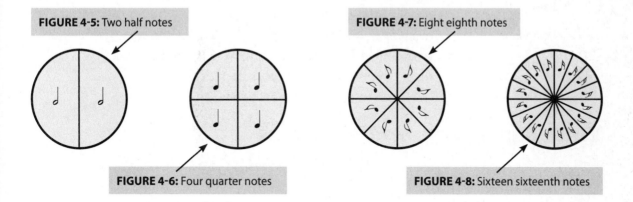

FIGURE 4-5: Two half notes

FIGURE 4-6: Four quarter notes

FIGURE 4-7: Eight eighth notes

FIGURE 4-8: Sixteen sixteenth notes

You can see that two half notes, four quarter notes, eight eighth notes, or sixteen sixteenth notes equal the whole pie. This is the mathematical backbone of notation.

Implementing Rests

Rests function exactly the same way as notes but with one key difference. While a note signifies sound, a rest indicates silence. A rest does not mean that the music pauses. The music continues whether you're resting or not (or whether there is sound or not). Think of a rest as a silent note.

When resting, always follow the music as if you were playing a note. Every note has a corresponding rest and rests have the same relationship to one another as notes do. Figure 4-9 shows each type of rest from whole to sixteenth.

As a composer, you'll want to think about "sound versus silence." Finding just the right balance is essential. In the end, this means knowing how to use rests effectively. There is nothing worse than music that sounds "busy" or "cluttered." If you try to create dense music, it will probably sound chaotic and muddy. Instead, strive to craft natural, flowing music using the fewest notes.

FIGURE 4-9: Divisional relationship of rests

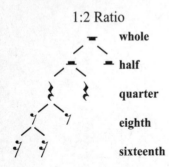

1:2 Ratio

Music that is thoughtfully pared down to its essentials is taut and eloquent. This doesn't mean that you should avoid thick layers or flurries of notes in your music. It simply means that, conceptually, you should have a good reason for choosing "notey" passages. Ultimately, let your instinct and ears guide you. The music of great composers never sounds forced, random, or mechanical. This can be achieved by implementing rests. Simply put, rests let your music *breathe*.

Time Signatures and Measures

Now that you have been exposed to notes and rests, you must piece them together to build rhythmical sentences. But in order to accomplish this, you must first learn about time signatures, which are also called *meters*. There are many time signatures used in music. However, most of this book will focus on four-four since this is the most common meter used in all styles. Figure 4-10 shows the time signature four-four as it appears on a staff.

All time signatures contain a top number and a bottom number. These numbers tell the musician two important things:

1. Number of beats in a measure
2. What note value equals one beat

FIGURE 4-10: Four-four time signature

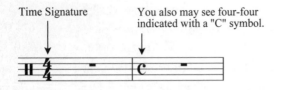

You're probably asking yourself, "What's a beat and what's a measure?" Most music is played in strict time. It has a pulse that, once started, continues until the composition or tune reaches its end. This pulse is the called the *beat*.

In written music, a series of notes and rests are segmented into smaller compartments of time. These boxes of time are called *measures* or *bars*. In other words, notes and rests are contained within measures, and measure lines are used to mark each measure's borders. As you will see in Figure 4-11, measure lines—usually called bar lines—are simple vertical lines used to separate or partition music into "chunks" or "pieces" of time.

FIGURE 4-11: Two blank measures with bar line

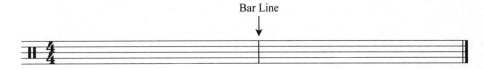

Music played with flexible or "free" time is called *rubato*. Rubato is often used in classical repertoire for slow movements or solo cadenzas. Also, pop intros and outros are sometimes played rubato. Lastly, you may hear rubato used by contemporary—usually experimental—jazz artists. Although rubato is not uncommon, you must first learn how to conceive of music *in time*.

Defining Four-Four

In standard notation, technically there is no line dividing the two numbers in a time signature. In four-four, for example, the fours merely sit on top of one another. However, for educational purposes, accept four-four as a legitimate fraction.

All fractions have a top number called a numerator and a bottom number called a denominator. In this case, the numerator tells you how many beats exist in a measure. Since there is a four in the numerator, there are four beats in each measure.

The denominator tells you the note value that equals one beat. In order to find this, temporarily replace the numerator with a one. Now, you have 1/4 or one quarter. This tells you that the quarter note equals one beat. So what does four-four really mean? *In four-four time, there are four beats in a measure and the quarter note represents (or equals) one beat.* In other words, quarter notes function as the pulse or beat in four-four time. In this sense, the quarter note acts as the heartbeat of the music. When you place four quarter notes into a measure of four-four, it is counted like Figure 4-12.

FIGURE 4-12: Four quarter notes

Each quarter note represents a *downbeat.* In four-four, downbeats equal the numbers: one, two, three, and four. If you divide quarter notes into eighth notes, you will have eight of them per measure. Figure 4-13 shows one measure of eighth notes.

In Figure 4-13 the beat was divided into two parts. It should be counted: "one-and, two-and, three-and, four-and." "Ands" are called *upbeats* and they are represented in the music with a plus sign (+). Upbeats represent the second half of a beat. Remember, for each note, there is a corresponding rest. In Figure 4-14, you'll see eighth notes with eighth rests indicated on the "ands." Now, eighth notes sound like short quarter notes!

FIGURE 4-13: One measure of eighth notes

FIGURE 4-14: Eighth rests on "ands"

Keeping Time and Counting Aloud

One of the most important facets of music is timekeeping. Music exists in time and space. Time refers to the pulse of the music, while space refers to the rhythmical components (notes and rests) that exist within a time span.

All musicians, including composers, should have good time sense. You won't be able to write music accurately if you don't have a solid sense of time. One of the best ways to improve your time is to count beats out loud. Counting will help you to make sense of the rhythms you're reading and writing.

FIGURE 4-15: Counting sixteenth notes

As previously stated, when you see four quarter notes you should count the downbeats 1, 2, 3, 4. Counting divisions and subdivisions are also helpful. For instance, you know that eighth notes are counted: 1 and, 2 and, 3 and, 4 and. Sixteenth notes are counted using the syllables: 1, e, and, ah—2, e, and, ah—3, e, and, ah—4, e, and, ah. Figure 4-15 illustrates this. Again, a plus (+) is used in place of the word "and."

If you combine sixteenth notes and eighth notes, rhythms become more elaborate. Moreover, if you use sixteenth rests, the rhythms really become knotty and difficult to play. When using these types of rests, you *must* be very diligent in your counting.

Other Time Signatures

In addition to four-four, there are many other time signatures. Three-four is a very popular meter. In this time signature, there are three beats in a measure, and like four-four, the quarter note receives the beat. Three-four is synonymous with the *waltz*. During the nineteenth century, it was also used for the *scherzo* movement in a symphony. Before that, three-four appeared in the *minuet and trio,* which comprised the third movement in classical-era symphonic form.

Two additional time signatures that use "4" in the denominator are five-four and seven-four. These time signatures tell you that there are five beats in a measure or seven beats in a measure, respectively. Again, the quarter

FIGURE 4-16: Five-four, seven-four, five-eight, and seven-eight time

FIGURE 4-17: Six-eight time

FIGURE 4-17: Six-eight time

FIGURE 4-18: Two-two time

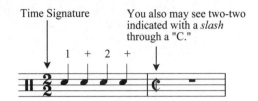

Two-two time is often called *alla breve* or *cut time.*

note receives the beat. Cousins to these odd meters are five-eight and seven-eight. Here, the *eighth* note receives the beat. These meters are used primarily in twentieth and twenty-first century composition (including rock and jazz). Figure 4-16 illustrates what these meters look like in notation.

Another very common time signature is six-eight time. This is often used in marches and occasionally in rock music, particularly heavy metal. It was also used for *gigues* (courtly baroque dances) and *jigs* (Celtic folk dances). This time signature tells you that there are six beats in a measure and that the eighth note receives the beat. Usually, however, six-eight is counted in "twos." In other words, the six beats in each measure are divided into two equal parts (3+3). This is illustrated in Figure 4-17.

Two-two is another widespread time signature. It is also sometimes referred to as cut time or *alla breve.* Here, the *half note* receives the beat and there are two beats in a measure. This meter is often used as a substitute for four-four when the tempo gets very fast. You'll see it used in marches, musical theatre, and *reels* (Celtic folk dance). Figure 4-18 shows what two-two time looks like in notation. Here, quarter notes are counted like eighth notes in four-four (with +'s).

Tempo, Expression, and Navigation Markings

Because western music is derived from European classical, most of the terms used in music are foreign to American speakers. Italy was the epicenter of the Renaissance in art and music and it spawned the majority of the musical terms in use today. Below is a list of key terminology you will need to know. These musical terms address:

1. Tempo (speed)
2. Expression (dynamics)
3. Navigation (the "road map" of a score)

In each case, practical definitions have been provided. As you learn about individual instruments later in this book, you will learn about other markings. For now, focus on the basics.

Tempo is the speed or pulse of the music. Sometimes exact tempos are shown in the top left corner of a score. An example of this is shown in Figure 4-19. Tempo can also be indicated using more generalized terms:

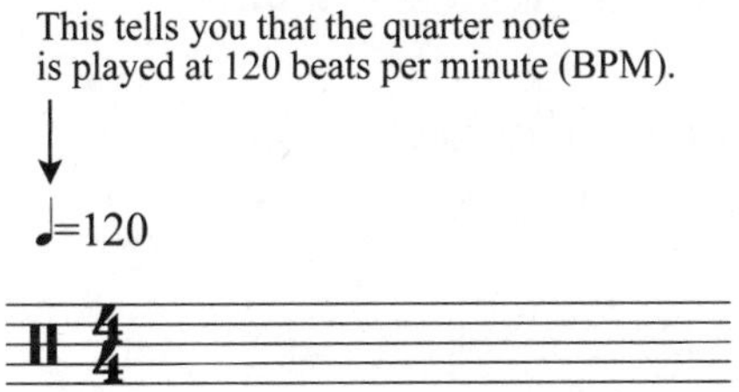

- **Largo:** Very slow (40–60 BPM [beats per minute])
- **Larghetto:** Slowly but faster than Largo (60–66 BPM)
- **Adagio:** Slow but faster than Larghetto (66–76 BPM)
- **Andante:** Faster than Adagio; often described as a "walking" speed (76–108 BPM)
- **Moderato:** Medium or moderate speed (108–120 BPM)
- **Allegro:** A lively or quick pace often described as "cheerful" (120–168BPM)
- **Presto:** Very Fast (168–200 BPM)
- **Prestissimo:** Extremely Fast (200+ BPM)

FIGURE 4-19: Tempo marking

This tells you that the quarter note is played at 120 beats per minute (BPM).

♩=120

In contemporary chart or lead sheet writing you may see other generic tempo designations, which indicate tempo *and* style. Examples include: "slow bossa," "fast bop," "pop ballad," or "medium rock." Lead sheets are simple renderings of a piece of music containing only the melody, lyrics (if applicable), and chord symbols. On occasion, fret diagrams for guitar may also appear. Charts are arrangements for jazz or pop ensembles.

FIGURE 4-20: Accents

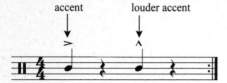

FIGURE 4-21: Crescendos and diminuendos

FIGURE 4-22: First and second endings

Terms used to indicate a change of tempo include:

- **Ritardando or Rallentando (these terms are interchangeable):** Gradual slowing of tempo usually written as the abbreviations *rit.* or *rall.*, respectively.
- **Accelerando:** Gradual increase in tempo usually written as the abbreviation *accel.*
- **A Tempo:** Return to the original or first tempo

The following terms are used to indicate expression (dynamics):

- **Pianissimo (*pp*):** Very soft
- **Piano (*p*):** Soft, a notch louder than pianissimo.
- **Mezzo Piano (*mp*):** Moderately soft, louder than "piano" but softer than "mezzo forte"
- **Mezzo Forte (*mf*):** Medium loud, usually a natural, unforced volume that exists in the middle of the dynamic spectrum
- **Forte (*f*):** Loudly
- **Fortissimo (*ff*):** Very loud

Accents are another expressive notation and mark a sudden increase in volume for specific notes. There are two main types of accents; both are seen as carets in the music. A caret that points upward is a strong or particularly forceful accent. Other terms such as "sforzando" (*sfz*) and "fortepiano" (*fp*) also tell you to give a note an extra emphasis or dynamic punch. Figure 4-20 shows what accents look like.

Other notations indicating a change in expression include:

- **Crescendo:** Gradual increase in volume. A widening "hairpin" symbol or the abbreviation *cresc* is used to denote crescendos.
- **Diminuendo or Decrescendo (these terms are interchangeable):** Gradual decrease in volume. A narrowing "hairpin" symbol or the abbreviation *decresc.* or *dim.* is used to denote decrescendos or diminuendos.

Figure 4-21 shows what a crescendo and a diminuendo (or decrescendo) look like.

The following terms relate to navigation:

- **First and Second Endings:** At the end of a musical passage, you may see two endings. In this case, the first ending always includes a repeat. After you take the repeat, you will play your way through the music again and take the second ending. Figure 4-22 shows what first and second endings look like.
- **D.C. al fine:** repeat to the beginning and end where you see the word "fine." Here, fine means "end" in Italian.
- **D.S. al Coda:** repeat to the "sign" then jump to the "coda" when indicated. You will end on the coda.

Chapter 5
Pitch and Scales

Now that you have studied rhythm, it's time to learn about pitch, intonation, clefs, keys, intervals, scales, equal temperament, and other related topics. This chapter is designed to school you in the basics of pitch and scales. If you're unsure about the fundamentals of pitch, be sure to study the material found here. The next several chapters assumes you know these concepts. If you don't, you're likely to become confused as the material gets more advanced.

Pitch Versus Intonation

In music, pitch corresponds with the notes found on the lines and spaces of a staff and/or the notes located on *ledger lines.* Ledger lines are small horizontal lines located above or below the staff. They appear only when a composer wishes to write a note outside the range of the staff. Figure 5-1 shows the pitch arrangements on the staff for the treble clef. Figure 5-2 details the same information on the bass clef.

FIGURE 5-1: Notes on the treble clef

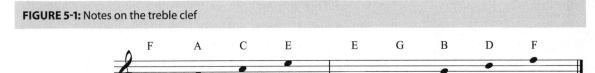

The spaces on the treble clef spell **FACE**. The lines can be remembered by using the mnemonic: **E**very **G**ood **B**oy **D**oes **F**ine.

FIGURE 5-2: Notes on the bass clef

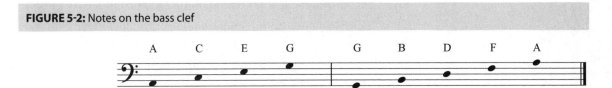

The spaces on the bass clef can be remembered by using the mnemonic: **A**ll **C**ows **E**at **G**rass. The lines can be remembered by using the mnemonic: **G**ood **B**oys **D**o **F**ine **A**lways.

Figure 5-3 shows where *Middle C* is located on the treble and bass clefs. Middle C is a frequently referenced pitch marker, especially for keyboard instruments. Ledger lines are used when writing Middle C in both the treble and bass clefs.

Whenever pitch is discussed, another term, *intonation,* often arises. Intonation refers to pitch correctness while playing an instrument. Poor intonation means that the instrument is "out of tune" and/or the musician lacks the skill to play "in tune." Intonation also applies to the human voice, which is an instrument unto itself.

Fretless string players, wind instrumentalists, and singers must all continuously control the pitch as they perform. If the musician can't manipulate one of these instruments very well, the notes will sound *flat* (below the

FIGURE 5-3: Middle C on the treble and bass clefs

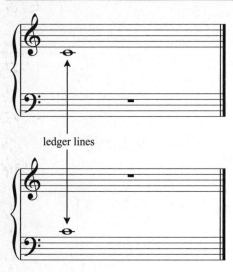

ledger lines

Middle C is also called C4.

intended pitch) or *sharp* (above the intended pitch). A pianist, on the other hand, is not concerned with intonation when performing since the intonation is fixed. (A professional tuner adjusts the piano strings in advance.) Other keyboard instruments such as a vibraphone, synthesizer, celesta, and harpsichord are also tuned in advance.

While intonation and pitch are often discussed as synonyms, they are not. This isn't to say that they aren't related. Pitch or frequency is one component of the physics of sound. Intonation refers to an instrumentalist's ability to generate precise pitches. As stated above, accuracy with intonation depends on the skill of the musician.

Today, pitch has been standardized under the rules of equal temperament, so that the A above middle C on the piano is set to 440 Hertz. This is also the tuning note for symphony orchestras.

Key Signatures

There are fifteen keys used in western, tonal music. These include seven sharp keys, seven flat keys, and one key without sharps or flats. Each key signature can be used to signify a *major* or a *minor* key depending on context. For example, if you see one sharp in the key signature, the music is either in the key of G major or E minor. You would need to look at the music itself— i.e., the harmonic structure—to determine whether or not the music is in a major or minor key.

What are flats and sharps? A flat lowers the pitch of a note by a half step, and a sharp raises it by a half step. Flats and sharps are written on the staff in a specific order. Key signatures contain either flats *or* sharps—not both. For example, you will never see a key with two flats and one sharp. In a key signature, the set of sharps or flats is written after the clef but before the time signature.

All notes written within the body of a piece must defer to the key signature. For instance, the key of G major contains an F♯. This means that *all* F's found in the composition will be played as F♯. In this context, if the composer wants the performer to play an F, a *natural sign* will be written to the left of the note. In this example, the F natural would be called an *accidental.*

An accidental refers to any note—sharp, flat, or natural—that is not included in the key signature. Figure 5-4 shows what a flat, a sharp, and a natural sign look like.

FIGURE 5-4: Flat, sharp, and natural sign

♭   ♯   ♮

FLAT   SHARP   NATURAL

To some listeners, each key bears a specific musical "color" or "personality." Because of this, composers and songwriters alike sometimes have favorite keys. Key signatures have practical value too. They are used to avoid writing lots of sharps or flats in the body of the music. Lots of sharps and flats can make a piece look messy. In turn, this makes it harder for musicians to play the music.

Ultimately, a key signature identifies a piece of music's *home base.* By its very nature, tonal music contains resolution points or musical periods. Also, a composition's conclusion usually matches the key. For example, if you're in the key of C major, the piece will likely end on a C major chord. Further, key signatures define the primary scale or mode of a piece. In turn, this scale defines the specific chord names (not types) used. As music gets more and more complex, exceptions to all of this may occur.

As previously mentioned, each key signature denotes two keys: a major key and a relative minor key. The relative minor key uses the same set of pitches as its major counterpart. The minor key is defined by three scales that begin and end a minor third below (or a major sixth above) the relative major. An example of this would be the relationship between "C" and "A." "A" is located a minor third below "C" and a major sixth above "C." The relative minor key also uses its own set of cadences (see Chapter 6).

In order to identify sharp keys, look at the last sharp then raise the pitch one half step. For example, the key of A major has three sharps (F♯, C♯, and G♯). One half step above G♯ is A.

In order to identify flat keys, look at the second to last flat. This flat identifies the key. For example, the key of A♭ major has four flats (B♭, E♭, A♭, and D♭). The second to last flat is A♭. Therefore, the key is A♭. You will need to memorize the major and minor key signatures with one flat. They are F major and D minor, respectively.

C major and A minor use all naturals (*no* sharps of flats) in their key signatures. However, as you will learn later on, the A harmonic minor scale and the A melodic minor scale both contain accidentals.

In each key, sharps and flats appear in a fixed order and position on the staff. You cannot alter this when writing out a key signature. There are a number of mnemonic devises used by students to remember the order of the sharps and flats on the staff. One memory tool for remembering sharps is: **F**at **C**ows **G**et **D**izzy **A**fter **E**ating **B**arley (F, C, G, D, A, E, B). A memory device for remembering the order of flats is: **BEAD G**o **C**all **F**red (B, E, A, D, G, C, D). Feel free to make up your own mnemonics too!

The Circle of Fifths

The circle of fifths is a common graphic model used to understand the relationship between keys and key signatures. The circle of fifths is a cycle that moves clockwise from C major (no sharps or flats) to G major (one sharp), to D major (two sharps), to A major (three sharps), to E major (four sharps), to B major (five sharps), and then to F♯ major (six sharps). At this halfway point, F♯ can also be written as G♭ major (six flats). (Note: The previous key, B major, can be spelled out as C♭ major but composers rarely use this key.) Continuing in a clockwise direction, the next key is D♭ major (five flats), which can also be spelled out as C♯ major, another largely obscure key. The circle continues with A♭ major (four flats), E♭ major (three flats), B♭ major (two flats), and finally F major (one flat). The next key, after F major, brings you full circle. This graph is shown in Figure 5-5.

FIGURE 5-5: Circle of fifths

Move through each key clockwise or counterclockwise!

As you can see, this circle always moves in *perfect fifths* (seven semitones). The same cycle can be applied to minor keys as well since every major key contains a relative minor. Also, since each successive key moving clockwise from C to C contains only *one* additional sharp or *one less* flat, respectively, the circle highlights familiar options for changing keys. For example, an effective yet easy modulation can be made between the keys of C major and G major since these keys share four of the same diatonic chords (see Chapter 6). Lastly, bear in mind that you can also move in a counterclockwise direction from C major to F major and so on. In this direction, the flats will increase by one and the sharps will decrease by one as you travel around the circle.

Melodic and Harmonic Intervals

An interval is the measured distance between any two notes. If two notes are played in succession, they form what is known as a melodic or linear interval. If these notes are played simultaneously, they form a harmonic or vertical interval. Melodic intervals can sometimes imply harmony, as you will learn later in the book. Figure 5-6 shows an example of melodic and harmonic intervals.

FIGURE 5-6: Melodic and harmonic intervals

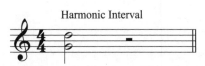

Figure 5-7 shows essential intervals. You will use these continually when you compose music. In this figure, you will see a perfect unison, a major second, a major third, a perfect fourth, a perfect fifth, a major sixth, a major seventh, and a perfect octave shown as melodic intervals. Other

FIGURE 5-7: Essential intervals

essential intervals include: minor second, minor third, minor sixth, minor seventh, augmented fourth, and diminished fifth; the last two intervals are also called *tri-tones*. These are shown in Figure 5-8.

FIGURE 5-8: Other essential intervals

There are still other intervallic relationships made possible through the beauty of *enharmonics*. Some of these include augmented unisons, augmented thirds, and diminished octaves. While these may be found in notation, the naming of intervals using these terms is more or less academic. In Chapter 6, you will encounter additional intervals in the form of harmonic extensions.

To understand what intervals really mean, count them using the smallest unit of measurement, which in western music are half steps or semi-tones. When you count intervals in this way you are moving *chromatically*. On a piano, chromatic movement means that you play every white and black key as you move up or down the keyboard. On a guitar, this means depressing every successive fret on any given string.

When determining intervals using half steps, you will see that a minor second contains two half steps, a major second contains three half steps, a minor third contains four half steps, a major third contains five half steps, a perfect fourth contains six half steps, and so on. In order to accurately count steps you *must* begin counting on the *first note*. For example, if you're moving up chromatically from C to A, you would count: C (1), C♯ (2), D (3), D♯ (4), E (5), F (6), F♯ (7), G (8), G♯ (9), A (10). There are a total of 10 half steps between C and A.

FACT

In equal temperament tuning—as defined later in the chapter—an enharmonic is any pair of notes that sound the same but are called two different names. For example, an F♯ may also be called a G♭ and a B♯ may be called a C natural. Enharmonic naming depends on musical context. Enharmonics may also be applied to key signatures.

You should also know how to count whole steps. Like half steps, when counting whole steps, you must begin on the first note. When you count whole steps, you will count *every other note* in the chromatic scale. For example, C to D is a whole step (skipping C♯). E to F♯ is another example (skipping F natural). Whole steps can also be called major seconds.

Major Scales

A scale is a predetermined set of intervals. The major scale, also called the Ionian mode, is composed of the following intervals: *whole, whole, half, whole, whole, whole, half.* The easiest scale to comprehend is C major since it contains no sharps or flats. The C major scale consists of the following notes: C, D, E, F, G, A, B, C. The interval between C and D and between D and E is a whole step. The interval between E and F is a half step. The interval between F and G, between G and A, and between A and B is a whole step. The interval between B and C is a half step.

You will use seven *scale degrees* to count the intervals in a major scale. The names of the seven scale degrees are outlined below:

- First degree: tonic
- Second degree: supertonic
- Third degree: mediant

- Fourth degree: sub-dominant
- Fifth degree: dominant
- Sixth degree: sub-mediant
- Seventh degree: sub-tonic (leading tone)

The ascending C major scale is shown in Figure 5-9. Whole steps, half steps, and scale degrees are also indicated.

FIGURE 5-9: Ascending C major scale

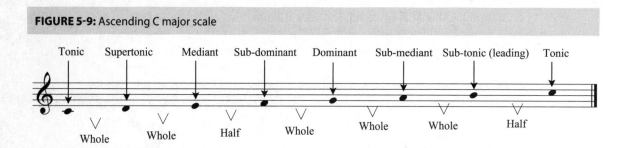

Minor Scales

The minor scale, also called the Aeolian mode, is closely related to the major scale. As you learned above, major and minor scales are "relative" keys. The difference lies in the start and stop points and in the positioning of the scale degrees. For example, the note E in the key of C major is a major third. The note E in the key of A minor (C major's relative minor key) is a perfect fifth.

Do not confuse relative minor/major with parallel minor/major. Parallel refers to two keys that have the *same* starting point or tonic (e.g., C major and C minor). However, parallel major/minor keys do not have the same intervallic relationships. In other words, their key signatures are not related. If you compare C major and C minor you will notice that C major contains no sharps of flats but C minor contains three flats.

Minor scales are divided into three categories:

- Natural Minor
- Harmonic Minor
- Melodic Minor

Beginning on the tonic, the natural minor scale consists of the following intervals: *whole, half, whole, whole, half, whole, whole*. Take a look at A minor on a piano or keyboard. This key uses all white notes. From A to B there is a whole step. From B to C there is a half step. From C to D and from D to E there is a whole step. From E to F there is a half step. From F to G and from G to A there is a whole step. This is shown in Figure 5-10.

FIGURE 5-10: Ascending A natural minor scale

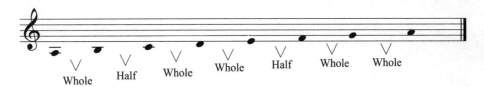

The harmonic minor is more exotic sounding since it includes one accidental. Instead of a minor seventh, the scale has a major seventh or leading tone. In the key of A minor the harmonic scale will include a G♯, resulting in the unusual interval of the augmented second; this interval creates the exotic sound. Figure 5-11 illustrates this.

FIGURE 5-11: Ascending A harmonic minor scale

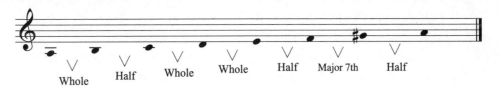

The melodic minor scale retains the minor third scale degree. However, it mimics a major scale on the sixth and seventh scale degrees. Traditionally, this occurs only when the scale ascends. In other words, the sixth and seventh scale degrees are altered only when you travel *up* the keyboard, guitar, etc. When descending, the natural minor scale is used.

In the modern era, the melodic minor may be used when improvising over specific chord types. In this setting, it can be used when ascending and descending. The melodic minor scale is particularly effective when solo-ing over minor-major chords, suspended (flat 9) chords, major (sharp five) chords, dominant seventh (sharp 11) chords, half-diminished chords, and minor seventh (flat 5) chords.

The chords described above are very advanced. At this point, you are not expected to know what these chords mean. However, they have been included above for future reference. (You will learn more about impro-visation in Chapter 15.) For now, just get acquainted with the melodic minor scale. Figure 5-12 shows an A minor melodic scale as it is written traditionally.

FIGURE 5-12: Ascending and descending A melodic minor scale

W=Whole Step
H=Half Step

Equal Temperament

In order to fully understand equal temperament, or any tuning system, you must posses some understanding of physics and mathematics. However, you do not necessarily need to understand the science of sound to com-pose. Despite this, you should know what equal temperament means so that you can better understand intervals and enharmonics.

Equal temperament is a system of tuning keyboard instruments that has now become the standard for interpreting intervals on any instrument. In layman's terms, equal temperament means that an octave—for example C to C on the piano—is divided into twelve equal semitones. In this twelve-tone system, each scale step contains the exact same frequency or pitch ratio. This allows composers to write music that can modulate (change keys) with-out worrying about unwanted intervallic dissonances or variances.

In other tuning systems, for example *meantone temperament* (which is constructed on a chain of ascending perfect fifths), a composer might inad-vertently confront a *wolf interval*. In a twelve tone system, this is a pair of per-fect fifths that sound sharper than another pair of perfect fifths. Wolf intervals (also called wolf fifths) occur because frequency ratios are unequal. Therefore, pure enharmonics do not really exist.

For example, a G♯ and an A♭ do not sound identical in meantone temperament. Consequently, if you pair up a G♯ with an E♭ the E♭ will sound *sharp*. (This interval is technically a diminished sixth. However, it is enharmonically the same as a perfect fifth.) Equal temperament resolves the dissonance of the wolf fifth by making these ratios the same. In other words, in equal temperament, a G♯ will sound identical to an A♭.

On the downside, equal temperament makes intervals sound generic, and for this reason, some scholars have challenged its supremacy. But whether you like it or not, equal temperament is here to stay. Unless you purposely seek out an alternative, you will compose in the twelve-tone equal temperament system by default.

Chapter 6

Exploring Harmony

This chapter outlines basic harmonic principles. On the following pages, you will discover major and minor triads, diminished and half-diminished chords, augmented chords, dominant seventh chords, borrowed chords, suspended chords, harmonic extensions, and much more. You will also learn about musical cadences. There are other more esoteric chords not included here. You will encounter some of these later in the book.

Triads and Inversions

A triad has three notes: a root, a third, and a fifth. The root of a chord *always* refers to the letter name of a chord. For example, the root of a C major chord is "C." Thirds and fifths refer to the intervals above the root.

Major and minor triads are widely used in tonal music. These chords sound very different from one another, yet they also share two of the same notes: the root and a perfect fifth. For example, in the keys of C major and C minor, the root and fifth combination of C and G outlines a I chord or a i chord (see E-ssential below). The difference between major and minor lies in the *third* interval.

As you might guess, the *major* triad contains a *major* third. If you're counting half steps or semitones, the major third is five steps (or five note names) away from the root. In this case, these steps are: C (1), C sharp (2), D (3), D sharp (4), and E (5). As you know from Chapter 5, the relationship between a C and an E is a major third (Figure 5-7).

The minor third contains only four half steps. This means that the third scale degree is flatted. In C major, the steps are: C (1), C sharp (2), D (3), E flat (4). Figure 5-8 illustrates a minor third interval.

Roman numerals are used to analyze chord functions. Uppercase numerals are used to indicate major chords (e.g., I, IV, and V). Lowercase numerals are used for minor chords (e.g., ii, iii, vi). Lowercase numerals with a degree symbol indicate diminished chords (e.g., vii°). In all cases, the numerals refer to the *scale degree* on which the chord is built. See Figure 6-3.

Figure 6-1 shows a C major and a C minor triad. Again, the only difference between these chords is the *third*. You will see an E-natural in the C major triad (major third) and an E♭ in the C minor triad (minor third).

Since these chords contain three notes, they can be written in three different positions. When C is in the bottom, as in Figure 6-1, the chords are in root position. When the third is on the bottom, these chords are written in first position. When the fifth is on the bottom, these chords

FIGURE 6-1: C major and C minor triads

FIGURE 6-2: Major and minor triadic inversions

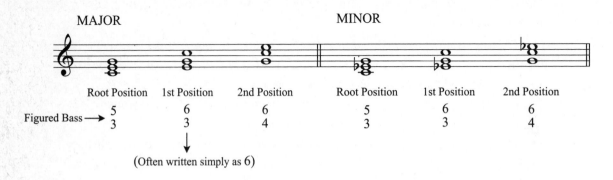

Figured bass integers refer to intervals above the bass.

are notated in second position. In general terms, first and second positions are called *inversions*. Figure 6-2 shows major and minor triadic inversions.

Diatonic Triads of the Major Scale

If you build a triad—on each scale degree in a major scale you get three types of chords. They are major, minor, and diminished, respectively. Simply stack thirds to create each chord. Chords stacked in thirds are called *tertian chords*. Figure 6-3, illustrates this in the key of C major.

The chords in Figure 6-3 are spelled out in root position and Roman numerals indicate each chord function. Like all chords, the triads of the major scale may be inverted. Since there are three notes in a triad, you can create two inversions. For example, a vi chord (A minor) can be inverted as seen in Figure 6-4.

FIGURE 6-3: Diatonic triads of the major scale

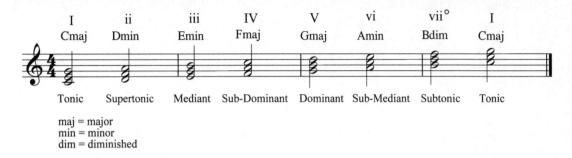

maj = major
min = minor
dim = diminished

FIGURE 6-4: vi Chord inversions

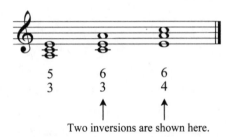

At this stage, your job is to get acquainted with each diatonic triad. These chords are the basis for thousands of chord progressions in thousands of compositions and songs. Once you learn them in C major, be sure to try them in other keys too.

Dominant Seventh, Diminished, and Augmented Chords

Dominant seventh chords are used in many styles of music. This chord type features a major triad plus a minor seventh. Technically speaking, this seventh is categorized as a harmonic *extension* (as defined later in the chapter). When you write the chord symbol for a dominant seventh, the chord will contain a letter name and the number seven. For example, you will see C7,

G7, or B7 etc. Once you add the seventh, you will have a four-note chord, and therefore, three possible inversions can be created. Regarding usage, the dominant seventh chord is used to add color to an otherwise plain V chord. Figure 6-5 shows a C7 chord and its three inversions.

FIGURE 6-5: C7 Chord and its inversions

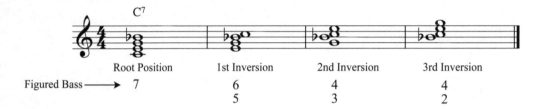

Root Position	1st Inversion	2nd Inversion	3rd Inversion
Figured Bass ⟶ 7	6 5	4 3	4 2

Diminished Chords

Diminished chords naturally occur on the leading tone (subtonic) of a major scale. For example, in the key of C major, a diminished chord is rooted on B, the seventh scale degree or leading tone. The diminished chord contains a double minor third interval. In other words, two minor thirds are stacked on top of one another creating a diminished chord quality.

A B diminished chord contains the intervals B to D (minor third) and D to F (minor third). The diminished chord gets its name from the interval created between the root and the flatted fifth (a diminished fifth). A B diminished chord is shown in Figure 6-6. The degree symbol is used to indicate the chord quality.

FIGURE 6-6: B diminished chord

Diminished Seventh Chords

Diminished seventh chords are often used as a substitute for V chords. (Again, since a seventh scale degree is used, this chord contains a harmonic extension.) As an unstable chord, they naturally lean in the direction

FIGURE 6-7: Diminished seventh chord

of the tonic. An unstable chord is a transitional chord. It cannot function as a *resting place* in the music. Instead, unstable chords gravitate toward stable chords such as I, i, or V. A diminished seventh stacks *three* minor third intervals on top of the root, making the interval between the root and seventh enharmonically the same as a major sixth. For example, a B dim7 chord contains an A-flat on top. If written as a G♯, the interval will be a major sixth. However, don't be confused by enharmonic naming. Just remember that a diminished seventh chord contains three stacked minor third intervals. The diminished seventh chord is shown in Figure 6-7.

Half Diminished Chord

The half diminished chord is a rather beautiful, impressionistic chord that can be used in a variety of ways. Often spelled out as a minor seven♭ five, the half diminished chord contains most of the same notes as a full-diminished seventh chord. The exception lies in the seventh (extension) itself. Instead of stacked minor thirds, the half diminished contains a *major third* on top. For example, a B half diminished contains the notes B, D, F, and A. The relationship between F and A is a major third. However, don't confuse this with the intervallic relationship between the root and the seventh, as this is a minor seventh. For example, B and A are minor sevenths. The half diminished chord is notated in Figure 6-8. The symbol for a half diminished chord is a degree symbol with a line or slash through it.

FIGURE 6-8: Half diminished chord

Augmented Chord

The augmented chord is a major triad with a sharp five. For example, a C augmented chord contains the notes C, E, and G♯. Enharmonically, this G♯ is also an A flat. As an A flat, this interval would be called a flatted thirteenth. Like the half diminished chord, the augmented chord was used primarily in music composed during the Romantic period and beyond. Figure 6-9 shows a C augmented chord and a C augmented seventh chord. A C augmented chord is usually written as C7#5 or C+7. The "+" symbol indicates the presence of a sharp five. Usually, augmented seventh chords are used to spice up V chords.

FIGURE 6-9: C augmented and C augmented seventh chords

Italian Sixth, French Sixth, and German Sixth Chords

From the baroque to the romantic periods, augmented sixth chords were commonly used as predominant chords (Predominant means any chord that precedes a V). Three common variants arose: the Italian sixth, the French sixth, and the German sixth. These are chromatically altered chords rooted on the ♭6 of the key (e.g. A♭ in the key of C major). The Italian sixth (It +⁶) derives from a iv⁶ chord, which is a minor triad build on the fourth scale degree in first inversion. For example, a iv⁶ chord in the key of C major is spelled: A♭ – C – F.

However, unlike its parent chord, the Italian sixth chord contains a ♯4. The ♯4 is perhaps the most defining element in this chord since it means that the root of the iv⁶ chord—in C major the note F—is thwarted altogether. Instead, the root replaced with a leading tone (F♯ in the key of C major). This leading tone then resolves neatly on the root of the V chord (e.g., F♯ to G). All totaled, the Italian sixth chord in the key of C major would then contain the notes: A♭, C (usually doubled because of its stability), and F♯.

French sixth (Fr +⁶) and German sixth (Gr +⁶) chords are both derived from the Italian sixth chord. The French sixth simply adds a fourth pitch: the second scale degree of the key (e.g., D in the key of C major). This means that, in C major, the notes for a French sixth would be: A♭, C, D, and F♯. Like the French sixth, the German sixth contains the same notes as an

Italian sixth but with an added fourth pitch. In this case, the German sixth adds a ♭3 (e.g., E♭ in the key of C major). Therefore, in C major, the German sixth chord would contain the notes: A♭, C, E♭, and F♯.

Secondary Dominant Chords

Secondary dominant chords are "V of __" Chords. When using Roman numerals secondary dominants are spelled out using slashes. For example, a V/V tells you to play the major chord that is five scale degrees above the dominant chord. In the key of C major, this means D major and G major, respectively. D is a perfect fifth above G.

Secondary dominant chords do not work well when paired with the seventh or leading tone scale degree. This is because the seventh scale degree forms a diminished triad, which is highly unstable. The secondary dominant should also never be associated with a I or tonic chord since the V of I is a *primary* dominant chord.

Secondary dominant chords are not limited to V chords. Figure 6-10 shows all of the secondary dominant chords you may use to enliven your chord progressions. In addition to V/V, you will see V/ii, V/iii, V/IV, and V/vi chords. In order to allow these chords to flow smoothly from one to the next, inversions have been used.

FIGURE 6-10: Secondary dominant chords

Inversions allow each chord to flow easily into the next.

Secondary dominants are interesting passageways between two diatonic triads. This is illustrated in Figure 6-11. Here, a V/ii spices up a simple I-ii-V7-I chord progression.

FIGURE 6-11: Secondary dominant chord progression

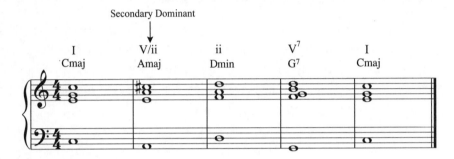

Borrowed Chords

Borrowed chords employ chords from the parallel key. For example, if you're in C major, the parallel minor key is C minor. This is not to be confused with the term "relative minor." Relative keys refer to keys that share the same sharps and flats in their key signatures. For example, F major and D minor are relative keys *not* parallel keys.

Borrowed chords can add excitement to any chord progression. Unlike some of the other chords discussed in this chapter, borrowed chords don't merely enhance a chord. In other words, they are not harmonic extensions or alterations like sevenths or sharp fives, etc. Instead, borrowed chords bend the ear in another direction entirely. When they are used, the music shifts gears altogether, taking the listener in an unanticipated harmonic direction. You might think of borrowed chords as musical portals into another key center.

Flat VI and flat VII chords are wonderful examples of borrowed chords. Figure 6-12 shows an approach to C major (I chord) using both the flat VI and the flat VII. In this example, diatonic VI and VII chords from C minor are used.

Figure 6-13 shows two minor iv borrowed chord progressions. Again, the minor iv comes from the parallel key not the relative key. In this instance, the two keys used are C major and C minor.

FIGURE 6-12: Borrowed chords

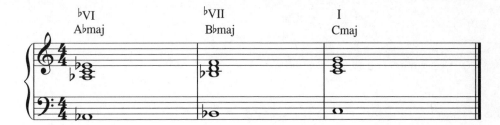

FIGURE 6-13: Minor iv borrowed chords

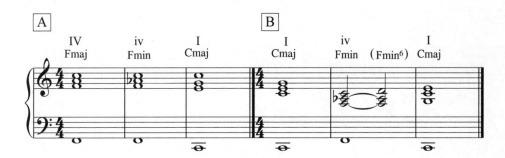

Experiment with your own progressions using borrowed chords. Make sure the borrowed chords act as an unexpected musical deviation. Then resolve it to the original key. If you don't return to diatonic chords, your music will simply wander without direction.

Chord Extensions

Although chordal extensions have been referenced earlier in the chapter, it's time to take a formal look at this musical element. A chord or harmonic extension refers to any scale degree added *above* the fifth scale degree of a triad. Adding a major sixth interval on top of a major or minor triad will create a four-note chord. These extended chords, known as major sixths or minor sixths, are shown in Figure 6-14.

Another common extension features a major seventh and minor seventh on top of major and minor triads, respectively. You may also use a minor

FIGURE 6-14: Major and minor sixth chords

FIGURE 6-15: Major, minor, and minor-major seventh chords

FIGURE 6-16: Major and minor ninth chords

FIGURE 6-17: Sharp eleven chord

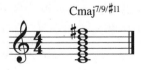

third together with a major seventh. The resulting major seventh, minor seventh, and minor-major seventh chords are illustrated in Figure 6-15. (Keep in mind that the dominant seventh, introduced earlier in the chapter, is a special kind of harmonic extension.)

Next, stack ninths on top of major and minor seventh chords. This creates major and minor ninth chords as seen in Figure 6-16.

You can also add sharp elevens on top of *major* chords. The sharp eleven implies the Lydian mode (See Chapter 15). This extension is shown in Figure 6-17.

FIGURE 6-18: Major six-nine chord

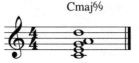

FIGURE 6-19: Spicing up a V chord

When considering extensions, many additional harmonic combinations and possibilities exist. Figure 6-18 shows one common example where a major sixth and a major ninth are used to spice up a I chord.

Several options exist for spicing up V chords. For example, you can create a chord with the following extensions: seventh, ninth, thirteenth. You may also use a seventh, a sharp nine, and a flatted thirteenth. These chords are notated in Figure 6-19.

Bear in mind that most of the chords shown in this section appear in root position. In real life, they *all* may be inverted. Moreover, select chord tones might be omitted (e.g., perfect fifths or major sevenths in a major ninth chord, etc.).

Suspended Chords

Suspensions add subtle tension and release to a musical passage. Suspensions usually last only a beat or two. When they do resolve, the resolution is more pronounced and noticeable given the "suspense" that preceded it.

There are two types of suspensions. They are:

1. Suspended seconds (sus2)
2. Suspended fourths (sus4)

This means that, in place of a major or minor third, a chord will contain the second scale degree or the fourth scale degree. In all cases, the chord will appear to "suspend" or freeze in time before it resolves to the tonic or major third.

Impressionistic pieces, modern jazz, and other contemporary settings sometimes use unresolved suspensions. Instead, the suspended chords seem to float in parallel motion over the music. This lack of resolution purposely obscures the key center. For now, you should focus on suspensions that resolve.

Figure 6-20 shows a variety of suspended second and fourth chords in C major. All of these examples resolve neatly and simply. The first example moves from a suspended second (D) to a major third (E). The second example moves from a suspended second (D) to the tonic (C). The third scale degree is not even used in this example. The next example moves from a suspended fourth (F) to a major third (E) and the last example incorporates both a suspended second (D) and a suspended fourth (F). In this case, the chord eventually resolves to a major third (E).

FIGURE 6-20: Suspended chords

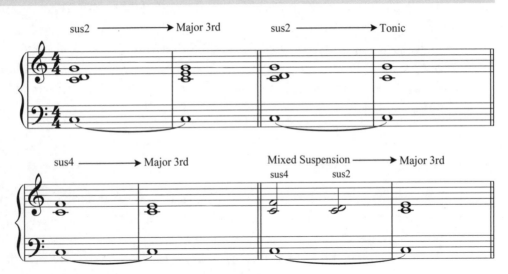

Alternate Roots

Alternate roots or bass notes can make chords, and indeed, compositions more adventurous. Like suspensions, alternate bass notes may sound unexpected to the listener. Because of this, they can add drama to a chord progression. Alternate roots are upper *chord tones* placed on the bottom of a chord. For example, an alternate bass note example might include Fmaj7 with a C in the bass. When using chord symbols, this appears as *slash chords*. This notation occurs frequently in jazz and popular music notation. With slash chords, the letter name written *after* the slash denotes the bass note. For instance, the chord Fmaj7/C means that the "C" is played in the bass.

With a four-note chord, you have three possible alternate bass notes. With a three-note chord, you have two possible bass notes, etc. Figure 6-21 shows alternate bass notes for an Fmaj7 chord. In the first measure, the chord is shown in root position. In the second measure, the third is indicated in the bass. In the third measure, the fifth is written in the bass. In the fourth measure, the seventh is notated in the bass. This concept can be applied to virtually *any* chord type.

FIGURE 6-21: Alternate bass notes

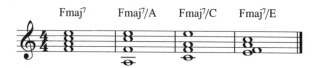

Cadences as Resolution

A cadence is a series of chords that signal the end of a phrase, and usually, the conclusion of a piece of music. Some cadences are obvious to listeners as they begin and end on I chords. However, music doesn't always fit this mold and cadence types can vary. In tonal music, cadences are necessary since they bring needed resolution. Without cadences, chords will simply hang in the air and there will be no musical closure.

Listeners crave resolution and finality. Cadences provide this. In Figures 6-22 and 6-23, you will find a myriad of cadences. There are four standard cadences notated in Figure 6-22. They are: authentic, half, plagal, and deceptive.

The authentic and plagal cadences are the most common cadences in western music, followed by the deceptive cadence, which is also quite universal. The authentic cadence is a simple chordal movement from V to I. The half cadence is a cadence that never resolves to a I chord. Instead, it hangs on a V chord indefinitely. Another type of half cadence is the Phrygian cadence. However, this cadence is not included here since it applies mostly to antiquated music.

FIGURE 6-22: Standard cadences

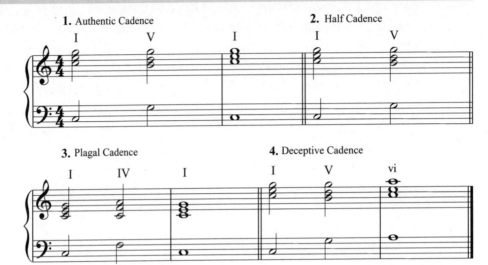

You may also add sevenths to the V chords in these cadences.

The plagal cadence moves from IV to I. This cadence is also known as the "Amen" cadence since it is used to sing amen in churches. The deceptive cadence is similar to the authentic cadence. However, instead of resolving on a I chord, it deceives the ear, and lands on a minor vi.

Figure 6-23 shows some examples of other more contemporary practical cadences. In most cases, these cadences do not have official names. Nonetheless, they are found in many styles of music.

The first cadence found in Figure 6-23 is a standard diminished cadence. Since the diminished vii° chord functions much the same way as a V^7 chord, you can use it as a chordal substitution when playing an authentic cadence. The Neapolitan major and minor cadences are more or less out-of-date. Yet, Neapolitan chords have an interesting color.

Cadences #4 and #5 from Figure 6-23 use borrowed chords to add a distinct harmonic twist to the plagal cadence and cadence #6 employs a suspended fourth (the note "F") in the top voice (beats three and four) of measure one. Lastly, the chord progressions illustrated in #7 and #8 of Figure 6-23 use slash chords (alternate bass notes). See how you can apply all of the above-mentioned cadences to pieces or songs you may be writing. If you use them wisely, your music will not only be well grounded, it will be filled with great color variety.

FIGURE 6-23: Other practical cadences

TRACK 4

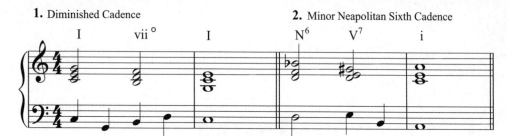

1. Diminished Cadence

2. Minor Neapolitan Sixth Cadence

3. Major Neapolitan Sixth Cadence

4. Minor iv Cadence

5. Minor iv and ♭VII Cadence

6. Suspended Fourth Cadence

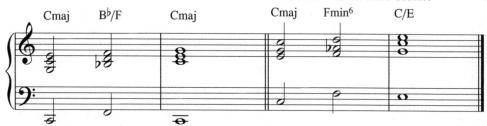

7. Slash Chord Cadence *

8. Another Slash Chord Cadence *

Note: This figure is written for the piano. It does *not* conform to the rules of four-part writing (see Chapter 13).

*Slash chords are used in popular music.

Chapter 7

Basic Melodic Construction

This chapter focuses solely on melody, and as such, does not contain chords or polyphony, etc. First, you will learn how to build melodies through simple intervallic leaps. Next, you will learn how to imply chords through arpeggios or broken chords. After this, you will experiment with accidentals and chromatic movement. Lastly, you will discover how to develop motives and phrases. Plus, you will explore techniques for varying melodies and learn what imitative counterpoint means. These melodic concepts can be applied when writing for all pitched instruments. For basic information on pitch see Chapter 5.

Using Seconds, Thirds, and Larger Jumps

A melody cannot exist without intervallic movement. In other words, you would never write one note over and over to create a melody. Melodies are like hikers trekking up hills and down into valleys, and good melodies usually span the staff. Sometimes they even move up and down into ledger line territory.

As a general rule, melodies should soar and climb over chords and they should never sound random or improvised. But where do you begin? First, take a look at melody from a simple intervallic perspective. Figure 7-1 shows a four-bar melodic snippet that uses only major and minor second intervals.

FIGURE 7-1: Melodic construction using major and minor seconds

To make your music more colorful, you can also use major and minor third jumps. This is shown in Figure 7-2. Notice that, in two instances, seconds are still used.

FIGURE 7-2: Melodic construction with major and minor thirds

Figure 7-3 adds perfect fourths to the mix. The perfect fourths give the music more lift in measure three.

FIGURE 7-3: Adding perfect fourths to your melody

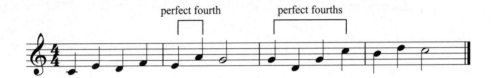

Now try working with perfect fifths. These are very consonant or stable intervals. Therefore, you will not want to use too many of them in a row, as good melodies contain a mix of consonance and dissonance. A simple melody containing perfect fifths is illustrated in Figure 7-4.

FIGURE 7-4: Adding perfect fifths to your melody

Next, add sixths and sevenths into the fold. These larger jumps are used sparingly on instruments such as trumpet, French horn, and the human voice in music at fast tempos. Additionally, the major seventh jump can be jarring to the ear. Therefore, it should be used for effect. Figure 7-5 shows a melody containing sixths and sevenths.

FIGURE 7-5: Adding major sixths and major sevenths to your melody

In Figures 7-1 through 7-6, the melody begins and ends on "C." Since the key signature is C major, "C" becomes a logical beginning and end point. However, once you add harmony, you needn't bookend your music this literally. While harmonic detours are desirable, you must still give the listener a sense of the *key* as your composition unfolds.

Lastly, add perfect octaves to a melody. These are extremely consonant. However, this big intervallic jump (up eight steps) can add excitement to any piece, without the jarring effects of the major seventh jump. One famous example of an octave jump occurs during the opening lines of "Somewhere Over the Rainbow." Figure 7-6 illustrates a melodic fragment with octave jumps.

FIGURE 7-6: Using octave jumps

In contemporary settings, no interval is *better* than another. It all comes down to personal preference, musical context, and harmonic restrictions (see Chapter 8). When writing simple melodies, such as the ones shown above, you should sing the notes. By vocalizing the melody, you will develop good relative pitch. You will also likely develop preferences for certain note pairings. This is good. In other words, this is a sign that you're establishing compositional sensibility (and sensitivity). Preferences are okay!

Arpeggios

Arpeggios are critical when developing both melodies and accompanying melodies. However, a melody rarely consists entirely of arpeggios. Instead, good melodies mix arpeggios and scale tones.

What is an arpeggio? An arpeggio is a *broken chord*. This means that the notes of a chord are separated and staggered one after another in succession. For example, a C major triad consists of the notes C, E, and G. Rather than writing all three of these notes on the same beat you can write them in rhythmical succession. This is shown in Figure 7-7. Here, the arpeggio begins on middle C (C4) and moves up the octave (to C5) then back down again to middle C.

FIGURE 7-7: C major arpeggio

In Chapter 6, you learned about a wide variety of chords. Now it's time to turn them into arpeggios. In addition to major arpeggios, you can build minor ones too. You may also build diminished and augmented arpeggios as well as arpeggios with extensions such as sevenths, ninths, elevenths, etc. Figure 7-8 shows minor, diminished, diminished seventh, half diminished, augmented, and augmented seventh arpeggios.

Figure 7-9 shows arpeggios with harmonic extensions. These include major and minor sixths, a dominant seven, a major and minor seven, a minor-major seven, a major and minor nine, a flat nine, a sharp nine – flat six combo, and a sharp eleven. In jazz, the flat six is often called a flat thirteen even though, technically speaking, the interval presented here is a flat six.

FIGURE 7-8: Minor, diminished, diminished seventh, half diminished, augmented, and augmented seventh arpeggios

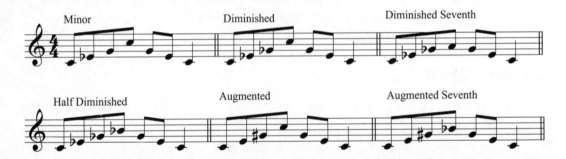

All of the arpeggios in Figures 7-8 and Figures 7-9 are notated in root position. However, inversions may be arpeggiated as well. Additionally, you can arpeggiate chords with suspensions and alternate roots. Literally, *any* chord can be turned into an arpeggio.

FIGURE 7-9: Arpeggios with harmonic extensions

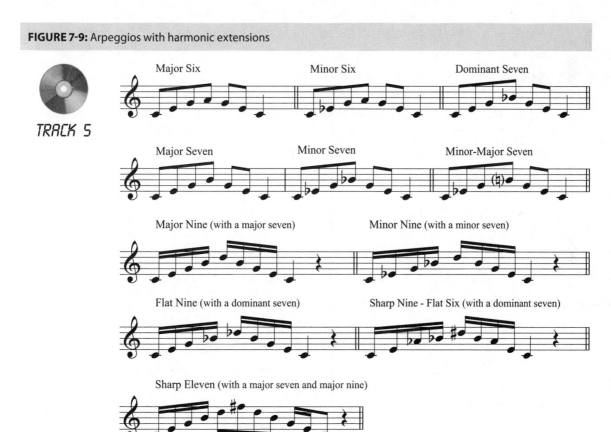

TRACK 5

Sharp and flat nines are almost always paired up with dominant seventh chords (V^7.)
Sharp nines also sound best with a flat six or flat thirteenth.

You will want to use arpeggios, or a segment of an arpeggio, to build melodies over specific, corresponding chords. Again, arpeggios rarely comprise entire melodies. However, they are often found along side scale tones in melodic construction.

Adding Accidentals and Chromatics

An accidental is any note *not* found in the key signature and corresponding major or minor scale. For example, if you write music in the key of C major, an accidental will include any note that has a sharp or flat next to it. In other keys, notes that contain a natural symbol may indicate an accidental. If you compose in the key of D major, for example, F-natural and C-natural become accidentals since this key naturally contains F♯ and C♯.

Accidentals are sometimes the result of harmonic twists from secondary dominant chords or borrowed chords. They also may derive from *blue notes*. Blue notes are minor thirds, flat fives, and minor sevenths played over dominant seventh chords (see Chapter 15).

Additionally, accidentals may derive from harmonic extensions (e.g., sharp nine or flat thirteen) or by pairing up certain modes with specific chords (e.g., a Lydian flourish over a I chord). Figure 7-10 shows a secondary dominant harmonic movement. This causes an accidental (F♯) in the melody. Notice that the melody uses arpeggios to outline the chords.

FIGURE 7-10: Accidental derived from a secondary dominant chord

Figure 7-11 shows accidentals created by blue notes. In this figure, you will see minor thirds sliding into major thirds. You will also encounter a minor seventh (outlining a dominant seventh chord) and a flatted five. The latter—G♭—is an especially dissonant accidental since it creates a tri-tone (in relation to the root of the chord).

Accidentals may also be used as passing tones in music. When you use accidentals in this way, *chromaticism* often results. Chromatic movement is ascent or descent in half steps (semitones). On the piano, this means playing every adjacent white and black note as you move up or down the keyboard.

FIGURE 7-11: Accidentals derived from using blue notes

Figure 7-12 illustrates chromatics by sliding between the pitches of a major chord (a root, major third, and perfect fifth). In this case, the chord is a C major triad. Notice how the chromatic line ascends then descends. The chord tones are accented to make them stand out. Chromatics often connect chord tones and they are most often used in conjunction with other scales.

FIGURE 7-12: Accidentals derived from chromatics

There are numerous accidentals in this example. Remember, in the key of C major, *all* sharped and flatted notes are considered accidentals.

Developing Motives

A *motive* (also called *motif)* is a melodic fragment that is memorable and ear catching. It is sometimes referred to as a *theme,* especially if it's several measures or phrases long and used as the basis for melodic variation (see Chapter 10).

A motive stands in contrast to a *figure*, which is a repeated pattern used to accompany. Motives, quite simply, give the ear something to latch onto. For this reason alone, they are vital elements in any composition.

Arguably the most famous motive in music is the opening four measures of Beethoven's Symphony No. 5 in C minor. Beethoven's motive contains a short-short-short-long rhythm between G and E (a minor third). It is then transposed down a whole step to F and D, respectively. This dark motive— often called the *fate motif*—is then used to build musical content for the entire first movement.

While motives are usually melodic in nature, they often rely on rhythm to bring themselves center stage. Such is the case with Beethoven's fate motif. As mentioned above, Beethoven's short-short-short-long rhythm (three eighth notes and a half note) is just as memorable as the pitches themselves. Ultimately, it is the *combination* of rhythm and melody that really brings this motive to life. If you listen to the first movement, Beethoven allows his motive to travel throughout the instruments of the orchestra with great ease. It is the pliable nature of his motive together with his use of repetition and reoccurrence (with subtle variation) that makes this symphony so powerful.

Motives comprise the heart or essence of a piece. Motives are often presented plainly at first then altered or varied in order to tell a vibrant musical story. Good motives have distinct melodic and rhythmical components. Moreover, they are harmonically flexible, elastic, and adaptable.

Figure 7-13 shows a motive with three options for developing it. The first two variations use only diatonic alterations (no accidentals). The third example employs a chromatic scale, which makes the motive busier and more ornate. In each case, the length of the motive remains intact. In other words, like the original, the motivic variations are all one measure long (ending on beat four).

FIGURE 7-13: Motivic example with variations

Creating Phrases

If you wish to compose expressive and lyrical tonal works you must learn how to use motives to build phrases. The most common phrase lengths are two and four measures but this is by no means an ironclad rule when writing phrases. In this chapter, you will explore two-bar phrasing. Again, harmony will not be applied here. Instead, you will focus all of your attention on single melodic lines.

Figure 7-14 shows a pair of two-measure phrases. In this case, a slur marking demarcates each phrase. Notice how the phrases *end*. In this example, the phrases end on beat four. Phrase endings *must* contain a musical breath or pause. Without this breath, the ear cannot detect phrasing and your music will sound like a mishmash of run-on sentences.

In Figure 7-15, a *faulty* phrase has been created. Here, the melodic line ends unexpectedly and quite haphazardly. This poorly composed phrase is

FIGURE 7-14: A pair of two measure phrases

Together these musical phrases form a musical *sentence*.

included in this chapter to show you what to avoid. Unlike Figure 7-15, proper phrases should contain a beginning (usually a chord tone) followed by a middle section (ascending or descending notes) and an ending that offers a musical *breath*. In Figure 7-15, the end of the phrase has been thwarted or left hanging.

Rhythm plays a critical role when beginning and ending phrases. As a novice composer, you should avoid beginning and ending phrases on "e's" and "ah's" as denoted by sixteenth notes. Instead, begin and end your phrase on a downbeat.

If you're brand new at composing, begin each phrase on beat one and end each phrase on beat four (like Figure 7-14). You may also begin each phrase on beat four and end each phrase on beat three. In this case, beat four acts as a *pickup* beat. Another common pickup can be written on the *and* (+) of beat four.

FIGURE 7-15: A faulty pair of phrases with no resolution

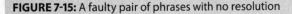

TRACK 8

Here, the phrase is left dangling.

Beginners should avoid ending or beginning a phrase on beat two, as this is an unstable beat and therefore an unsteady point of departure. Also, unless you're composing the final phrase of a song, avoid ending phrases on beat one. If you do this, your next phrase will begin on beat two, which again, you will want to avoid. If you do find yourself in this predicament, you may use rests so that your next phrase begins on a strong beat. However, you should first to learn how to create phrases without breaks or rests in the music.

Repetition and Near Repetition

When composing virtually any style of music, repetition and near repetition become important elements. Listeners expect repetition. Without it, your music will likely sound unorganized, ill conceived, and even confusing. There *are* examples of music that does not use any repetition, near repetition, or repeats. However, you do not want to emulate these exceptions—at least not in the beginning.

Repetition does not mean that you need to simply reiterate motives and phrases exactly as they were previously heard (although this is not wrong to do). You may wish to slightly alter or modify the melodic content but still retain the basic contour of the melody. Or you may wish to introduce your motive, develop it, and then return to it. Such is the case with the recapitulation section in *sonata form*. The recap brings symmetry and balance to the music by reintroducing the thematic (motivic) material found earlier in the composition. See Chapter 19 for a full definition and description of sonata form.

On a much simpler level, you can get a lot of mileage out of a musical idea simply by using repetition and near repetition in the phrase itself. The bottom line: *Don't impatiently move on to new ideas without first fully exploring your current motive or theme.*

Exact repetition is pretty self-explanatory but near repetition means that there is a slight difference each time a motive appears in the music. Figure 7-16 shows three different "near repetition" approaches when repeating a basic motivic phrase in B minor. Notice how the melody does not change

FIGURE 7-16: Phrase with near repetition options

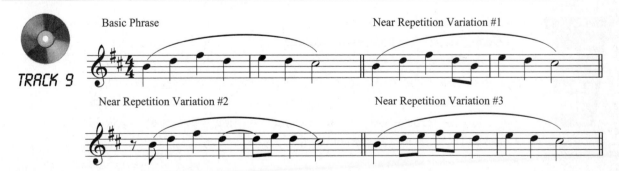

dramatically. Instead, subtle intervallic and rhythmical variances add color and heterogeneity to a single two-bar phrase. Space is left in the figure for you to write two of your own near repetition variations.

Other Ways to Vary a Melody

There are some tried and true methods for varying a melody, which have been handed down through time. Much of this comes from the practice of *imitative counterpoint*. In its simplest form, counterpoint is the use of two or more complementary melodic lines. These lines or "voices" are played simultaneously and they may imitate one another since they share the same motivic material (Think: Row, row, row your boat). Such is the case with rounds, canons, and the granddaddy of them all: the fugue.

The fugue is a highly sophisticated composition that uses complex imitative counterpoint and several independent voices. In this form, the primary thematic material is called the *subject*. When multiple subjects are employed, a double, triple, or quadruple fugue is formed.

Structurally, a fugue is designed around the *subject* (theme), an *answer* (restated theme in a different voice part), with *episodes* (connecting passages), and *further entries*. With each successive entry, the composer develops and varies the initial subject(s), often by introducing countersubject(s). The result is a "subject and answer" musical dialog. New entries typically cycle through keys using the circle of fifths. Fugues then close with a *coda*, which reverts back to the original key. J.S. Bach is best known for his fugal masterpieces especially The Well Tempered Clavier (Books 1 and 2) and late uncompleted work, The Art of Fugue.

A canon is a contrapuntal composition that begins with a single melody called a *leader*. After a specified duration of time, an imitative voice(s) enters called a *follower*. Follower voices may appear altered or varied in more advanced canons. The simplest form of a canon is a *round*. In a round, the voices enter on separate beats or measures (i.e., staggered) but the melody remains unvaried.

Contrapuntal voices are connected harmonically. However, they maintain melodic independence. Sometimes lines move in parallel motion (up and down together). However, composers generally prefer to write voices moving in contrary motion (away from one another). This means that one line will ascend while another descends. During the Renaissance and baroque periods, five devices evolved to vary a melody or line. When set against the primary theme or motive, all of these variances encourage contrary motion and line independence. These devices are:

1. Melodic inversion
2. Retrograde
3. Retrograde inversion
4. Augmentation
5. Diminution

With *melodic inversion*, the melody is turned upside down. For example, if the original melody jumps up a major third, in the inversion, it will now jump down a major third. If it raises a perfect fifth, it will now drop a perfect fifth, etc. Often, however, the contour of the melody is simply flipped upside down but the diatonic quality is maintained (see Figure 7-17).

FIGURE 7-17: Using melodic inversion, retrograde, retrograde inversion, augmentation, and diminution

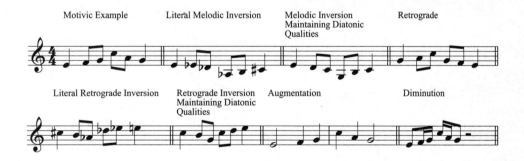

When the motive is played backward it's called *retrograde*. For example, if you have the notes C, E, A, D, a retrograde treatment would mean that

the notes appear as D, A, E, C. In counterpoint, retrograde is typically used in the imitative voice (often the second voice that enters in a round). *Retrograde inversion* means that the melodic line is turned backward and upside down. It's really a combination of retrograde and melodic inversion.

Augmentation means that the melody is stretched out rhythmically. In other words, the rhythms—not the tempo—are slowed down or lengthened in some way. For example, you might have quarter notes shifting to half notes or eighth notes shifting to quarter notes. You may also use ties to expand the duration of each note.

Diminution is the reverse of augmentation. Here, the notes are sped up. Typically, quarter notes become eighth notes, eighth notes becomes sixteenth notes, etc. In all cases, you must first introduce the melody plainly or unadorned then build variations from this. The ultimate goal with melodic variation in any form—round, canon, fugue, or modern usage—is to show juxtaposition, development, and contrast. Figure 7-17 shows the original motive used in Figure 7-13. However, now it is varied using melodic inversion, retrograde, retrograde inversion, augmentation, and diminution, respectively.

Chapter 8

Combining Melody, Harmony, and Rhythm

Previously, melody, harmony, and rhythm have been discussed independently. Now, you will get the opportunity to coalesce your knowledge and see how these musical elements are both distinct yet interrelated. Accordingly, you will explore melodic construction using chord tones, diatonic passing tones, harmonic extensions, and chromatics. This chapter will also delve into modulation and end with general pointers designed to keep you productive.

Using Chord Tones

When writing tonal music, your primary concern should be the marriage of melody and harmony. Rhythm's job is to assist in this union by delineating phrases, framing motifs and themes, and creating a sense of activity. Rhythm also contributes to the overall mood of the piece (see Chapter 9).

If you're a beginner composer, the easiest way to create cohesion between melody and harmony is to build a melody from notes found in the harmony. To do this, use *chord tones.* For example, the chord tones in a C7 chord are C, E, G, and B♭. Professional composers almost never write a melody consisting of *only* chord tones. However, they use them often, especially at the end of phrases when the melodic "journey" comes to a logical pause.

Chord tones are similar to arpeggios. However, an arpeggio is a fixed sequence of notes played one after the other, either ascending or descending. In other words, the notes of an arpeggio are played in an uninterrupted, contiguous manner. For example, a C7 arpeggio would be played: C, E, G, B♭, C (ascending) and C, B♭, G, E, C (descending). See Figure 8-1, example "A."

Unless you're composing monophonic or atonal music, you must *always* think about how melody and harmony are interconnected. On every beat of your music, you should be able to hear the harmonic link between the melody and the harmony. You may compose the chords first, the melody first, or you may work on both simultaneously.

When using chord tones, you should not restrict yourself to a pure arpeggiated ordering of notes. For instance, if you were to write a melody based on a C7 chord, you might write: G, G, E, B♭, C, G, E, G, C (see Figure 8-1, example "B"). You may also omit one or more of these five chord tones. There is no rule that says you must incorporate every chord tone into your melody.

FIGURE 8-1: Arpeggios versus chord tones

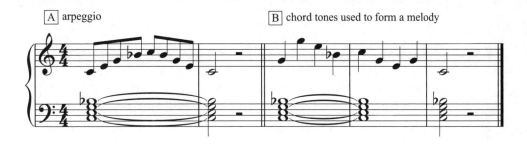

To be absolutely clear: When composing with chord tones, you do not need to move systematically up or down the staff like arpeggios. If an arpeggio feels right, use it—see measure four of Figure 8-2—but don't focus on them. Instead, feel free to change direction at any time and even employ octave jumps. This will add more excitement to your melody.

As an exercise, use the harmonic progression in Figure 8-2 to write a melody(s) consisting only of chord tones. Use only half notes, quarter notes, and/or eighth notes on your initial attempt(s). After some practice, you may use more advanced rhythms. One possible realization is shown in Figure 8-2.

FIGURE 8-2: Using chord tones to create a melody

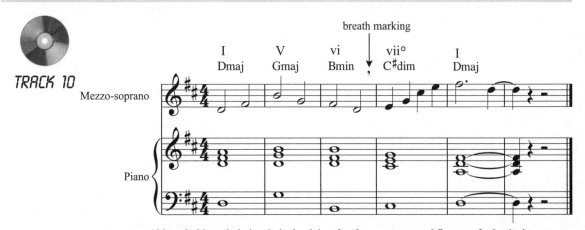

Although this melody is relatively plain, *chord tones* are a good first step for beginning composers.

If this exercise goes well, try writing your own chord progression. If you do this, use only diatonic chords. Later, you can branch out harmonically.

Non-Chord Tones and Scalar Melodies

Once you learn how to manipulate chord tones, you may expand your horizons by implementing diatonic non-chord tones and scalar melodies. Non-chord tones act as *passing tones* in music. They add variety and color to your melody by allowing you to use "stepwise" movement (i.e., approached by step and left by step in the same direction.)

As mentioned earlier, effective melodies must go on a "journey." They must travel over a harmonic terrain and communicate something unique and captivating to the listener. Chord tones alone rarely make this journey eventful. However, non-chord tones help to make your melody more lyrical and flowing.

Think of non-chord tones as musical bridges. Simply put, non-chord tones connect chord tones. As passing tones, they should usually occur on weak beats or offbeats. In 4/4, this means beats two and four. Offbeats are also used for passing tones when employing eighth and sixteenth notes. Figure 8-3 shows a musical example that includes non-chord tones. Notice that this figure uses the harmony from Figure 8-2. After you've analyzed the given melody, write your own melody with non-chord tones.

Melodies that are overtly scalar are also meaningful, though you should use scalar melodies sensibly. If you're not careful, scalar melodies can sound more like exercises rather than music. This is because, in major keys, scalar melodies move in whole and half steps only. (Slightly larger intervals occur with some other modalities.)

When composing a melody, intervallic leaps larger than half and whole steps are needed to make the melody more eventful, exciting and expressive. Despite this, scalar melodies can be rewarding, especially in small doses. For instance, fast scalar lines create intense musical momentum.

Figure 8-4 shows an example of a scalar melody based on a D major scale. In this figure, chord tones appear on downbeats (counted numbers 1, 2, 3, and 4) while non-chord tones appear on upbeats (ands). Larger

FIGURE 8-3: Using non-chord tones

TRACK 11

The notes in parentheses are non-chord tones.

FIGURE 8-4: Scalar melody

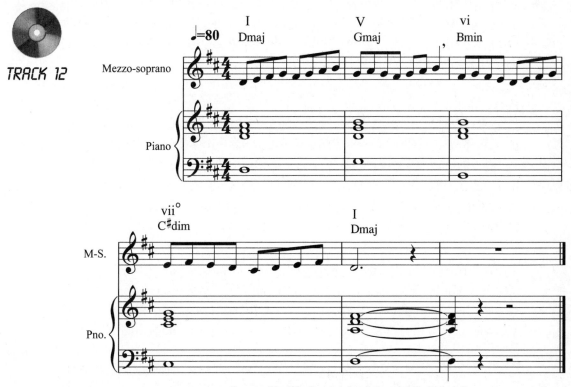

TRACK 12

Can you identify the non-chord tones in this melody?

intervallic jumps occur between beats four and one of each measure (excepting the first measure). This allows the strong beats to remain on chord tones. It also avoids the monotony of using whole and half steps exclusively. Again, the chord progression from Figure 8-2 is implemented here. As before, review the given melody, then compose your own scalar passage.

Harmonic Extensions in the Melody

Sometimes a melody note is not found in the underlying chords and it isn't a passing tone. If this is the case, it's probably a harmonic extension. Don't be fooled; these pitches are still part of the harmony even though they are not played by the harmony instrument(s). For example, a C7 chord (C, E, G, B♭) with a D♭ in the melody becomes a slightly different chord. Specifically, it becomes a C7 flat-9 chord. The chord or accompaniment instrument(s) needn't play the extension, but if it appears in the melody it must be considered part of the harmonic content. Moreover, harmonic extensions may occur on strong or weak beats.

E-QUESTION

Can a harmonic extension also be a chord tone?
Absolutely. If the accompanying instrument(s) doubles the extension being played or sung in the melody, it may be called a chord tone. If the note merely floats above the chordal accompaniment it is not a chord tone, simply an extension.

The bottom line: Tonal composers use harmonic extensions regularly. In other words, professional music is not limited, by any means, to chordal triads and passing tones. Sometimes, the extended note appears *only* in the melody line. If this is the case, it cannot technically be called a chord tone.

FIGURE 8-5: Examples of harmonic extensions in the melody line

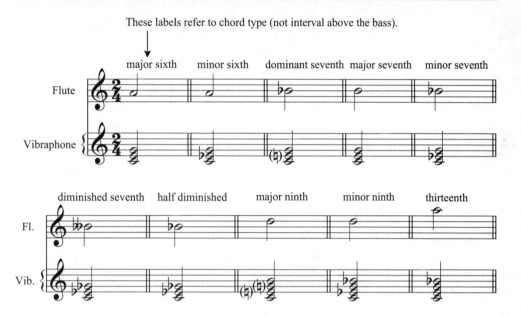

In each of these examples, the extension occurs only in the melody line (flute).
The B-double flat shown in measure six is enharmonically the same as A natural.

Figure 8-5 shows a myriad of harmonic extensions written in the melody line but not in the accompaniment.

Alone, the harmonic extensions seen in Figure 8-5 don't tell the full story. In order to understand their purpose, study a musical example that features an actual chord progression. This is illustrated in Figure 8-6.

In Figure 8-6, the melody line uses chord tones, passing tones, and extensions. Analyze each measure and determine where each of these three elements appears. After this, create your own melody that incorporates chord tones, passing tones, and extensions.

Remember, without harmonic extensions, your work may sound plain, so get used to using them in both the melody and harmony parts.

FIGURE 8-6: Progression using harmonic extensions, chord tones, and passing tones

ASSIGNMENT ——→ 1. Label harmonic extensions, chord tones, and passing tones *under* the melody line.
2. Write in the chord symbols for each measure *above* the melody.

TRACK 13

After you've analyzed this example, check your work with Figure 8-7. The Roman numerals purposely do not reflect the extended harmonies produced by the melody line.

If you don't know how to pair up extensions with specific chords types, see Chapter 6. Overall, extensions add depth and color to your work often by invoking the concept of *tension and release*. As you will learn in Chapter 10, tension and release is a critical component in the telling of a musical story. Once you've analyzed Figure 8-6 see Figure 8-7 to check your work.

FIGURE 8-7: Analysis of Figure 8-6

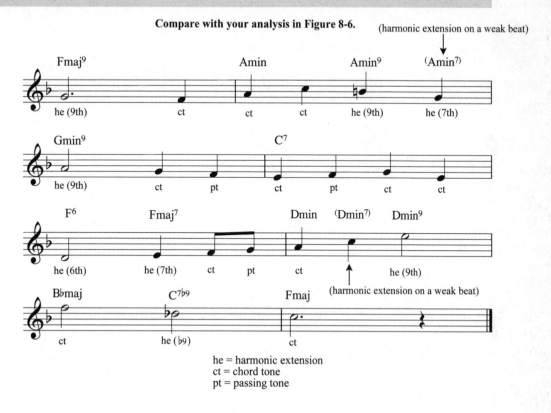

Compare with your analysis in Figure 8-6.

he = harmonic extension
ct = chord tone
pt = passing tone

Applying Chromatics

Harmonic extensions often require the use of accidentals in music. However, accidentals occur through other means too, namely through chromatic passing tones. You will hear chromaticism, sometimes reflected in the use of passing tones, employed more extensively from about 1820 onward. In fact, one telltale sign of romantic period music is a shift toward chromaticism. For example, the middle sequence of young Frederic Chopin's

FIGURE 8-8: Progression using chromatic passing tones

FIGURE 8-9: Atonal use of chromatics

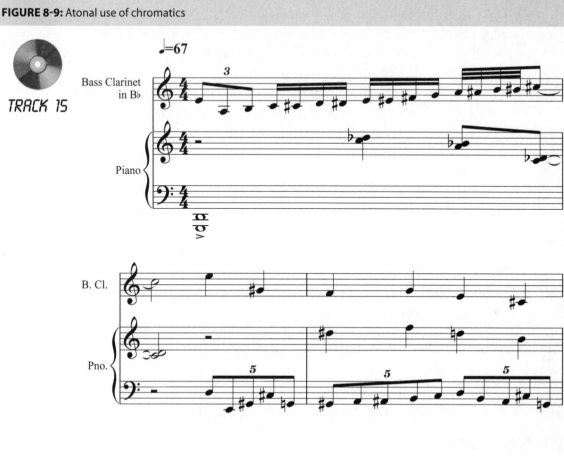

Etude No. 3 in E Major, Opus 10, composed in 1832, features chromatic dissonance that falls like a torrent. Nevertheless, you should avoid excessive, cascading chromatics if you're a beginning composer. If not used properly, they can clutter and even obscure your work.

Start by using occasional chromatics as passing tones on offbeats or weak beats. This often means implementing them on "ands," "e's," and "ah's"; see Chapter 4. You may use chromatics in an ascending or descending fashion, but for now, keep chord tones and other diatonic pitches on strong beats.

Figure 8-8 shows an elegant, jazzy musical example that features chromatics. Remember, like other passing tones, chromatics ultimately serve as a bridge between more consonant, stable pitches. They are a vital element in most contemporary composition, whether it's tonal or atonal music.

Figure 8-9 shows a brief passage that features chromatics in an atonal setting. The severe dissonance found in atonal styles encourages the use of snaky chromatic musings and you will hear them implemented by dozens of twentieth and twenty-first century composers.

How to Create Meaningful Chord Progressions

So far, you have focused on developing melodies over a chord progression. But where do these progressions come from and how do you go about creating them? These are not easy questions to answer and whole books could be dedicated to this subject. For now, simplify the process so that you get started on the right foot. In the beginning, you should make sure that what you write is rooted in the theoretical "laws" of music. Sometimes novices attempt to do too much too soon. As a result, their music sounds disorganized or chaotic. It's best to start with "easy" music then gradually advance from there.

In this context, what does easy mean? Easy means to use *only* diatonic chords. These are the chords that naturally occur in the key signature. At first, use only diatonic triads. Add sevenths, other extensions, suspensions, etc. once you become comfortable manipulating diatonic chord types. Most of all, don't meddle with borrowed chords or "outside" harmonies until you're adept with diatonic chordal movement.

Diatonic chords of the major scale were delineated in Chapter 6. In natural minor, they are: i, ii°, III, iv, v, VI, VII, I (see Figure 8-10). When writing in minor keys, however, the v chord is converted to a major V for cadential reasons. (If you review Figures 6-22 and 6-23, you'll notice that when the V chord is invoked it is major.) Also, remember that there are two additional minor key variations. Specifically, the harmonic minor may be used, raising the seventh scale degree to create a diminished triad. Moreover, the melodic minor may be used, raising the sixth and seventh scale degrees (mimicking the parallel major). In this case, the chord built on the sixth scale degree becomes minor.

FIGURE 8-10: Diatonic chords of the natural minor scale

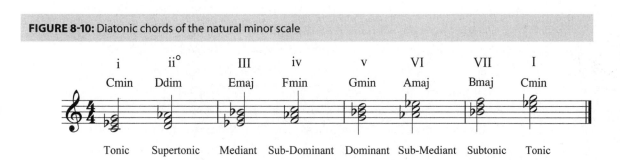

But the million-dollar question is "What order should I put these chords in?" You can know every chord type that exists (see Chapter 6 for many of them). However, if you don't know how to group them together to create a cohesive, listenable, chord progression, you can't call yourself a composer. Therein lies the art of composition! Yes, there are common chord progressions, clichés, and models (see Chapter 11 for some). But ultimately, you must use your own judgment and instinct in order to create meaningful chord progressions. Much of this comes from trial and error and from extensive listening. If you actively listen to music and study scores, in time, you will develop a taste or feel for which chords go together and which don't.

Additional Tips for Writing Chord Progressions

Music is an art form with many exceptions, deviations, and aberrations. Therefore, you must ultimately trust your own musical instincts. As mentioned above, this should be informed by your listening experience. Also, the more scores you analyze the better. It's helpful to *see* what the great masters have written in addition to hearing what they have composed.

When writing chord progressions, remember the following tips:

- You don't necessarily have to start your piece on a I or i chord. You should end your piece on the tonic chord though (I or i). This will ensure that the music "comes home."
- Once you arrive at a V or vii° chord, write a I, i, or vi chord next. By using a vi chord, you invoke a deceptive cadence.
- If you arrive on a IV or iv chord, you may either go to a V chord or back to a I or i chord. By using a I or i chord, you invoke a plagal cadence. Another approach is to drop the bass note down to the second scale degree while maintaining the voicing of the IV chord. When you do this in a major key, you will create a ii minor seventh chord, which is quite beautiful. From here, it's best to move to a V-I or V-vi cadence. Similarly, when you drop the bass note down in a minor key, the iv chord becomes a ii half diminished chord. From here, you may move to the relative major (III chord) or, more predictably, to a i chord.
- Depending on the modality (major or minor), use ii, ii°, iii, and III in the beginning of each new phrase or passage. Remember, once you invoke a dominant (V) chord you're required to resolve it in some fashion (see above.) Also, traditionally speaking, once you play a ii, ii°, iii, III, vi or VI chord, you shouldn't use them again until you've completed the phrase or section with a cadence or resolution. In other words, it would be rare to go ii-iii-ii-iii in a back and forth, parallel manner. It *can* be done but beginners should generally avoid this.

Voicing refers to the way pitches are ordered in a chord. A voicing may omit notes (often fifths) or double others (often octaves). A voicing may also refer to the way in which a chord is spelled out between instruments or singers in an ensemble setting. Bear in mind that harmonic instruments (e.g. piano and guitar) voice chords differently based on the construction of the instrument and the methods and techniques used to play each instrument.

Modulating to a New Key

If you're a beginning composer, you should avoid modulations or key changes. Why? If you don't understand how to modulate, key changes can complicate matters and make your music sound confused and directionless. After you've written a few well-structured pieces in one key, and boned up on music theory, you will be ready to use modulation.

There are many ways to modulate. As a beginner, when modulating use a *pivot chord* to move to the subdominant or dominant key (e.g., C major to G major or C major to F major). When you do this, you are invoking the symmetry of the circle of fifths (see Chapter 5). You may also use a pivot chord to modulate to the relative minor key (e.g., C major to A minor). A pivot is any chord that is shared by both current and upcoming keys (i.e., a common chord) and can be given Roman numeral identification in both keys. Common pivot chords include: ii, iii, IV, and vi.

Be careful when transitioning from one key to another. You cannot use the above-mentioned ii, iii, IV, and vi pivot chords freely. It all depends on where you are and where you're headed! For instance, if you modulate to the dominant key, you would not use a ii chord because it's not a shared chord. Likewise, if you modulate to the subdominant key, you would not use a iii chord because this is not a shared chord. When in doubt, vi chords are always safe bets as pivot points when moving to dominant keys, subdominant keys, or relative minor keys. Figure 8-11

TRACK 16

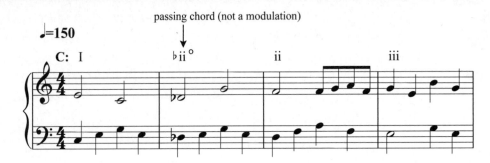

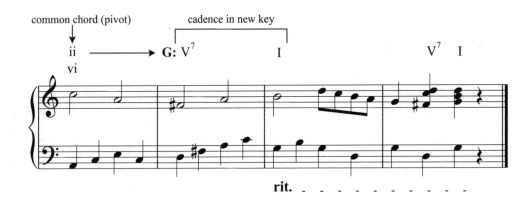

shows a dominant key modulation using a vi chord as a pivot. (It will be a ii chord in G major.)

Another common modulation is to the parallel—not relative—major or minor key. To do this, composers will often cadence—on the V chord. The V chord is a convenient springboard because both major and minor keys use it regularly and you can move from a V chord directly to a minor i chord without any additional set-up. If you're in a minor key, you can also end your piece or passage with a (major) I chord. This unexpected raised third is called a Picardy third or *tierce de Picardie*.

Leave modulations to *remote keys* to the pros. In other words, for now, modulate only to a parallel minor key or to an adjacent key on the circle of fifths. Figure 8-12 illustrates a modulation to a parallel minor key.

FIGURE 8-12: Modulation to a parallel minor key

TRACK 17

In this figure, the chord progression begins in major then mirrors itself in minor.

At the end of the form, or during another logical pause in the music, you may modulate to a new key without any set-up. Though this type of modulation, sometimes referred to as a phrase modulation, is abrupt, it is used in a variety of musical styles. Sometimes these "unprepared modulations" are employed to accommodate technical or range considerations. Other times, they are used to "lift" or energize the piece.

Final Pointers

If you're having a difficult time developing coherent musical statements or integrating melody, harmony, and rhythm try the following, general tips:

1. Sing along with your chord progressions. This will help you to build natural, lyrical melodies. If you sing something you like, write it down before you forget it.

2. If you're still confused about chord progressions after you've worked your way through this book, try using a "chord wheel." This moveable chord diagram gives you a basic sense for when and how to use diatonic chords; see Appendix B for a web link.

3. Meticulousness is critical when voicing chords. See piano voicings in Chapter 12, part writing in Chapter 13, guitar voicings in Chapter 14, and jazz voicings in Chapter 15. First and foremost, do not limit yourself to root position chords. Also, unless you're writing suspended chords, or power chords for the guitar, always make sure the third scale degree is present in your chords, as this ultimately defines the chord type. If you omit any pitch, choose the fifth, except when writing diminished and augmented chords; these chords cannot be properly formed without the diminished fifth or augmented fifth, respectively.

4. Use rhythms that you're comfortable with and ones that will best propel your melodic and harmonic content. Don't needlessly employ complex rhythms just to make your music appear fancy or sophisticated. Some of the most profound music uses a simple, repetitive rhythmical underpinning. Convoluted rhythms do not necessarily equal brilliance in composition.

Chapter 9
Texture and Mood in Music

Instruments and voices produce a variety of musical textures. As you will learn, monophony, polyphony, and homophony create distinct textures. Part of this is due to the layering (or lack of layering) of sound. Mood is defined, to some extent, by the textures and colors you present to the listener. Lastly, rhythms play a key role in determining both the texture and mood of a piece. Be sure to see Chapter 10 for further thoughts on harmony and its role in defining mood.

Understanding Timbre

You will often hear timbre referenced or implied in this book because it's such an essential component to composition. The composer Maurice Ravel was one of the finest orchestrators in history. He was so successful, in part, because he was a magnificent *colorist*. Composers get used to making timbral judgments even when they're not specifically pondering it. In truth, timbral decisions are both conscious and unconscious.

But what is timbre? Pronounced "tam-ber," timbre is the *sound quality or sound color* of a pitch. Timbre does not necessarily have any connection to expression markings such as accents or dynamics, nor does it concern itself specifically with pitch. Also, it's not connected to various techniques (e.g., col legno or fluttertonguing, etc.), although these techniques do produce a wide range of timbral variants. Such is the paradox with timbre.

Timbre is best understood through comparison and contrast. For example, pretend a glockenspiel and a clarinet are to play the exact same half note in succession at the same volume. While the pitches and dynamics are equal, the sensation each instrument produces is different. The glockenspiel has a sharper, metallic tone while the clarinet sounds breathy and woody (see Figure 9-1). This color difference is identified as *timbre*.

An instrument can also produce different timbres. For example, if a violin plucks an open A-string, then bows the same string, the pitch has not been altered. However, the timbre has varied considerably. The plucked note has a short, percussive attack while the bowed note is long and droning. Notes played in different octaves can also produce different

---

FIGURE 9-1: Timbral differences between a glockenspiel and a clarinet

TRACK 18

Listen to the CD to hear the difference in timbre.

timbres. For example, a low note on a flute sounds dark and silky while an upper harmonic sounds shrill and piercing.

Because of timbre, the sounds that come from instruments can be described in a variety of ways. Common descriptions include: dark, light, bright, dull, delicate, brittle, robust, full-bodied, harsh, gentle, coarse, smooth, scratchy, velvety, mellow, abrasive, etc.

Monophony

Monophony (sometimes called *monody)* refers to music with a single melody line, and is the oldest and "simplest" form of composition. The texture created by monophonic music is incisive and singular. It's as if the music has only *one* discernable activity.

In monophonic composition, the ear can easily zero in on phrasing and melodic content. This is because monophony is *all* melody. This usually takes the form of unison singing where the vocalists all sing the exact same part. Some forms of monophony may also feature a melody in perfect octaves but if harmony is present it cannot be called monophonic. True monophony has no underlying chords, no counterpoint, and no competing melodic threads (polyphony).

Despite its relative simplicity, monophony can be very powerful music. In the west, monophony is best epitomized by the liturgical music of the Catholic Church. This monophonic style is still sung today but it reached its zenith during the early middle ages. The broad term for ecclesiastical, monophonic singing is *plainchant* and the most famous version of plainchant is *Gregorian Chant*, named after Pope Gregory I (590–604). Among many others, the Kyrie eleison is a monophonic chant featured in the Ordinary of the Mass.

By the High Middle Ages, monophonic forms of music began to be replaced by multiple, independent voices, and by the early baroque period, homophonic texture began to be used (e.g., composers Giulio Caccini and Jacopo Peri). However, monophony can be effective in modern music, principally if you wish to simulate medieval composition (which *is* becoming popular again).

Monophony has other uses too. For example, unison parts offer great musical clarity for listeners, especially if they are played (or sung) in contrast with musical passages that feature dense harmonies. If you wish to write a simple, unadorned tune or song monophony may also be implemented. As you will learn later in this chapter, unison writing also has its uses in *minimalism*. The bottom line is: Don't categorically discard monophony. Monophony can impress listeners and have a powerful effect on the mood or overall "feeling" of your music. Figure 9-2 shows an example of monophony using tenor and baritone voices.

FIGURE 9-2: Musical example of monophony

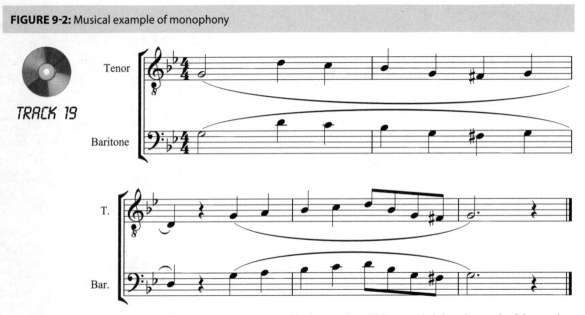

TRACK 19

Exact unisons between the tenor and baritone voices. This example is based around a G harmonic minor scale.

Polyphony

Stated simply, polyphony has four main tenets:

1. Two or more non-unison lines or "voices."
2. Each line shares the same key signature, but otherwise, they remain independent.
3. There is melodic equality between each line. Polyphony does not feature a central melody with accompaniment.

4. Polyphonic lines can but do not necessarily illuminate an underlying or hidden harmonic structure.

Scholars and composers have long argued about the definition of true polyphony, with some experts calling certain polyphonic compositions "disguised homophony." One of the earliest forms of polyphony is called *organum*. Throughout history, polyphony has been a skill that composers have cultivated in varying degrees. Polyphony can range from passages that are very dense to passages that are quite clear. Polyphony becomes even more complex when you consider modern usage, especially the work of György Ligeti whose music is sometimes labeled *micropolyphony*.

Some compositions also fall into the category of *heterophony*. In heterophony, you vary or ornament the *same* melodic line. True polyphonic music features multiple, independent lines.

Polyphony is similar to another term, counterpoint. But historically, the latter suggests a hierarchy of lines, while the former implies pure linear equality. Due to the independence built into polyphonic lines, the rhythms differ too. However, you may see lines mirroring or copying one another in some staggered fashion. Just beware: If your lines resemble one another too closely, you're probably writing heterophony.

FIGURE 9-3: Musical example of two-voice polyphony

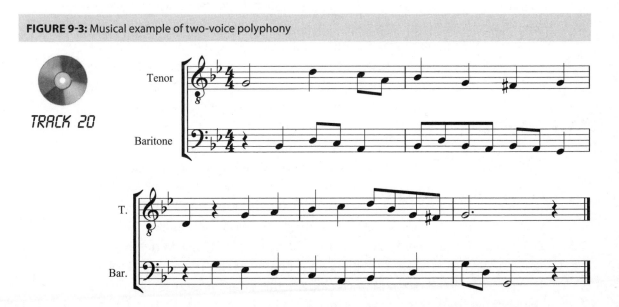

TRACK 20

As a beginning composer, you may find limited use for true polyphony. By default, most contemporary music features a central melody with accompaniment. This is simply the norm in the modern era. However, it's a good idea to experiment with equal, independent voices in your compositions. This will develop a more acute sense of melody. If anything, you will learn how to create more imaginative and complementary modal patterns. It could also be a way to introduce various themes in a novel, creative manner. Figure 9-3 shows a simple example of two-voice polyphony using tenor and baritone voices.

Homophony

Homophony, a single melodic line with noncompeting, supporting accompaniment, has dominated musical output in the West since around the middle of the baroque era. As mentioned above, by default, you will likely compose homophonic music unless you purposely seek out another texture. Homophony is centered on harmonic association rather than independent scalar lines (strict polyphony). The most salient element in homophony is musical "sameness." (The prefix *homo* means *same*.)

Older styles of homophony use strict part writing (see Chapter 13) as developed by J.S. Bach and other baroque period composers. This style—usually four voice compositions—contains rhythms that move together with little or no deviation between the parts. For example, all four voices (soprano, alto, tenor, bass) might contain a dotted half note and a quarter note in measure one followed by three quarter notes and a quarter rest in measure two. Because the rhythms in each part are identical, the music is called *homorhythmic*. Additionally, with homophony, the four voices merge together to create a discernable harmonic progression, which includes the use of cadences.

More contemporary forms of homophony feature chordal accompaniment with a lead voice (or line) soliloquizing overtop. Like earlier styles though, the music still moves in a kind of "lock-step" even if homorhythms are not used. In this case, the melody is almost always found on top. In other words, the highest pitches in the music are reserved for the melody line. Most of the time, voice leading is also employed so that the chords don't inadvertently jump into the range of the melody. With melody-dominated homophony, the role of harmony is simply to support the melody. In this case, harmonies may be colorful but they must never overwhelm the lead voice.

FIGURE 9-4: Melody-dominated homophony

TRACK 21

Melody-dominated homophony is often seen in piano music. For example, listen to Frederic Chopin's Nocturne Op. 9 No. 2 in E♭ Major. In this piece, you will hear low bass notes followed by chords in the middle register and a single melody line on top. This practice is exceedingly common in western music including popular genres. Figure 9-4 illustrates melody-dominated homophony as described above.

Atonality

As discussed in Chapter 2, atonal music does not contain a tonal center or key. However, misconceptions and inaccuracies have long plagued atonal music. First, it's sometimes assumed that atonal music is just a series of random notes. Rarely is this the case. Even with *free atonality*, composers generally develop motifs, even if they are camouflaged by intense dissonance and/or rhythmical complexity.

FACT

Milton Babbitt (b. 1916) is an American composer who developed total serialism based on the concepts and theories of *The Second Viennese School*. His 1947 piece, Three Compositions for Piano, best epitomizes this style of atonality. A mathematician, Babbitt used formal numerical approaches to classify and categorize pitch class sets, rhythms, dynamics, and articulations. After codifying serial theory, Babbitt applied his twelve-tone ideas to electronic music.

Some styles of atonality, in fact, are quite rigid in their use of compositional rules. Often, these rules have mathematical underpinnings, and atonal composers have been known to be preoccupied with symmetry, logic, and even the science of music. This is especially true of the twelve-tone compositional method, which was introduced by Arnold Schoenberg and his followers in the early twentieth century.

In general, this style of composition features the twelve chromatic notes of the keyboard arranged in *sets* or *rows*. These notes are called *pitch classes* and they are usually numbered zero to eleven with "C" commonly designated as zero. Each of the twelve notes found in these sets of note configurations share equal emphasis and importance. This stands in contrast to the hierarchy of notes found in tonal music. For example, in the key of C major, the note "B" is a subordinate leading tone. In other words, in tonal music, functionality creates harmonic ranking of notes derived from key centers. Not so in twelve-tone music because, again, keys do not exist.

Musical ideas are developed quite differently in twelve-tone serialism. In this style, composers first determine a *prime set* of notes. They then go about expounding on this set through transposition, retrograde, inversion, and retrograde inversion. In practice, multiple sets are usually devised and passages of *free atonality* can also be found in much of the repertoire.

Most of all, keep in mind that atonality and tonality don't have to be at loggerheads with one another. Atonality can be the perfect foil to a sugary tonal passage. In reverse, tonality can be the ideal antidote to a passage of mysterious, inexplicable atonality.

Minimalism

Minimalism is a style of music that developed in New York City and San Francisco in the early 1960s. Terry Riley, Steven Reich, Philip Glass, and La Monte Young became its chief architects. Broadly speaking, minimalism is marked by a stripped down, austere use of notes, chords, themes, and variations. In fact, it consciously avoids the harmonic formulas and models of European classical music. Nonetheless, minimalism is largely tonal, eschewing twelve-tone technique and serialism as well as John Cage's chance music.

Although the pioneers of minimalism were not openly influenced by European forerunners, early experiments with minimalism can be heard in Richard Wagner's opera *Das Reingold*, which features an undulating E♭ major chord for 136 measures and Eric Satie's *Vexations,* which is built on a theme and variation with 840 repeats.

Minimalism uses repetitive (often modal) patterns that evolve slowly. However, because change is so gradual, the listener may perceive the music to be largely static. Minimalism is often described as hypnotic or meditative, and rhythm usually plays a role in mesmerizing or lulling the audience. For example, Reich's use of *phasing* allows melodic ostinatos, or short repeating patterns, to move in and out of synchronization with one another making the music feel as though it's slowly peeling apart, or perhaps, echoing around the room.

With the exception of pop music genres, minimalism is the most accepted style of new music to emerge in the twentieth century. Glass's film soundtracks *Kundun, The Hours,* and *No Reservations* likely played a role in this, as did the music of rock icons Brian Eno and Robert Fripp, who drew heavily from Reich's work. As a student of composition, you may find that minimalist experiments provide the opportunity to explore motivic development. You may also find that writing minimalist exercises stimulates your creative mind in ways that traditional composition does not.

Syncopations, Hemiolas, and Polyrhythms

Syncopation is a class of rhythms that stress upbeats (the note that comes just before a downbeat) and offbeats (any note in the measure except the downbeat). In order to be labeled as syncopation, the rhythmical pattern must avoid most, but not all, downbeats. This makes the music feel jagged and even, in some cases, purposely unstable. Figure 9-5 illustrates an example of syncopation.

FIGURE 9-5: Syncopated rhythms

TRACK 22

Syncopation is largely associated with jazz music. However, it can be found often in twentieth century symphonic and chamber music and even in romantic era compositions. For example, Ludwig Van Beethoven's Piano Sonata in A♭ Op. 110 features a passage (in movement three) that stresses sixteenth notes on the "e." Remember, sixteenth notes are counted: 1, e, and, ah, 2, e, and, ah, 3, e, and, ah, etc.

Hemiolas

Centuries ago, the term *hemiola* referred to the pitch ratio 3:2. In modern times, hemiola is synonymous with rhythm. The hemiola rhythm is a kind of "over the bar line" pattern that offsets the usual stress points in a time signature. Specifically, the hemiola is two measures of simple *triple* time phrased to sound like three measures of simple *duple* time. Simple duple time refers to time signatures such as 2/4 or 4/4. Simple triple time refers to meters such as 3/2 or 3/4. In order to create this rhythm, the downbeat in the music is temporarily suspended.

The best way to understand this is through example. Tap out the rhythm in Figure 9-6 and listen to the CD track to hear how this sounds. To really understand this pattern you must hear it in juxtaposition. Therefore, two measures of regularly stressed time are included here too.

You will find hemiola rhythms used in many pieces dating back to the classical era. For example, W. A. Mozart's Piano Sonata No. 12 in F Major K. 332 employs this exact rhythm (in measures sixty-four and sixty-five of movement one). Among others, Johannes Brahms employed this rhythm too. One example is found in the first movement of Symphony No. 3 in the opening string passage after the menacing horn chords.

FIGURE 9-6: Hemiola pattern

Measures three and four are felt like 1 2, 1 2, 1 2 even though the meter is 3/4.

FIGURE 9-7: "America" rhythm

The most famous example of a hemiola—albeit one built on a mixed meter—is the pattern in Leonard Bernstein's "America" from *West Side Story*. In this song, the rhythm moves from 6/8 to 3/4, creating the same effect as Figure 9-6. Bernstein's ostinato is illustrated in Figure 9-7.

Polyrhythms

A polyrhythm is a complex rhythmic weave that can be difficult for musicians to play, so be judicious in your use of this device. A polyrhythm consists of two independent lines superimposed on top of one another. Simultaneous quarter notes and eighth notes, for instance, are *not* polyrhythms because the eighth note is merely a division of the quarter note. In order to create a polyrhythm, you must superimpose two opposing patterns of different beat divisions on top of one another so that an "x against y" rhythm is produced.

FIGURE 9-8: "Two against three" polyrhythm

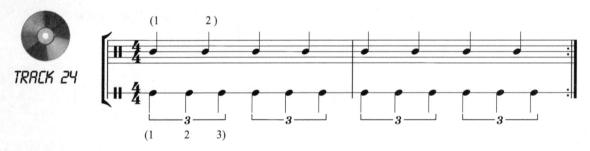

TRACK 24

FIGURE 9-9: Complex polyrhythms

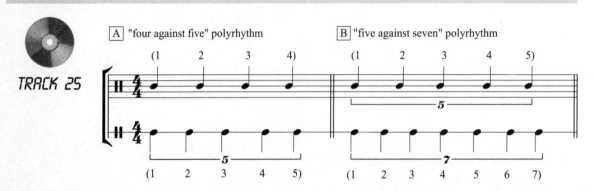

TRACK 25

The simplest example of this is a "two against three" polyrhythm. This is illustrated in Figure 9-8.

Other more complex polyrhythms might include "four against five" and "five against seven." These are shown in Figure 9-9. Many more polyrhythmic options exist. Can you come up with your own?

Polyrhythms are generally associated with modern music, especially the music of Béla Bartók, Igor Stravinsky, Paul Hindemith, and a whole host of jazz composers/performers. However, it is also found in polyphonic music of the Middle Ages (e.g., French secular song). Superimposition may also be applied to meters.

Overall, syncopations, hemiolas, and polyrhythms will alter the texture and mood of your music in unique ways. Experiment with these patterns where you might otherwise fall back on unimaginative, plain, and stable rhythms.

Chapter 10
Telling a Story

In this chapter, you will learn how to tell a musical story. It begins with an explanation of program music versus absolute music. Next, it details how to choose the best instrument(s) and ensembles to bring your story to life. From there, this chapter offers you key information on building themes and variations, creating an expressive musical dialogue between instruments, and how to employ tension and release to add excitement to your compositions. The chapter ends with a musical excerpt designed to show you how to create musical peaks through tension and release.

Program Music Versus Absolute Music

Composing music is a process. Sometimes it is a known, discernable one; other times it is inscrutable and mystifying. One thing is certain; the notes that appear on the page are the visible manifestation of internal decision-making. Sometimes composers find themselves ruminating on a particular subject. For example, Ottorino Respighi's *Pini di Roma* is about pine trees in Rome, and Claude Debussy's *La Mer* is about the sea: likely the English Channel. These famous works are based on specific subject matters and therefore are programmatic.

Any time a specific subject matter (person, place, object, scene, action, or image) drives the compositional process, the composer is writing program music. If the music does not draw from extra-musical sources, it is said to be absolute music; both terms stem from the Romantic period. With absolute music, the composition has no intentional connection to anything else. It makes no external references nor does it contain specific subject matter. Many symphonies that use number categorizations (e.g., Symphony No. 3) tend to be absolute in design though this is not always the case. For instance, Beethoven's Symphony No. 6 contains many programmatic elements despite his claims to the contrary.

Franz Liszt was the first to use the term program music to describe compositions with a "poetical idea." The term is typically, but not exclusively, applied to music of the nineteenth century (e.g., Hector Berlioz symphonies). However, this approach to composition was in use long before the romantic period. As early as 1700, Johann Kuhnau published six Bible sonatas, which are unquestionably programmatic.

Program music is marked by three elements:

1. It uses extra-musical sources as its inspiration.
2. It seeks to illuminate these sources through a musical narrative.
3. The story is told without the use of words or lyrics. Instead, it is woven through sound and silence, harmony, melody, rhythm, counterpoint,

timbre, texture, instrumentation, and the expressiveness of the musicians themselves.

Initially, program music (such as Hector Berlioz's Symphonie Fantastique) included a written preface by the composer detailing the extra-musical sources upon which the music was based. Today, this preface is not always included.

The definition of program music, as elucidated above, is sometimes debated, especially when trying to categorize music throughout history. Two questions often arise:

1. Is imitation synonymous with program music? For example, if a piccolo imitates the chirping of a bird or a bass drum imitates the boom of a cannon, does this indicate the presence of a narrative?
2. If the music is based around a specific character (e.g., Strauss's *Don Quixote)* is it automatically programmatic?

The answer to these questions depends on the work. Analysis from a variety of perspectives must be taken into account when making such distinctions. However, as a composer, you needn't concern yourself too deeply with this matter. Leave these questions to the music historians. Instead, you should focus on telling *your* story. It may be programmatic or absolute but it must take the listener on a journey of some sort and it must engage their imagination on some level.

Choosing the Right Instrument(s)

The first step in telling a story is to determine the right instruments and ensemble size for your composition.

You must revisit the concept of timbre (see Chapter 9) to properly determine what instruments to use. You must also consider range and the limitations of each instrument. For example, a harp is not designed to play fast chromatic passages. It just can't be done on that instrument. Similarly, you wouldn't create a trumpet part that jumps in large intervals from the top to the bottom of that instrument's range. However, these jumps can be performed on a tenor saxophone, for instance, although you'd still want to be judicious in your usage.

Essential Chamber Ensembles

It's highly recommended that you write for just one instrument before you try writing for an ensemble. Your primary instrument is certainly a logical choice. From there, you may "up the ante" and focus on chamber settings. Common chamber ensembles are:

- **Piano and voice** (piano with any voice type; see Chapter 13)
- **Piano trio** (piano, violin, violoncello)
- **String trio** (violin, viola, violoncello)
- **String quartet** (violin I, violin II, viola, violoncello)
- **Piano quartet** (violin, viola, violoncello, piano)
- **Saxophone quartet** (soprano sax, alto sax, tenor sax, baritone sax or double the alto sax)
- **Piano quintet** (violin I, violin II, viola, violoncello, piano *or* piano, violin, viola, violoncello, and double bass—as in the famous Trout Quintet by Franz Schubert)
- **String quintet** (violin I, violin II, viola, violoncello with either an extra viola, violoncello, or a double bass)
- **Brass quintet** (two trumpets or cornets, French horn, trombone, tuba or bass trombone)

These ensembles are shown in Figures 10-1 through 10-9. In each case, very similar measures of music are used to highlight the timbral and textural differences between each group. Note: due to the shift in instrument types and ensemble sizes, it would be impossible to literally transfer each measure exactly, although in some instances (like the melody line) this has been achieved. Listen to the CD to hear the difference between each passage.

FIGURE 10-1: Piano and voice phrase

TRACK 26

FIGURE 10-2: Piano trio phrase

TRACK 27

FIGURE 10-3: String trio phrase

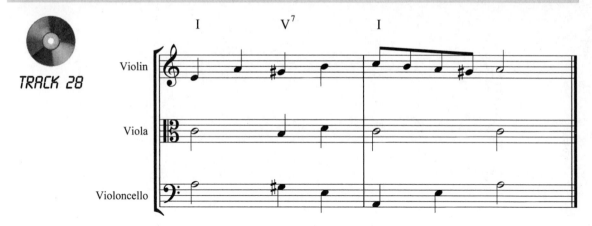

TRACK 28

FIGURE 10-4: String quartet phrase

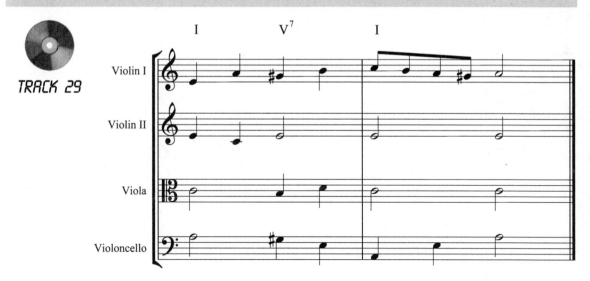

TRACK 29

FIGURE 10-5: Piano quartet phrase

FIGURE 10-5: Piano quartet phrase

TRACK 30

FIGURE 10-6: Saxophone quartet phrase

TRACK 31

FIGURE 10-7: Piano quintet phrase

TRACK 32

This example uses the same instrumentation as Schubert's "The Trout."

FIGURE 10-8: String quintet phrase

TRACK 33

FIGURE 10-9: Brass quintet phrase

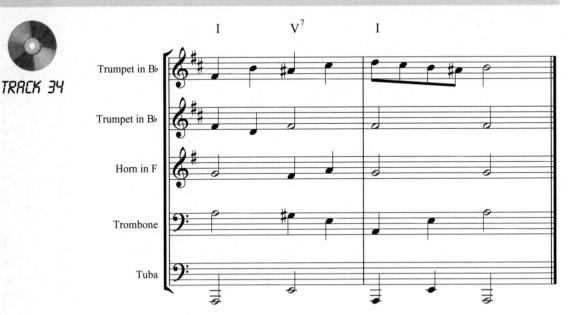

TRACK 34

Theme and Variation

Theme and variation is the hallmark of *most* composition in the West. The two are also inextricably connected. In fact, without the use of variation, a theme is nothing more than a passing melody. The Italian composer and theorist, Gioseffo Zarlino, first introduced theme as a term in his 1558 book *Le istitutioni harmoniche.* By his definition, theme is a repetitious melody that is varied during the course of the piece. Themes may also be called *subjects,* and in the baroque era, these subjects became the basis for fugal composition by J.S. Bach and others.

Lengthy, multimovement works such as symphonies, operas, and most chamber pieces contain numerous themes, counter-themes, and secondary themes. Music with multiple themes is called *polythematic.* Music with a singular theme is called *monothematic.* The latter is generally employed on shorter, less involved works that contain a performance time fewer than ten minutes. Large-scale symphonies, for example, simply cannot be sustained by one theme alone. Atonal music—especially the early compositions of the Second Viennese School—is *athematic*. This means that no discernable themes are employed.

When they were first used, themes were presented at the beginning of a composition. They were also similar if not synonymous with motives (see Chapter 7). Lastly, composers didn't necessarily call attention to their themes. In other words, composers were not necessarily concerned with making their themes stand out as prominent, identifiable features. Instead, themes were seen more as an objective function of the music. This was especially true in the fugue, where themes or motives became simple vehicles for variation.

By the nineteenth century, and the arrival of the romantic period, themes became more recognizable, striking, and dramatic. They were also not necessarily presented in the opening passages of a piece. Instead, they could appear after long introductory sections. Additional themes might also pop up throughout the movement. Moreover, from the romantic period onward, thematic design focused on longer melodies with multiple phrases. Overall, themes became complete musical statements, not merely outstanding melodic snippets (motives). Lastly, by the middle of the nineteenth century, thematic variation also included modulation to remote keys. And by the twentieth century, atonal themes, and bitonality (themes in simultaneously different keys) were created.

Figure 10-10 shows a simple example of a theme and variation. This figure uses only diatonic chords as denoted by Roman numerals. In this case, the theme is fourteen measures long. In a real composition, however, the theme may be considerably longer.

Take the piano melody and harmony in Figure 10-10 and transform it in some way using your own staff paper or score writing software. You may want to use the methods for variation detailed in Chapter 7. This means using one or more of the following:

- Melodic inversion
- Retrograde
- Retrograde inversion
- Augmentation
- Diminution
- Repetition and near repetition

FIGURE 10-10: Theme and variation example

TRACK 35

You may also:

- Modulate to a new key (see Chapter 8)
- Change or add instruments
- Add embellishments or ornaments around the theme (see the scalar patterns used in variation #1)
- Alter the harmony (supporting chords)

Question and Answer

In many styles of music, the concept of question and answer is employed. Also termed "call and response," this technique makes a composition sound conversational. Very often question and answer is used in jazz and blues. For example, blues artists will often use question and answer between voice and an instrument. Usually, they will sing a phrase then answer it on a guitar or piano.

In jazz, it's common for musicians to "trade fours" or "trade eights." This means that one soloist will improvise over four or eight measures, then another soloist will improvise over the next four or eight measures. In this back and forth manner, the soloists continue to "trade" until they've improvised over the entire form. This type of soloing creates an attractive musical dialog between instruments. In general, it's compelling for listeners because question and answer encourages coherence in music. For example, when great jazz musicians "trade" they borrow ideas from one another and the music flows with magnificent balance and congruity.

In classical music, question and answer is also used even though it is not always mentioned in musical analyses. Bach's two part inventions, for example, are based largely on question and answer between the voices. In these etudes, motivic variations (usually transposed an octave apart) engage in a fast paced conversation. This occurs because each line is independent and songlike. In fact, Bach used the musical term *cantabile* to describe his inventions. This translates as "singable."

Bach's playful, linear music is not the only example of question and answer found in classical repertoire. The concept is often used freely in symphonic design, especially between the four—sometimes five if there are keyboards present—families of the contemporary orchestra. (The four families of the orchestra are: strings, brass, woodwinds, and percussion.)

For instance, the brass might play a motive or theme. The composer then transfers this same material to the woodwinds or to the strings, etc. often with some variation. At the least, timbral variation is incorporated by default.

You might also hear a theme played by one instrument family followed by a counter-theme in another instrument family. Or you might hear short back and forth phrases much like the ones illustrated in Figure 10-11. Overall, this kind of conversational writing encourages an articulate musical dialog between the colorful instrument families of the orchestra. This concept may also be applied to any chamber group.

One superb, yet often overlooked, example of musical dialogue is Maurice Ravel's orchestrated version of *Pavane pour une infante défunte*. This piece is built upon one of the most haunting main themes in classical music history. In this piece, the French horn first renders the theme in plaintive, legato phrases. Later, emotional violin swells bring this theme to a dramatic conclusion. When listening to the piece, one can't help feeling a kind of long distance conversation between the French horn and the strings, whose shared themes bookend the piece so powerfully. Ultimately, *Pavane* unfolds as a bleak yet poignant tale of mortality and sorrow. It is a successful work because it tells its story of death so vividly.

The most obvious piece in the classical canon that employs question and answer is *The Unanswered Question* by Charles Ives. This composition features slow and contemplative long tones in the string section. On top of these laconic chords, a solo trumpet asks a musical question seven times. After each question, the woodwinds answer the trumpet with impatient, atonal phrases. In this piece, the musical tableau quickly shifts from pastoral to edgy as the trumpet and woodwinds engage in a tense call and response.

Figure 10-11 shows an example of question and answer as seen between an alto flute and a bassoon. A string quartet maintains the chordal underpinning with whole notes played arco (using a bow).

FIGURE 10-11A: Question and answer example

TRACK 36

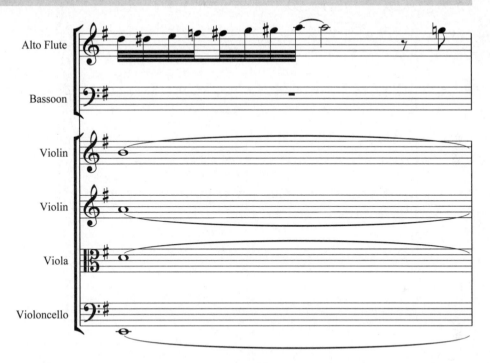

FIGURE 10-11B-: Question and answer example

TRACK 36

Tension and Release

Tension and release is another common technique used in music to weave a tale. Tension and release help to build plotline in music through a series of ups and downs, conflicts and resolutions. It can be achieved through harmony, through rhythm, or through a combination of both. Melody can assist in this, but on its own, it does not invoke tension and release with the same efficacy.

Tension may build over the course of a chord progression. Depending on the piece, tense chordal movements may be long-winded or brief. Release often occurs at cadential points. Therefore, release usually comes in the form of major or minor chords. Tonic (I or i) chords are especially good releasers. They may or may not have extensions added to them; it depends on context, period, and style of music. Extensions (such as major sevenths and ninths) will make the release less resounding but they do not hinder the objective, which is an easing of tension.

E-QUESTION

Must I always use climactic build-ups in my music?
Yes and no. You should employ tension and release, including climaxes *most* of the time and in varying degree. However, it's not absolutely necessary. Certain styles such as serialism, minimalism, ambient music, and liturgical music do not contain strong elements of tension and release. And on occasion, static pieces can be successful too (e.g., Erik Satie's slow and doleful *Trois Gymnopédies*).

Tension comes from dissonance. It could be argued that a V^7 chord provides tension, which is then relieved by a I or vi chord. However, the tension between a $V^7 - I$ or a $V^7 - vi$ cadence is light: to modern ears anyway. Therefore, simple cadences like this might be better described as an anticipation. Greater dissonance is needed to invoke a more potent version of tension and release. In the aforementioned case, you would alter the V^7 chord to make it more pronounced, harmonically unstable, and tense.

Ultimately, tension and release is much more arresting when the tension is built up over the course of many measures. In other words, tension becomes more musically valuable when it climaxes to a veritable breaking point. When you compose music, use tension and release where applicable. It will make your musical story much more expressive, expansive, and memorable.

Chapter 11

Musical Forms

Most music has a predetermined form. Even when music is free of form, it's due to a conscious attempt to avoid musical structure. Therefore, in a sense, form is always a consideration. There are many forms used in western music. You may also create your own musical structures. In this chapter, you will learn about some common forms used throughout history, but bear in mind that still others exist.

Strophic Form

Strophic form is a common structure employed in many styles and eras of music from American folk music to church hymnals to nineteenth century German *lieder*. It is primarily used for music with poetry or lyrics, though rare instrumental varieties do exist. Strophic form is the opposite of *through-composed* music. Through-composed music constantly changes and evolves to complement such text as is found in sixteenth century madrigals. In other words, through-composed music does not use repetition.

In contrast, strophic form uses the same music, or music with only slight variations, to accompany numerous verses or stanzas called *strophes*. This means that the melody and harmony are reiterated throughout the piece with little or no change. In this form, the only element that uses significant alteration is the lyrics themselves. The form therefore is denoted as: A, A, A, etc. If there are slight variations it may be analyzed as A, A^1, A^2, A^3, A^4, etc.

You may be wondering about the significance of all those "A's." When outlining musical form, letters are used to signify each new section of a piece. If a section contains only a slight variation, usually melodically, the letter will have a number attached to it. Since music written in strophic form contains ostensibly only one section, this form is designated with A's exclusively.

Sometimes, strophic music is made complex by the reiteration of vocal phrases inside each verse. When this occurs, the repeated pattern acts as a refrain. Such is the case with late medieval and renaissance *chanson* from France. The music of Guillaume de Machaut is the finest example of this.

Typically, however, strophic form is used in simpler, shorter music. In other words, you generally will not find it employed in lengthy, elaborate works. Instead, it is a great vehicle for straightforward song styling. It is particularly effective when a composer wishes to weave a narrative (often about romance or heartache). If you are writing devotional music that contains prayers or supplications, strophic form may also be a good choice. Historically, hymnal composers have preferred it.

Binary Form

Today, binary form is more or less academic. However, it does have historical significance as the antecedent to sonata form (see Chapter 19). Binary form gradually evolved during the Renaissance and became common during the end of the 1600s. In the baroque era, it was often used for instrumental *suites* especially during dance movements. Dances of the day included the gigue, the bourrée, the minuet, the sarabande, the courante, the allemande, and the hornpipe.

By the late baroque period, composers such as J.S. Bach and George Frideric Handel regularly used binary form, and increasingly, it appeared in chorales and arias. For instance, Bach uses binary form for his Chorale No.38: *Straf mich nicht in deinem Zorn* and Handel used binary form for the memorable tenor aria, "No, no cruel father, no!" from his oratorio *Saul*. During the classical era, binary form was replaced by sonata form but this newer structure culled directly from binary principles. This link is reflected in sonata form's alternate name: compound binary form (see Chapter 19).

A perfect cadence uses V-I in root position with the top voice sounding the tonic in a four-voice I chord. The opposite of this is an *imperfect cadence,* which employs chordal inversions. Historically, perfect cadences are considered to be more stable and decisive but they are not always practical or idiomatic.

As the word indicates, *binary* form has two parts: A and B. This form always includes a modulation to another key followed by a return to the original key. There are a number of binary varieties such as "simple," "rounded," "sectional," "continuous," "symmetrical," "asymmetrical" and "balanced." In the strictest sense, the A and B forms are about the same length (symmetrical) and both contain a repeat at the end of the form. Thus, AABB becomes the literal structure of most binary compositions. When the form is asymmetrical, the B section is usually longer.

With regard to modulation, if the piece is written in major, the B section typically shifts to the dominant key. If the piece is written in minor, this B section will usually modulate to the relative major key. Sometimes the motivic material presented in the A section will appear again toward the end of the B section. This is called rounded binary and an ABA structure is created. If material from the A section does not appear toward the conclusion of B, the piece is written in simple binary.

If a perfect authentic cadence ends the A section, the piece is called sectional binary. In this case, A is commonly referred to as harmonically "closed." If other cadential varieties are used at the end of A, there will likely be a continuation of the material previously established (albeit in a new key). In this case, you have continuous or "open" binary form.

Lastly, with balanced binary, harmonic and melodic material presented at the end of each section mirror one another. This is called "rhyming." This technique brings equilibrium to each section by highlighting the harmonic and thematic relationship between the two parts.

Ternary Form

Ternary form is denoted as ABA. Early versions of this form date back as far as the thirteenth century. However, it has been used primarily as a vehicle for homophonic composition. During the middle and late baroque eras, sharp harmonic, textural, and tempo distinctions were made between A and B sections.

In this period, ternary form was especially popular in vocal idioms (oratorios, cantatas, and operas). Specifically, *da capo arias* were structured around the well-balanced bookends of A reprises, or repetitions. The second A section, however, required the soloist to ad-lib using melodic ornaments. This was done so that the two "A" sections wouldn't be identical. When this improvisatory skill fell out of favor with opera singers and composers, so too did the da capo aria. (The first movement of Bach's cantata *Jauchzet Gott in allen Landen* is a superlative example of this baroque singing style.)

However, ternary form would continue to be used in the minuet and trio, a triple meter—usually 6/8—third movement used in classical symphonies, string quartet music, and sonatas. Employing an ABA form consisting of three parts, the trio or B section initially featured three instrumentalists while the rest of the ensemble rested (tacit). In the symphonies of Mozart and Haydn, this movement harkened back to baroque courtliness. In practical terms, it provided a release from the more complex, dramatic movements that preceded and followed it.

With the emergence of Ludwig Van Beethoven, symphonies would eventually drop the minuet in favor of a similar device, the scherzo. Translated as "joke" or "game," scherzos were generally faster than minuets. However, they retained the trio portion of the movement, and therefore, ternary form continued to be implemented. In some instances, a kind of "double ternary" form (ABABA) was also used.

FACT

Although Beethoven is largely credited with the development of the scherzo movement in symphonic design, Franz Joseph Haydn was the first to use the marking "scherzi" in his music. Specifically, he used it for his Opus 33 set of "Russian" quartets. In some of these quartets, the scherzo movement appears second rather than third. Robert Schumann's second and third symphonies would emulate this ordering.

Twelve-Bar Blues

Every musician and composer should be aware of the blues. It's simply omnipresent in contemporary music. From New York to Moscow, Johannesburg to London, you'll find musicians everywhere using this form. In fact, it's arguably the most widespread and universally recognized form in popular music. Thousands of songs/compositions use this form and more and more are being penned every day.

The blues is a type of strophic form since it only uses a single repetitive "A" section. The blues has a fixed length of twelve measures, which repeats on loop a dozen times or more depending on the composition. The blues also uses a predetermined set of chord changes. These chords may be altered slightly but the main harmonic tenets of the form must always be maintained. These are I, IV, and V chords. These chords make up the "meat and potatoes" of this form; you simply cannot have a blues piece without them. See Figure 12-16 for basic blues form.

The scales most associated with the blues are called, not surprisingly, blues scales. The basic scale is shown in Figure 11-1, while the more advanced version is illustrated in Figure 11-2.

FIGURE 11-1: Basic C blues scale

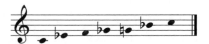

In this key, *blue notes* are E-flat, G-flat, and B-flat. Blue notes are the salient elements of a blues scale.

FIGURE 11-2: Full C blues scale

When composing a blues piece, you should focus on melodic motifs just like any other style of music. Moreover, repetition and near repetition (see Chapter 7) are common in blues melodies. Rhythm is a key element in the blues as well. In fact, there are many blues grooves you will want to research. The three most common types are: the shuffle, the 12/8 ballad, and the "straight eighth" rock beat. For the latter, see Figure 18-10. Figures 11-3 and 11-4 show the rhythmical underpinning (drumbeats) for a shuffle pattern and a 12/8 ballad, respectively. In Figure 11-3, the "x" note head on the top line tells the drummer to play on

FIGURE 11-3: Shuffle rhythm

FIGURE 11-4: 12/8 ballad

the ride cymbal. In Figure 11-4, the "x" note head on top space tells the drummer to play on the hi-hat.

The blues is also a superb vehicle for improvisation. All composers should have some improvisatory skill since improvisation is really "spontaneous composition." Therefore, as an exercise you should:

- Improvise over the blues on your primary instrument using the scales notated in Figures 11-1 and 11-2, *and*
- Compose a melody over a blues chord progression. Again, use the scales illustrated in Figures 11-1 and 11-2.

See Figures 12-16, 15-17, and 15-18 for various blues forms and chordal options. For more about this important form, see *The Everything® Rock and Blues Piano Book*. Moreover, study recordings by prominent artists in this style.

In Chapter 15, you will explore some of the chordal substitutions and embellishments used in jazz blues. However, even in the jazz variety, I, IV, and V chords remain at the core of the form. The same is true of minor blues keys. However, when in minor, chord qualities (not functions) must be adjusted accordingly.

The Great American Songbook

The Great American Songbook is not literally a book, but rather, a style of songwriting that was adopted by many New York and Los Angeles songwriters from about 1925 to 1960. Music written by Tin Pan Alley "song pluggers" and Broadway show composers make up the vast majority of compositions found in this style.

However, songs penned by Hollywood film composers are also found in the songbook. For example, the perennial favorite "Have Yourself a Merry Little Christmas" by Hugh Martin and Ralph Blane was originally composed for the MGM film *Meet Me in St. Louis*.

Music from The Great American Songbook is often referred to as "standards." Prominent composers include Irving Berlin, George Gershwin, Hoagy Charmichael, Duke Ellington, Jerome Kern, Cole Porter, Richard Rodgers, and Johnny Mercer. (This list is by no means exhaustive.) Songs from the Great American Songbook have also had a profound effect on popular culture and many of the most famous tunes have been recorded and interpreted by a multiplicity of artists of varied backgrounds: from pop to jazz, country to symphonic. Instrumental and vocal jazz is especially preoccupied with The Great American Songbook. Additionally, crossover artists such as Michael Buble, Tony Bennett, and Diana Krall—among many others—have dedicated their careers to keeping this historic music alive.

The Great American Songbook is built on a thirty-two bar form. This structure contains four sections of eight bars each organized in an AABA format better known as a *chorus*.

Additionally, many songs from the "songbook" also contain an introductory verse, usually sung rubato. However, the verse is often omitted in jazz performance and in less formal contexts. Within the chorus, the B section is typically referred to as the *bridge* or *middle eight* and it usually features a brief harmonic detour of some kind (e.g., a modulation).

Almost always, standards are notated using lead sheets. Lead sheets feature chord symbols, a melody, and a lyric. They do not literally spell out what the chordal instrument(s) will play as accompaniment. It's up to pianists or guitarists to voice chords in a way that's idiomatic to their instruments and to the style of song being performed. However, any additional orchestrations, such as string or brass parts, would be written out literally (i.e., note for note) exactly like classical score writing.

Virtually any chord progression is fair game in this style as long as it contains cadences or resolutions and it doesn't wander too far from the home key. On your first attempt you may want to use a preponderance of ii-V-I changes (see Chapter 15). This chord progression is employed over and over again in the Great American Songbook. Nevertheless, it would be a gross oversimplification to imply that these songs *only* use ii-V-I variations. Whatever chords you choose, again, make sure you don't stray too far from your key center. If you're not careful, you could write a series of ii-V-I's that merely wander through various keys and lead to nowhere meaningful.

Pick up a copy of the *Real Book* (see Appendix B) or another *fake book* to see examples of real standards.

Form in Modern Rock

There are many song forms used in modern rock. However, each song is a combination of the basic elements detailed below. Keep in mind that you will not find all of these elements in every single song. For example, some songs have introductions while others don't. The elements of modern rock are:

- Introduction
- Verses
- Pre-choruses
- Choruses
- Re-introduction(s)
- Bridge or Middle eight
- Solo section(s)
- Outro or Coda

There are four additional types of songs that may not use the elements bulleted above. These songs are:

- Built on a riff or single motif
- Ever evolving and building with no repeated sections (through-composed)
- Stories (usually spoken word) set to music
- Structured around older forms such as the twelve-bar blues

Again, it would be rare to find a song that uses *all* of these elements.

An introduction is a short musical prologue or opening passage. Verses tell the story of the song. In most cases, the first verse begins when the lyrics enter. Pre-choruses are optional. They are usually a harmonic variation on the verse designed to make the song build seamlessly into the chorus. The chorus almost always contains the hook, which is a "catchy" melodic fragment designed to "hook" the listener in. Without a doubt, the chorus is the most important song element in modern rock.

When the chorus is sung, you will often hear the song title. If there is a re-introduction, it will be used to loop you back to the beginning of the song. You can bet that after a re-introduction another verse will follow.

A bridge is a sudden shift in the song's mood. Bridges often connect a chorus to a third verse or a chorus to another more dramatic chorus. Key changes are common in bridges but they are not required. A middle eight is a type of bridge that contains eight measures; this is the only section in modern rock structure that culls directly from The Great American Songbook.

ALERT!

The word "chorus" is used differently in contemporary pop and rock. In these genres, a chorus is the main section of the song where the hook is commonly found. In older traditions, such as blues and jazz, a chorus refers to a complete song form such as a twelve-bar blues or a thirty-two-bar (AABA) bebop or show tune.

Solo sections sometimes act as bridges too. In this case, they give instrumentalists a chance to show off their wares. Solo sections can occur over introduction, verse, or chorus chord progressions. They also may occur over completely new chord changes. Last but not least, outros or codas are end pieces. Often, they mirror the song's introduction but, on rare occasion, they can also introduce new musical ideas. Such is the case with the famous Celtic inspired violin solo on the coda of The Who's "Baba O'Riley."

Chapter 12

Writing for the Piano

Many composers use the piano as their compositional tool, even when writing for other instruments (winds, voice, mallet percussion, etc.). Of course, you don't have to use piano to write, but if there's one instrument you should know how to play, at least a little, it's the piano. You'd be hard pressed to find a credible composer—or musician for that matter—who wouldn't agree with this sentiment. This chapter outlines the most salient elements of the piano together with some suggestions on how to write piano music in a variety of styles.

The Versatile Piano

The piano is notated on the *grand staff*. This is made up of the G or treble clef and the F or bass clef. Due to its octave range, the piano is widely considered to be "a symphony at your fingertips."

The piano is featured in virtually all styles of music: from rock-n-roll to jazz, Latin to contemporary pop. In the classical tradition, the piano is the centerpiece of hundreds of concertos and sonatas and it has produced dozens of icons including Franz Liszt, Frederic Chopin, Sergei Rachmaninoff, Vladimir Horowitz, Arthur Rubinstein, Józef Hofmann, and Glenn Gould, among others.

Italian harpsichord tuner, Bartolomeo Cristofori invented the piano around 1700 while in the employ of Grand Prince Ferdinando de' Medici in Florence. His early models culled from clavichord and harpsichord design but there was one fundamental innovation: this new instrument used *hammers*. Clavichords employed tangents or metal tips to strike the strings (without rebound) and harpsichords used quills to pluck the strings.

Cristofori's piano hammers were made from soft leather and coiled paper. Moreover, after they hit the strings they bounced back. This rebound allowed for a fast sequence of notes to be played and "hammer-action" also made dynamics possible. Dynamic expression on keyboards, prior to the piano, was crude or nonexistent. Because you could play loud and soft, Cristofori's invention was dubbed a *pianoforte*. Remember, "piano" means soft and "forte" means loud.

Around 1732, German piano maker, Gottfried Silbermann, added a sustain pedal to Cristofori's prototype and J.S. Bach began composing for the instrument toward the end of his life. By the 1760s, the pianoforte became less alien to musicians and a growing number of composers, including Haydn and Mozart, began featuring this instrument in their work. The modern piano, as we know it, became standardized around the late nineteenth century due in large part to Steinway & Sons piano manufacturers.

Keyboard Layout

The piano keyboard is laid out in a structured fashion with notes repeating themselves every twelve keys. When a key is pressed, a hammer strikes a series of strings (one, two, or three strings depending on the note's position on the piano) and a pitch sounds. The pitches move from low to high, left to right. In other words, when you sit at the piano, the lowest pitch will be to your left and the highest pitch will be to your right. If you're sitting at your piano now, strike the highest and lowest keys. You will hear a distinct difference between them. Modern pianos and most professional digital pianos contain eighty-eight keys.

The keys on a piano are white and black and they each have letter names. The white keys are: A, B, C, D, E, F, and G. Collectively, these notes are called "naturals." After G, the lettering begins again with A. This A to G sequence occurs seven full times on an eighty-eight keyed piano. After these seven octaves, three additional notes remain. They are A, B, and C.

It's important to note that each key on the keyboard has been assigned a numerical name. These numbers correspond to the placement of the note on the piano. The numbering system begins with zero. The first or lowest note on the keyboard is A0. The top note is C8 since it is the eighth C to appear on the keyboard (see Figure 12-1). The twenty-fourth note up from the bottom, when counting only white keys, is middle C. This is called C4 since it is the fourth C on the keyboard (traveling up the keyboard from left to right). This numerical method of determining octaves can also applied to other instruments (e.g., violin, marimba, flute, etc.).

FIGURE 12-1: The range of the piano on the grand staff

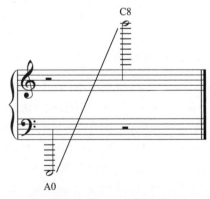

The modern piano has 52 white keys and
36 black keys. This equals 88 keys in total.

Visualizing the Keyboard

Keyboard layout can be visualized in two distinct groups or clusters. The first group consists of C, C♯ (also called D♭), D, D♯ (also called E♭), and E. Visually, this layout contains three white keys and two black keys: five keys total. This configuration appears on an eighty-eight keyed piano seven full times. It is shown in Figure 12-2.

The next group of notes includes F, F♯ (also called G♭), G, G♯ (also called A♭), A, A♯ (also called B♭), and B: seven keys total. Like the previous note group, this configuration appears on an eighty-eight keyboard seven full times. This is illustrated in Figure 12-3.

When you put these two groups together you have twelve keys total. That's five plus seven. If you include one more note on the top—a C—the cycle will be complete. That same C also signals the beginning of a new cycle. A full note cycle from C to C is indicated in Figure 12-4. This cycle is called an octave.

FIGURE 12-2: C – E keyboard layout

FIGURE 12-3: F – B keyboard layout

FIGURE 12-4: C – C keyboard layout

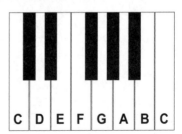

FIGURE 12-5: Fingering chart

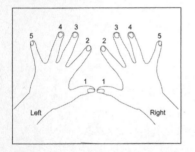

Fingering Considerations

When writing for piano, you do not need to indicate fingering unless you're composing music for children, amateurs, or beginning method books. However, you should be aware of fingering concerns and even sit at the piano to experience the technical requirements of playing this instrument. How does it work? In both hands, the thumbs are called finger one, the index fingers are called finger two, the middle fingers are called finger three, the ring fingers are called finger four, and the pinky fingers are called finger five. This is illustrated in Figure 12-5.

Each finger has its strengths and weaknesses. Since the thumb is situated on the side of the hand it must cross under the fingers to maneuver up the keyboard. This can be tricky and this movement requires practice. The index and middle fingers are the strongest. The ring fingers are least coordinated, and the pinky fingers are usually the weakest. Sit at the piano and practice the C major scale to get a sense of fingering on the instrument. When playing this scale, the thumbs must cross *under* the other fingers. Moreover, the third fingers and, in the left hand, the fourth finger must cross *over* the other digits to render the scale (see Figure 12-6).

FIGURE 12-6: Fingering for a C major scale

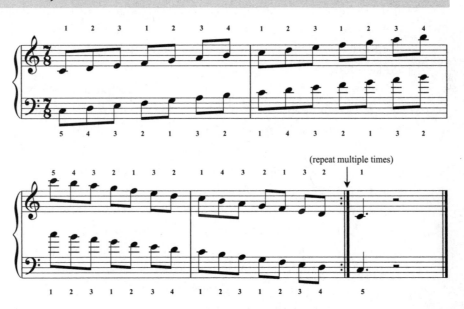

Fingering is shown here for two octaves.

Piano Pedaling

Grand and baby grand pianos contain three pedals. They are called the sustain, sostenuto, and the una corda pedals. The sostenuto pedal allows notes in the bass register to sustain while the middle and upper registers remain

FIGURE 12-7: Piano pedals

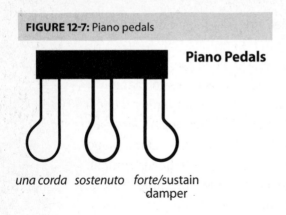

Piano Pedals

una corda   *sostenuto*   *forte/sustain damper*

untouched. The una corda pedal shifts the hammers on the piano so that they strike only one or two of the strings rather than all three. The result is a muffled or softer sound.

The sustain pedal—also called the loud pedal, the forte pedal, or damper pedal—has the widest applications in music. This pedal creates a full-bodied tone on the piano and it allows pianists to play beautiful, legato phrases. Figure 12-7 shows the three pedals as they appear on the piano. Note: Not all pianos contain a sostenuto pedal.

When you press down on the sustain pedal, the dampening mechanism lifts so that the strings can vibrate freely. Because of this, the pianist must be deft at coordinating his keyboard playing with his pedaling. Simply put, if your pedal markings are sloppy, your music will sound sloppy. As a composer, you must write specific, well-conceived pedaling or suffer the consequences.

Pedaling on the sustain pedal comes down to three words: before, with, or after. Sometimes, you will want to anticipate your pedaling. This means that the pianist will press the pedal down before he strikes the keys. Other times, you will want to press the pedal down as you strike the keys. Lastly, pianists will sometimes strike the keys then press the pedal down. This is called syncopated pedaling.

How does the pianist know when to use each technique? It all depends on context. Phrasing, rhythm, and harmonic clarity affect these decisions the most. Obviously, the goal is a sharp, articulate interpretation of your work. Consequently, it's important to work with pianists to determine the best pedaling options for your music.

In notation, pedaling is indicated below the bass clef. There are different symbols used to denote sustain. Sometimes, the abbreviation "Ped" is used in conjunction with an oversized asterisk, which tells you to lift up on the pedal. The use of brackets is easier to read and more prevalent today.

There are three bracket options to choose from. Figure 12-8 shows bracketed pedaling varieties as well as the aforementioned asterisk version. The first two examples are the recommended symbols. The first

FIGURE 12-8: Sustain pedal symbols

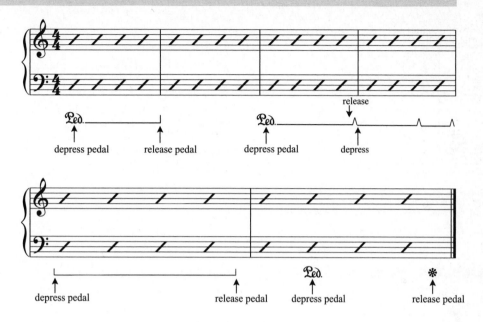

shows you where to release the pedal, as denoted by the end of the bracket. The second is best used when writing lots of limited duration, tricky, or subtle pedaling indications. Here, the up-arrows tell you when to depress and release the pedal.

Basic Chord Voicings

The pianist can play single lines, basic two or three note chords, or dense chords using upwards of eight notes. If a pedal is used—and a pianist plays arpeggios with hand crossing—a dozen or more notes may be included in a chord (see Figure 12-9).

Usually, when playing both melody and harmony, the pianist will play three or four-note chords in the left hand and a melody line in the right. However, the role of each hand may also be reversed (chords in the right hand) or the hands could be integrated, sharing the task of both melody and harmony.

Unlike the guitar, the piano generally features chords with close intervallic relationships including major seconds and even semitones. Chords

FIGURE 12-9: Huge Arpeggiated chord on the piano

The squiggle indicates an arpeggio. All arpeggios are played ascending unless you write a down arrow. You must use "hand crossing" to play this fifteen note chord.

FIGURE 12-10: Voicings for C maj and C min chords in root position

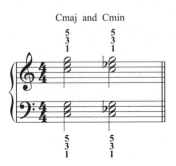

FIGURE 12-11: G⁷ to Cmaj voicings

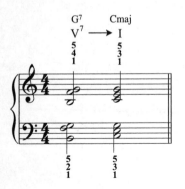

FIGURE 12-12: F maj to C maj voicings

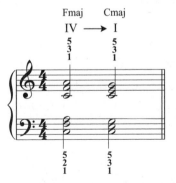

with stacked thirds are very common, especially when playing major and minor chords. In this case, you will see the root, third, and fifth featured in each chord. Figure 12-10 shows voicings for C major and C minor triads. These chords may also be arpeggiated. Notice how fingers one, three, and five are used in both hands.

Another common "shape" on the piano utilizes fingers one, four, and five in the right hand and finger one, two, and five in the left hand. These voicings are commonly used for inverted V^7 chords (dominant sevenths). Figure 12-11 shows you how to voice the movement from G^7

to C major. Notice how the fifth of the chord is left out of the voicing. For instance, in the first example you see the notes B, F, and G (no D). In each case, the third of the chord is always on the bottom (first inversion).

Lastly, IV chords typically use a voicing that features the fifth of the chord on the bottom (second inversion). The most common voice leading for this type of chord employs fingers one, three, and five in the right hand and fingers one, two, and five in the left hand. Remember, IV chords are major when played in *major* keys (see Figure 12-12). For more information on piano chords, including more advanced, hip voicings, see Chapter 15.

Composing Piano Music for Students

Student or amateur level music is especially popular on piano since thousands of kids (and other beginners) take piano lessons every day. As you might imagine, student level music is marked by simplicity. If you're a beginning composer, you may find that writing simpler music allows you to "get your feet wet" without the strain and headaches involved in writing and arranging professional level scores.

This concept doesn't just apply to piano music, but can be applied to *any* instrument. So before you try your hand at composing pro-level music, explore simpler formats first. In time, you can work your way up to more sophisticated material.

When writing beginner level piano music keep in mind the following rules:

- For absolute beginners, always write in the key of C major.
- For absolute beginners, only use 4/4 time.
- For absolute beginners, use whole notes, half notes, and quarter notes together with corresponding rests. For more advanced beginners, you may use dotted half notes, eighth notes, and eighth rests. Generally avoid sixteenth notes and eighth note triplets. Thirty-second notes, quarter note triplets, sextuplets, and especially, polyrhythms are to be avoided.

FIGURE 12-13: Etude for thumbs on middle C position

TRACK 37

This etude is designed for beginners. Make sure middle C is played with the correct hand.

FIGURE 12-14: Etude for C and C octaves position

TRACK 38

This etude is designed for beginners.

- For more advanced—but still beginner level—pianists, avoid keys with four or more sharps and flats. For example, keys like C♯ minor or A♭ major should not be used.
- For absolute beginners, do not use excessive intervallic leaps. Instead, focus on adjacent notes (i.e., no changes in hand position).
- In all beginner music, do not use excessive expression markings.
- Do not write music to be played at allegro or presto tempos.
- For absolute beginners, do not write music that is longer than eight measures.
- When using fixed hand positions, the best positions to use are: "thumbs on middle C position" or "C and C octaves position." "Thumbs on middle C position" means that the thumbs of *both* hands are positioned on middle C. In the right hand, the only notes available to you then become: C, D, E, F, and G. In the left hand, the only notes available to you become C, B, A, G, and F. "C and C octaves position" is used for slightly more advanced beginners. In the left hand, finger number five (pinky) is positioned on C3 (one octave below middle C). In the right hand, finger one (thumb) is positioned on C4: middle C. When in this position, the only notes available to you in the left hand are C, D, E, F and G. In the right hand, the same set of notes is available to you but they are located one octave higher. See Figures 12-13 and 12-14 for examples of "thumbs on middle C position" and "C and C octaves position."

Piano in Popular Music

As mentioned earlier, the piano is used in dozens of styles of music. As a composer, you should learn a little bit about how the piano is implemented in many of these settings. For instance, Latin music often features the piano. In the 1960s, the bossa nova emerged in Brazil. Its most important composer, Antonio Carlos Jobim, combined relaxed samba rhythms with cool jazz. He found the perfect blend in tunes such as "Desafinado" and "One Note Samba," which became hits in the United States.

A common bossa nova pattern uses bass notes played in perfect fifths. Traditionally, an acoustic guitar would "comp" the chords, but in its absence, the piano performs this role.

In salsa music and Afro-Cuban jazz, pianists often play a two or four measure repeating pattern (ostinato) called a *montuno*. Also known as a *guajeo*, the montuno is used as a refrain or vamp in music. Moreover, it usually appears as a syncopated accompaniment. For example, a timbale or conga player may solo freely over a montuno ostinato. Figure 12-15 shows two examples of montunos.

Shifting gears altogether, the piano was an integral part of 1950s rock-n-roll as evidenced by such stars as Little Richard, Jerry Lee Lewis, Fats Domino, and others. Although rock music has changed considerably over the last fifty years, this style of piano playing is still popular today. Centered on the blues, rock-n-roll piano remains an indelible part of the pianistic canon. Figure 12-16 shows an example of a rock-n-roll piano music.

FIGURE 12-15: Montuno patterns

TRACK 39

Notice the use of major and minor tenths in example A.

Lastly, no chapter on piano would be complete without a nod to the contemporary piano ballad. You will hear rock, pop, new age, country, and other types of artists using this "style" of reflective piano composition. Artists include Elton John, Billy Joel, Tori Amos, Joe Jackson, and George Winston. Arguably, George Winston best represents this type of piano music.

Figure 12-17 emulates the feel and mood of the contemporary pop ballad. Overall, think about how you can implement the disparate piano styles presented in this chapter in your work. For more examples of rock and blues piano, see *The Everything® Rock and Blues Piano Book*.

FIGURE 12-16: Rock-n-roll piano pattern

TRACK 40

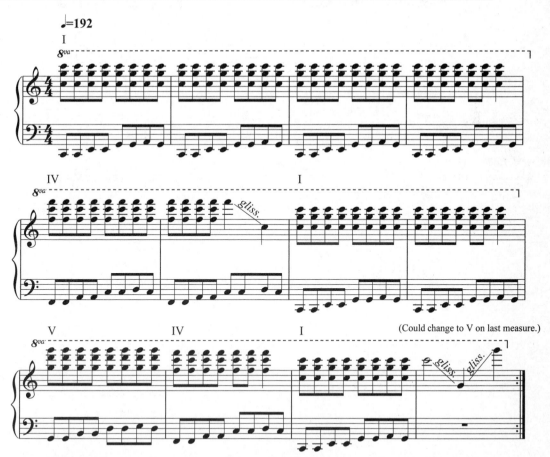

Like many '50's rock-n-roll songs, this example is a twelve-bar blues; the form is delineated by Roman numerals. See Chapter 15 for more about the blues.

FIGURE 12-17: Pop ballad

TRACK 41

Chapter 13
Writing for Singers

In this chapter, you will explore the human voice. A fundamental ingredient in western music, voice has not only been used in so-called classical music but also popular genres, where it has largely dominated. On the following pages, you will learn about vocal classifications, ranges, and registers, and the voice's early role in western music. Furthermore, you will meet the great composers of the operatic tradition and learn about Bach chorales and four-part writing. The latter is a critical skill for *all* composers, arrangers, and orchestrators to possess.

The Human Voice

In music, the human voice is viewed as an instrument, and is considered to be the oldest. It is also responsible for the very development of music. Additionally, the human voice is the most expressive instrument. Instruments manufactured throughout history such as the violin, trombone, and saxophone, were designed to emulate the tone and euphony of the human voice.

Singing is at once a simple act yet a complex physical process involving many anatomical components in the thorax and head regions of the body. This includes the larynx (voice box), vocal folds (vocal chords), the trachea (windpipe), lungs, the tongue, cheeks, palate, and lips. The vocal folds produce sound when air is expelled and they vibrate. Men and women have different sized folds accounting for the difference in pitch range between the two genders. As you might guess, vocal folds in men are larger creating a deeper tone and lower range. The physical appearance (size and shape) of any individual may also contribute to the timbre and range of one's voice. For example, you might notice a significant timbral difference between very tall men and unusually short men.

Professional singers train hard to control the pitch, tone, timbre, and the range of their voice. Voice instruction is often two-fold, concentrating on both the science *and* the art of sound production. Major areas of study include:

- **Breath control** (respiration)
- **Posture** (position of the body, particularly the upper torso)
- **Phonetics** (speech, articulation, elocution)
- **Resonance** (using sympathetic vibrations in the pharynx, collar of the larynx, oral and nasal cavities to enhance tone color and sound quality)
- **Projection** (using the diaphragm muscle, throat, and lungs to sing dynamically; related to breath control)
- **Ear training** (focuses on intonation or pitch accuracy)
- **Music reading skills** (reading and interpreting musical notation)
- **Singing techniques** (legato, vibrato, coloratura, and more; related to singing styles)
- **Singing styles** (opera seria, opera buffa, bel canto, verismo, singspiel, opéra comique and more; related to singing techniques)

Early Uses of Voice

In western history, the voice became the primary instrument of Ancient Greece, Rome, and the Middle Ages. Written vocal music first flourished in the liturgy of the Christian church. Early vocal music called plainsong was originally sung in unison (monophony) without the use of instrumental accompaniment. By the end of the ninth century, a style of chant called *organum* developed. This featured two-voices and polyphonic texture.

Around the eighth century, the most popular version of plainsong became Gregorian chant, a style that dominated Western Europe until roughly the eleventh century. Charlemagne, who is largely credited with uniting Western Europe in the 800s, vigorously promoted this style of chant. Due to Charlemagne's influence as well as the Roman Pope, Gregorian chant ultimately replaced other forms of plainsong such as Ambrosian and Mozarabic chant.

FACT

Around 700, the Holy See officially established a singing organization called the Schola Cantorum. This papal choir was one of the first well-trained singing ensembles. Some contemporary music schools have modeled their institutions after the innovations of the original schola cantorum, including La Schola Cantorum in Paris.

From the Middle Ages into the Renaissance, vocal music remained the primary method of expression for many composers. This included multi-voice polyphonic compositions set to either religious or secular text. The secular madrigal (often with text about love) and the canon became the Renaissance's most durable contributions. Recently, there has also been a revival of British lute song, primarily the music of John Dowland, whose work spans the late Renaissance and early baroque periods.

The Emergence of Opera

Around the end of the 1500s, *opera in musica* emerged in Florence. Jacopo Peri and Giulio Caccini were on the forefront of this new dramatic form that combined music and theatre. The Camerata (Italian for circle) was a group of intellectuals in Florence that included Peri and Caccini. This group was dedicated to the research of ancient Greek theater and the role that music (singing) played in the dramas of Sophocles and Aeschylus. Through their research, they believed that this ancient music had the capacity to stir human emotions and wanted to find a way to transfer that power to the music of their era. It is believed that this resulted in the realization of one of the first operas, Peri's *Dafne*, which was staged in 1597. Unfortunately, however, much of Peri's manuscripts no longer exist.

Claudio Monteverdi's *L'Orfeo* (1607) is one of the earliest operas still performed today. A celebrated composer of his day, the Italian Monteverdi was a great innovator, helping to usher in the baroque era itself. The Renaissance madrigal and Venetian church music were Monteverdi's main influences. Yet, his operas were more than a mere reiteration of older forms. Embracing ornamentation and forging new stylistic models particularly for the voice, Monteverdi's work is seen as nothing short of revolutionary by many scholars.

Yet, Monteverdi's aesthetic was not the only catalyst for change during the seventeenth century. Later in the century, French composers Jean Philippe Rameau and Jean-Baptiste Lully wrote compelling operas as well as Reinhard Keiser and Heinrich Schütz in Germany. And by the end of the century, Henry Purcell, England's first major composer, composed six operas of historical significance.

In the eighteenth century, opera became "all the rage," as two forms burgeoned: *opera seria* (serious opera) and *opera buffa* (comic opera). The librettist Metastasio epitomized the former until Christoph Willibald Gluck brought reform to the Germanic operatic tradition. One sweeping change was the omission of the *da capo aria* (see Chapter 11). Gluck and his predecessors believed that narrative in opera was being stifled and that singers were taking advantage of their prominent position. Moreover, the shape of the da capo aria restricted story-telling and character development. The changes imparted by Gluck allowed for all of the diverse elements of opera to coalesce around a taut narrative. With this precedent, it was Wolfgang Amadeus Mozart who best defined the classical era opera. This is exemplified by his *seria* offering *Idomeneo* and his indelible *buffa* operas *The Marriage of Figaro, Don Giovanni, Così Fan Tutte,* and *The Magic Flute.*

Like Gluck, Mozart's mature operas illuminate the characters on the stage through vivid orchestral colors and deft melodic invention. Mozart referred to the text that was sung by the singers (the *libretto*) as "the obedient daughter of the music." Further, Mozart believed that music could project narrative and characterization whether you heard the words or not.

Beethoven's Fidelio

As a new century dawned, Ludwig Van Beethoven began work on *Fidelio,* his first and only opera (1805). A political statement, it is a story of heroism and torment, *Fidelio*—or rather *Leonore*—as Beethoven preferred it to be called (and as early versions corroborate) marks the middle period for Beethoven who was not only losing his hearing but also living in a period of political unrest in Europe. (When the opera was premiered, Vienna was occupied by 10,000 of Napoleon's troops.) Undergoing many rewrites and even two librettos (German and French versions), *Fidelio* nonetheless proved Beethoven's prowess in the operatic idiom.

Bel Canto, Verdi, and Puccini

Bel Canto (meaning beautiful singing) is a vocal technique that was popular in the Italian operas of the late eighteenth and early nineteenth centuries. In this vocal style, the singer remains at the forefront of the musical presentation. Beautiful singing was understood to mean gorgeous lyrical passages with virtuosic displays of skill and technique. Three operatic composers typify this movement: Gioachino Rossini, Vincenzo Bellini, and Gaetano Donizetti. More than any other, Rossini's *Barber of Seville* is the most enduring work of this period and his baritone aria "Largo al factotum" remains well known even among lay listeners.

By the middle of nineteenth century, Italian opera reached its zenith with Giuseppe Verdi who wrote such masterpieces as *Rigoletto, Il Trovatore,* and *La Traviata.* Only the younger Giacomo Puccini rivals Verdi (in terms of brilliance and popularity) in the romantic Italian operatic tradition. However, until Puccini's rise around the turn of the century, Verdi was unparalleled in Italy. This was due to Verdi's ability to write emotionally charged arias and soaring, heartrending melodies.

Like Gluck, Puccini was interested in the unbroken, sweeping narrative of the story. On the other hand, Verdi was entrenched in the Italian tradition, where the voice remained the focal point. However, like Verdi, Puccini's masterworks, *La Bohème, Tosca,* and *Madama Butterfly* would further the Italian tradition and earn him lasting international acclaim.

Russian Nationalism produced many operatic icons during the late nineteenth century. Seen as the "Golden Age" of opera, the most significant Russian works of this period include Mikhail Glinka's *A Life for the Tsar,* Modest Mussorgsky's *Boris Godunov,* Pyotr Tchaikovsky's *Eugene Onegin,* and Alexander Borodin's *Prince Igor.*

Richard Wagner

While Italian operas may be passionate, Richard Wagner's operas are nothing short of fanatical. An eccentric genius that, along with Verdi, dominated opera in the mid to late 1800s, Wagner's mature work is best summed up by his own term *Gesamtkunstwerk,* which translates as "total artwork." For Wagner, this meant the union of musical, literary, visual, and theatrical elements: many of which Wagner controlled himself. In Wagner's music, the voice was sublimated into the texture so that the instruments (the orchestra) and the voice were considered equal constituent parts. These parts take on the function of "inner music" (orchestra) and "outer music" (voice) so that the voice projects the narrative while the orchestra projects the inner spirit, thoughts, and mood of the characters.

Wagner's imaginative librettos were often influenced by Greek mythology, and of his ten masterpieces, *Der Ring des Nibelungen* (The Ring Cycle) is his most ambitious—so ambitious, he even designed an opera house in Bayreuth, Germany to premier it. A collection of four distinct yet interlocking operas, The Ring is usually performed as separate works today.

Opera in the Twentieth and Twenty-First Centuries

Opera in the twentieth and twenty-first centuries is extremely varied. Output depends largely on the period, the nationality of the composer, and the influences of each composer. You will see a great contrast between operas from the twentieth and twenty-first centuries and earlier periods simply because modern composers may now use bitonality and atonality, in addition to traditional tonality, in their work. Moreover, the contemporary composer has greater access to ethnic musical styles from around the globe, and therefore, regionalism plays less of a role in the work of the living masters.

The most important operas of the twentieth century include Richard Strauss's one-act *Elektra*, Alban Berg's *Wozzeck,* and Arnold Schoenberg's *Moses und Aron.* The last two incorporate a musical device known as *Sprechstimme* or "spoken song." In the post-war era, Benjamin Britten's operas *Peter Grimes* and *The Rape of Lucretia* are also cited as groundbreaking works. Stravinsky's *The Rakes Progress* is an example of the neo-classical twentieth century movement where the composer redefines and reinterprets formal and material elements from the past. In Stravinsky's case, this meant using the operas of Mozart as a model.

Additionally, in the United States, opera has flourished since the 1930s. For example, George Gershwin's *Porgy and Bess* brought jazz and blues into the opera house. Other American styles such as minimalism have found their way into opera too. Philip Glass's opera's *Einstein on the Beach* and *Satyagraha* and John Adams' *Nixon in China* best epitomize this. Robert Ashley's *Perfect Lives (Private Parts)* is also an example of the American operatic tradition.

Like so many styles discussed in this book, opera is a *vast* musical form with over four centuries of development. Due to this, use this chapter strictly as point of departure for your own research.

Vocal Classifications, Ranges, and Registers

There are seven *basic* vocal classifications used today. Due to musical concerns, chiefly the projection of notes, the usable range for opera singers and soloists differs from the usable range in a vocal choir. This is because certain notes (extreme low or high notes) may not be sung loud enough to carry over an orchestra when sung by a soloist. However, these same pitches, when sung by a group of singers, may project over the orchestra quite pleasingly. Despite this, operatic soloists usually have a larger compass because aria writing tends to push the limits of the voice.

Countertenors are also sometimes referred to as "male alto" voices. These vocalists use an artificial singing voice to sing parts originally written for castratos. To do this, the countertenor will sing in the falsetto register. These singers are not necessarily endowed with an extremely high natural voice. In contrast, most countertenors are actually baritone singers. Much of the music that countertenors perform comes from the early baroque period, a time when the practice of castration to preserve a high register male voice was common.

There are many sub-types of vocalists, and vocal range, timbre, and ability vary depending on each sub-type. For example, lyric tenors and spinto tenors have slightly different ranges and the tones of their voices are noticeably different. (The tone of the former is lighter while the latter is weightier.) Leggiero tenors or *tenore di grazia* are even more specialized. These singers have the ability to sing florid, coloratura lines and extend their range past their lyric and spinto counterparts. Female voices (especially the soprano) break down into a variety of sub-types too.

Additionally, some singers possess a slightly decreased or slightly extended range depending on natural ability and/or training. Because of this, a soprano who can sing above C#6 is called a sopranino and a bass singer who can singer lower than G1 is called a basso profundo or contrabass.

Vocal Classifications

The three basic types of female singers are: soprano, mezzo-soprano or alto, and contralto. The four basic types of male singers are: countertenor, tenor, baritone, and bass. Mezzo-soprano and altos are *gener-*

ally synonymous. The term alto is used in choral settings and the term mezzo-soprano is used in operatic settings where reference is being made to a soloist.

See Figures 13-1 through 13-6 for approximate vocal ranges for six of the seven types listed above. (The countertenor's range is the same as a mezzo-soprano or soprano depending on the singer.) In each case, the range is given for both a choral singer and an opera soloist.

FIGURE 13-1: Soprano range

Choral Range:

Operatic Range:

FIGURE 13-2: Mezzo soprano and alto ranges

Choral Range for Alto:

Operatic Range for Mezzo-soprano:

FIGURE 13-3: Contralto range

Operatic Range (classification not used in choral music):

FIGURE 13-4: Tenor range

The "8" tells you that the notes are written one octave higher than they sound.

Choral Range:

Operatic Range:

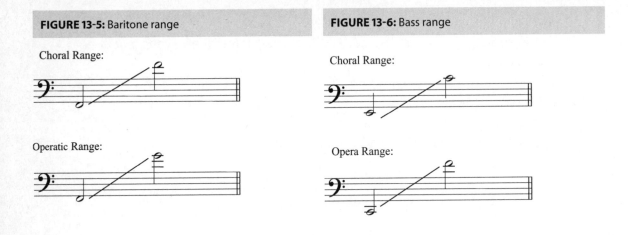

FIGURE 13-5: Baritone range

Choral Range:

Operatic Range:

FIGURE 13-6: Bass range

Choral Range:

Opera Range:

Vocal Registers

There are four vocal registers used by the human voice. From highest to lowest these are:

- Whistle (flageolet)
- Falsetto
- Modal
- Vocal fry

On the lowest end, the vocal fry is sometimes employed in deep bass parts written for gospel quartets. Occasionally, bass parts in choral repertoire may also dip into this register. The sound produced in this register is a "froggy" tone that may even pop or rattle if sustained.

The Modal register is the most comfortable, unforced, and useful register for most singers. Here, the voice is heard in its natural state. The falsetto register is used either by countertenors to simulate the voice of a castrato or by other singers to hit notes too high for the so-called "chest voice." It is the chest region where vocal resonances in the modal register are often felt. Falsetto singing produces a very clear pitch but the tone is thinner. Lastly, the whistle register is so named because its high pitch resembles a shrill whistle. This register is mostly limited to coloratura sopranos.

Bach Chorales

Virtually all music majors in all music schools are required to study four-part writing. Why is this so important and what *is* part writing anyway? Part writing is derived from four-voice chorales written by J.S. Bach. The late baroque era composer wrote a total of 371 harmonized chorales. Today, most students' reference Albert Riemenschneider's 1941 compilation of Bach chorales (see Appendix B).

Most of Bach's chorales are settings of Protestant (Lutheran) hymns. The German chorale tradition goes back to the Reformation Period in the early 1500s. Johann Walter and Martin Luther himself were key pioneers and they wrote chorales from a borrowed or preexisting melody called a *cantus firmus* (fixed song). Despite its initial popularity, by the first quarter of the eighteenth century, Bach was the only major baroque composer to concentrate on this unique form of sacred music.

Bach's chorales are not independent pieces. Rather, they are musical passages, often whole movements, applied to larger works such as the motet, the passion, the oratorio, and most poignantly, the cantata. Eighteen of Bach's chorales also cull from his organ repertoire. According to Riemenschneider, the source material for most of Bach's chorales is folk music and Gregorian chant.

What's more, Bach's four-part chorale style does not just apply to vocal music. It may be used when arranging music for most keyboard instruments, string quartet, brass quartet, and virtually any other mixed quartet. By extension, Bach's methods may also apply to other ensemble settings as well.

The Rules of Four-Part Chorale Style

Traditional four-part exercises use soprano, alto, tenor, and bass voices. The exercises are typically four to eight measures long, but in real composition, the Bach chorale may be much more elaborate. The four voices are written on treble and bass clefs, with the soprano and tenor note stems pointing upward and the alto and bass note stems pointing downward. Chordal functions are usually written in Roman numerals above, below, or in the middle of the staff along with the key signature(s).

Students learn four-part writing in varied stages depending on the instructor. Advanced students are usually given a set of Roman numerals or figured bass markings together with a fixed melody or *cantus firmus* in the soprano voice. In other instances, the bass voice may be provided instead of the soprano voice. In all cases, the student's job is to create a "mini composition" using the rules of four-part writing. This is commonly referred to as "setting a melody."

When setting a melody, you have four options with regard to *movement*:

1. Parallel motion
2. Similar motion
3. Contrary motion
4. Oblique motion

These linear motions are shown in Figure 13-7. Be sure to see the "rules" below for restrictions on all of these motions.

When writing in chorale style, the student must also observe the following rules very closely. Most of these rules pertain to voice leading;

- Write within the range of each voice; see Figures 13-1, 13-2, 13-4 and 13-6.
- Use chord tones on downbeats, passing tones on upbeats only; the only exceptions to this are suspensions, which must always be resolved (scale degrees: 4-3, 2-1, 6-5, 9-8, or 7-6).
- Avoid crossing voices. For example, the tenor should rarely move higher than the alto voice.
- Soprano and alto voices must be written within one octave of one another and alto and tenor must be written within one octave of one another.
- Never leave out the root and third of chords.

FIGURE 13-7: Linear motion in chorale style

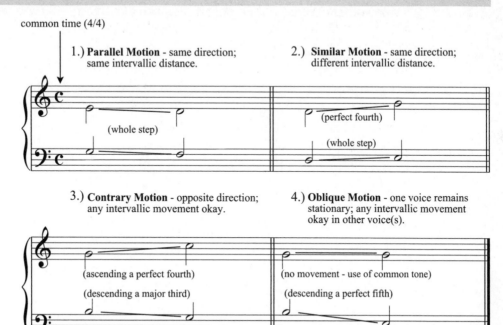

common time (4/4)

1.) **Parallel Motion** - same direction; same intervallic distance.

2.) **Similar Motion** - same direction; different intervallic distance.

(whole step)

(perfect fourth)

(whole step)

3.) **Contrary Motion** - opposite direction; any intervallic movement okay.

4.) **Oblique Motion** - one voice remains stationary; any intervallic movement okay in other voice(s).

(ascending a perfect fourth)

(descending a major third)

(no movement - use of common tone)

(descending a perfect fifth)

For ease in reading, only the alto and tenor voices are shown here.

Whenever possible, contrary and oblique motion are always advised.

- Avoid parallel (perfect) fifths (a very common mistake) (see Figure 13-8).
- Avoid parallel octaves (another very common mistake) (see Figure 13-8).
- When possible, maintain "common tones" (especially in inner voices) as you move from one chord to another.
- Use contrary motion when possible (especially in relation to the bass).
- Leading tones should always resolve *up* to the tonic.
- If you employ chromatic alterations or accidentals, move in the same direction to resolve them (i.e., sharps resolve up and flats resolve down).

- Unless you're writing a V⁷ chord, you will need to use doublings since other chords contain only three pitch classes; in this case,

FIGURE 13-8: Parallel fifths and parallel octaves

1. Parallel Fifths - **ALWAYS AVOID**

2. Parallel Octaves - **ALWAYS AVOID**

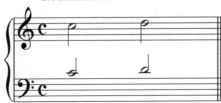

"Hidden" parallel fifths and octaves between the alto and tenor voices often plague students.

FIGURE 13-9: Four-part writing example #1

TRACK 42

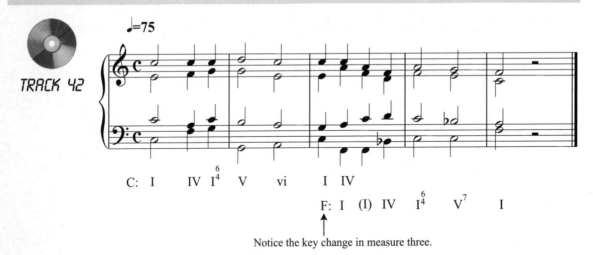

Notice the key change in measure three.

double the root when possible.
- Never double the leading tone of the home key.

Figure 13-8 shows the two most common errors: parallel fifths and parallel octaves.

FIGURE 13-10: Four-part writing example #2

TRACK 43

6 = chord in first inversion (third in bass)

$\frac{6}{4}$ = chord in second inversion (fifth in bass)

Figures 13-9 and 13-10 show two examples of four-part writing, as it should be done. Look for strict observance of the above-mentioned rules in both examples. Then, using staff paper or score writing software, write your own four-part exercises. You may use the soprano or bass lines from Figures 13-9 and 13-10 as templates.

For the beginner, four-part writing can be tricky and even confusing. Bear in mind that it's best learned under the watchful eye of an instructor. For a comprehensive, step-by-step analysis of this subject matter, see the additional resources listed in Appendix B.

Chapter 14

Writing for Guitars and Electronic Media

This chapter provides insights into writing for guitars and electronic media. It begins with information about acoustic guitars, including information about nylon and steel stringed instruments and the development of the classical guitar. Next, the chapter moves into popular milieus exploring a style of notation called tablature, followed by information on the electric guitar and bass guitar. Along the way you will learn how to voice chords and build bass lines. Lastly, this chapter ends with an overview of electronic music, including a look at synthesizers and keyboards.

Acoustic Guitars

Although the exact origins of the guitar are not fully known, musicologists hypothesize that this instrument has its roots in both ancient Greece and Mesopotamia. The acoustic guitar is used in many styles of music from folk to rock-n-roll, country and western to jazz. It's also used in select ethnic styles, such as Irish music, and it has a deep European classical music tradition.

All acoustic guitars use a soundboard and a sound box to amplify the vibrations. For this reason, all acoustic guitars have hollow bodies and their *basic* design is not unlike instruments in the violin family (see Chapter 16). One major difference, however, is the fretted neck, which is a feature on virtually all guitars. Frets are thin metal strips that are built into the fingerboard on the guitar's neck. Frets divide the fingerboard into precise half steps or semitones. Because of this, each string on the neck may be played chromatically. The number of frets on a guitar can vary and you may find anywhere between seventeen and twenty-four frets on any given instrument. Acoustic guitars usually have nineteen frets.

When a string is depressed or "stopped," it temporarily shortens its length and this results in a higher pitch. Given this, the lowest note on any string is an *open* string. Strings are strummed or plucked by the fingers—usually in the right hand—and there are many styles of finger picking used today. (Non-classical guitarists often use a plectrum or pick instead of their fingers.) The open strings of the guitar are shown in Figure 14-1.

FIGURE 14-1: Open strings on a six-string guitar in standard tuning

Acoustic guitars fall into two general categories:

- Steel string
- Nylon (occasionally gut strings but these are rare today)

Steel string acoustic guitars are used in folk, rock, Celtic, gypsy jazz, and other popular genres where a brighter, louder, or more biting tone is desired. The attack of nylon stringed guitars is not as sharp. Instead, the sound is more rounded and full-bodied.

Nylon stringed guitars are also referred to as classical guitars, but these types of guitars are also used in many styles of music outside of classical. This includes the Brazilian bossa nova, the Spanish flamenco, and even pop music. In pop music, the classical guitar is often used when a Latin or Spanish "vibe" is desired in a tune. The practical range of the guitar is shown in Figure 14-2. This compass does not include natural and false harmonics (see Chapter 16), which may be used to extend the range on most stringed instruments.

FIGURE 14-2: Range of the guitar in standard tuning

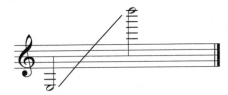

Music for guitar is notated one octave *higher* than it sounds. Also, the upper range may very slightly depending on the make and model of the guitar.

Modern Classical Guitar

There are many precursors to the modern classical guitar. However, during the Romantic period the guitar, as we know it, began to take shape. The first six-string instrument was produced in 1779 by Italian luthier Gaetano Vinaccia and the first music for the six-string guitar was published in 1780. During the nineteenth century, a number of European composers became fascinated by this instrument and began writing for it. In virtually all cases, these composers were also guitarists themselves. The most important composers of this pivotal era were: Mauro Giuliani, Johann Kaspar, Giulio Regondi, and "The Beethoven of the Guitar," Fernando Sor.

The violin virtuoso Niccolò Paganini and the programmatic composer Hector Berlioz also composed for guitar. In fact, Berlioz was reputed to

FIGURE 14-3: Neck diagram up to the twelfth fret

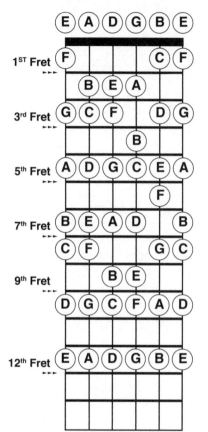

be a very good guitarist. He also wrote in *Treatise on Instrumentation* that the guitar is almost impossible to write for unless you know how to play it. This is a very true assessment! Therefore, if you wish to compose for this instrument, you should learn how to play it.

Start by learning where naturals—as opposed to sharps and flats—are found on the strings. A neck diagram has been provided in Figure 14-3 to acquaint you with the modern guitar. You'll notice that on fret twelve, the open string pitches (E, A, D, G, B, E) are repeated one octave higher. This same symmetrical pattern continues as you ascend the fretboard.

In the twentieth century, the guitar fully bloomed as a recital instrument. Additionally, in this period performance techniques were codified as well as teaching approaches. In this century, beautiful works by Enrique Granados, Heitor Villa-Lobos, Manuel de Falla, Joaquín Rodrigo and many others ensured the classical guitar's lasting role on the concert stage. In most cases, the repertoire contained ethnic musical elements from Spain, Brazil, or Argentina.

Although several virtuosi emerged in the twentieth century, the undisputed legend of this era was the Spaniard Andrés Segovia who brought great acclaim to the instrument. Figure 14-4 shows a brief example of a nylon stringed classical guitar performing with a string orchestra. You might hear something like this in a movie soundtrack with a romantic "Spanish" feel.

The modern classical guitar has been used, quite successfully, to interpret various keyboard, violin, and cello works from the baroque period as well as repertoire for lute. It's also been used to play music written for predecessors of the modern guitar such as the Spanish Vihuela.

FIGURE 14-4A: Classical guitar example

TRACK 44

FIGURE 14-4B: Classical guitar example

TRACK 44

rit.

The Electric Guitar

Few instruments, if any, are so pervasive in contemporary music. Without a doubt, the electric guitar is at the epicenter of popular music and it's rare to find a band that does not contain at least one guitarist. The electric guitar also has a rich history in jazz music from the swing era onward.

What you may not know is that the electric guitar has also been used in contemporary classical or "new music." Beginning in the 1950s, composers such as Karlheinz Stockhausen, Donald Erb, Morton Feldman, George Crumb, Leonard Bernstein, Steve Reich, Arvo Pärt, and others have successfully employed this instrument in formal concert settings.

For example, Steve Reich's three-movement minimalist work, Electric Counterpoint, brilliantly combines tape loops and samples with layers of guitar chords, single-line motifs, and pulsating rhythms. It was written for and recorded by jazz guitarist Pat Metheny in 1987.

Pick-Ups

The electric guitar comes in many different incarnations. Virtually all of the components of this instrument may vary considerably. This includes the wood(s) used, the body shape, the electronics, the strings, the finish, and the actual size. However, one element that distinguishes the acoustic guitar from the electric guitar is the use of pick-ups. In fact, pick-ups are responsible for electrifying the instrument.

When the strings of the guitar vibrate, the pick-ups, acting as electromagnetic transducers, capture the sound. This is then transformed into an electronic signal. From here, the signal is converted into sound via the amplifier and speaker cabinet. Many different pick-ups exist. However, the classic pickup found on most electric guitars is passive (as opposed to active circuitry, which requires battery power). Examples of passive magnetic pickups include the humbucker, championed by the Gibson Company, and the single coil, championed by the Fender Company.

Tablature

Often referred to as Tab, tablature is a system of notation used for fretted string instruments such as guitar and electric bass. Tab is a relatively easy way to communicate the intricacies of neck positioning and note selection. Because there are so many options regarding where to play a note on a guitar, a notation system, such as Tab, can help solve this dilemma. Tab tells you the precise order of the notes and the exact string and fret to play them on. Numbers correspond to frets (e.g., 3 means third fret) while the lines correspond to the guitar strings themselves; the number zero means an open string.

For the rock guitarist or bassist, Tab is most commonly used to figure out chords, leads, and bass lines from a favorite recording. Tab is helpful because it communicates the best path and position(s) on the fretboard based on context. Standard notation cannot communicate this. On the downside, tab does not always include rhythms or time signatures. Figure 14-5 shows you four non-contextual examples of tablature written for a six-string guitar. The goal here is to simply acquaint you with the basics of this very useful form of notation.

FIGURE 14-5: Understanding tablature

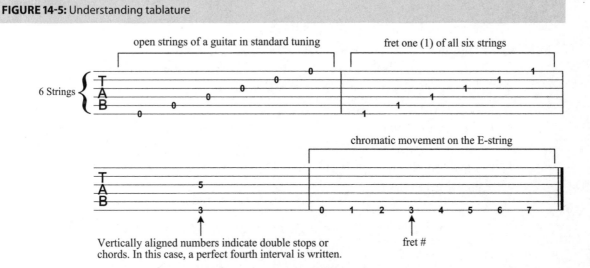

Note: Bass tablature is identical to guitar tab except only four strings are shown.

Tab is an ever-evolving, creative, and dynamic tool. Increasingly, there are new ways to communicate complex and intricate performance techniques and articulations such as bends, slides, pull-offs, etc. To learn these techniques and use them in your compositions, you should study guitar method books and/or take a handful of lessons from a qualified guitar instructor.

Scales and Chords

There is a relational aspect to all scales and keys that makes them essentially the same on guitars (including bass guitars). This is due to the way the neck is constructed, especially the frets, which neatly organize intervals along the fretboard.

All major and minor keys and scales are based on the same exact recipe, relatively speaking. As mentioned in Chapter 5, that recipe is composed of whole steps intervals (two frets apart) and half step intervals (one fret apart). For example, if you wish to play a *major* scale, the intervallic model "whole, whole, half, whole, whole, whole, half" is translated as such:

1. Play the tonic (first note of the scale).
2. Go up one whole step (two frets) and play that note.
3. Go up another whole step (two frets) and play that note.
4. Go up a half step (one fret) and play that note.
5. Go up a whole step (two frets) and play that note.
6. Go up a whole step (two frets) and play that note.
7. Go up a whole step (two frets) and play that note.
8. Go up a half step (one fret) play that note. You have now reached the octave (tonic) pitch.

If you follow rules one through eight above, you will play a scale on one string. This is an important first step toward understanding the fretboard of the guitar. However, this is not practical in a real musical context. Why? This kind of horizontal movement means that the guitarist must constantly change positions and this is not the most efficient way to play a scale. Instead, guitarists typically change strings to build scales and other linear patterns. Figure 14-6 shows the first set of scales that are usually taught to students. These scales are G major and E minor, respectively.

If you're a piano player, guitar chord voicings are particularly foreign. Rarely do pianists play non-arpeggiated chords with such a wide compass unless they use two-handed accompaniment sans melody. This is the beauty of guitar chords: the wide breadth of intervals. For example, a typical E major open chord contains a fifteenth interval (two octaves) between the lowest note and the highest note.

What is an open chord? Open chords are chord positions that contain one or more open strings. This is designated by an "o" in a chord diagram. Figure 14-7 shows the fifteen most common open chords on guitar. They appear in three groups: major chords, minor chords, and seventh chords. Many more advanced chords can be created and jazz guitarists, in particular, have turned voicing chords into an art form; see Chapter 15.

FIGURE 14-6: Ascending G major and E minor scales

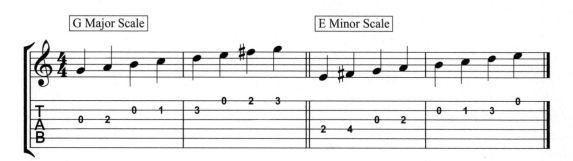

FIGURE 14-7: Open chords on the guitar

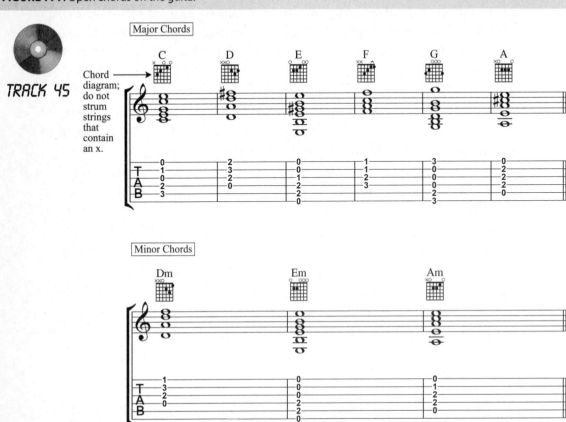

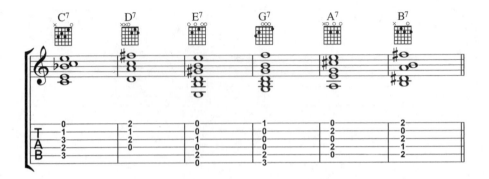

The Electric Bass

The electric bass is employed in many styles of popular music. From rock to country, Latin to hip-hop, the electric bass is a key feature. The electric bass is also sometimes used in jazz in place of the upright bass. In these situations, the fretless bass is sometimes preferred. As you might guess, the fretless bass does not contain frets. Rather, the neck resembles the fingerboard on instruments in the violin family; see Chapter 16.

The electric bass comes in many styles, shapes, and colors (finishes). This includes various specifications for: wood, electronics, strings, size, scale, neck, and body contours. A more recent development is the addition of supplemental strings. The standard electric bass has four strings. However, five and six string models are now commonplace. These additional strings add extra range to the instrument. Generally, the addition of strings, beyond four, is a special case and it represents the need for increased range. When extra strings are used, bassists will sometimes experiment with alternate tunings as well.

Unless you plan to write for a souped-up bass, you only need to be aware of the range and tuning for the standard four-string instrument. This is shown in Figures 14-8 and 14-9, respectively.

FIGURE 14-8: The open strings of a bass guitar in standard tuning

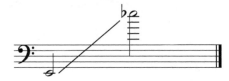

Music for bass guitar is notated one octave higher than it sounds.

FIGURE 14-9: The open strings of a bass guitar in standard tuning

The Role of the Bass

The role of the bass in the rhythm section is two-fold:

- To define and maintain the pulse and groove of the music
- To highlight the roots of each chord

If the bass part does not focus on roots (usually played on downbeats), your music will lose its anchor and drift into a state of ambiguity, even confusion.

The bassist must also work as a team with the drummer. The drummer is the timekeeper. Together with the bass, the drums "hold down the fort." The bass and drums work together to ensure steadiness and forward momentum in the music. In rock and pop, the bass and the bass drum even play in sync most of the time. Because of this, bass players and drummers share a special, symbiotic relationship. If you hear a band that's really "grooving," you can bet the bassist and drummer are locked rhythmically. Always strive for this *locked* sound in your music.

FACT

Like the electric guitar, the electric bass must be plugged into an amplifier. The amp has the ability to modify the sound of the bass by changing its tone, volume and, in some cases, adding distortion, reverb, or other effects. The same is true of amps designed for electric guitars.

Building Bass Lines

A bass line is any pattern played by a bassist that is designed to accompany chords, a drum set groove, a melody line, or all of the above. Bass lines are usually single note patterns, and often, they comprise the root and fifth of the chord. Bass lines may also include passing tones or thirds, sixths, and sevenths. Occasionally, alternate roots are also used. There are many types of bass lines. For example, if the bass part features small intervallic leaps—usually half, whole, and third intervals—together with pulsating quarter notes it's called a "walking" bass line; see Chapter 15.

The best bass lines employ rhythmical repetition. If a bass line contains too many rhythmical shifts or changes it could obstruct the melody line. In contrast, bass lines should assume a supportive role. With few exceptions, the listener should not be drawn to the bass line, but rather, the melody or soloist, etc. Figure 14-10 shows a typical rock bass line that uses eighth notes. In this case, the eighth notes really drive the music.

Figure 14-11 shows another common bass line. In this case, you will see a generic Latin pattern that could be applied to both salsa and samba

FIGURE 14-10: Eighth note rock bass line

TRACK 46

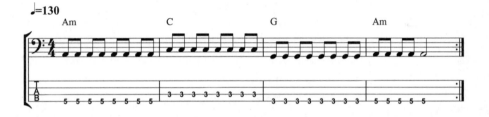

FIGURE 14-11: Up-tempo Latin featuring roots and fifths

TRACK 47

music. Here, the bass plays roots and fifths exclusively. For many more bass lines, see *The Everything® Bass Guitar Book.*

Electronic Music

In case you were wondering, composition is not limited to acoustic instruments. In fact, such an attitude would be very old-fashioned. Keyboards, synthesizers, computers, and MIDI instruments are being used all the time to write music for television, film, video games, popular genres, and even "contemporary classical."

Beginning in the 1960s, compositions for electronic media really boomed. This was due, in large part, to the development of the Moog synthesizer. Wendy (aka Walter) Carlos' seminal album *Switched-On Bach* (1968) featured electronic interpretations of J.S. Bach's music as performed on a Moog modular synthesizer. This top selling album best captures the brief but exciting Moog revolution. Figure 14-12 is a synthesizer example inspired by baroque music and the pioneering spirit of Wendy Carlos, even though it is decidedly more "pop."

In the 1980s and 1990s, digital technology and MIDI (Musical Instrument Digital Interface) gradually replaced analog keyboards and synthesizers. This culminated in pieces written for the Fairlight CMI and Synclavier sampling synthesizers. One example of the latter is Frank Zappa's groundbreaking *Civilization Phaze III,* posthumously released in 1994 by the Zappa Family Trust.

Modern Uses of Keyboards

In the new millennium, the trend is to create electronic samples that authentically capture the rich timbres of acoustic instruments (e.g., sampled grand piano). Virtually every instrument in western music now has a keyboard equivalent. For example, most keyboards can simulate the human voice, harpsichords, organs, string orchestras, guitars, flutes, clarinets, harps, banjos, French horns, glockenspiels and much, much more.

FIGURE 14-12: Wendy Carlos-inspired synthesizer example

TRACK 48

Other common sounds include bongo and conga drums, timpani, clapping, ocean waves, gunshots, car horns, animal noises, glass breaking, and other sound effects. Many companies even offer whole sound libraries, which contain hundreds of carefully engineered presets.

FACT

A sample is a small portion of music (or sound clip) that has been taken from one sound source and applied to another. In the pre-digital era, these clips were captured through the use of magnetic tape. Tape loops were then created so that the sample could be applied to a new setting. Today, samples are made using computer technology.

Keyboard Sound Quality

How good are the sounds on contemporary keyboards? It depends on the company and the products themselves. Not all samples are created equal and there are many variables that contribute to a sound's quality. As of this writing, certain wind instruments such as trumpet and saxophone are generally poor. However, instruments such as the piano, flute, vibraphone, glockenspiel, and drum kit tend to be good enough to deceive the ear in certain contexts. These technological advancements have been fully exploited by composers who have scored music for "virtual orchestras" or other "virtual" ensembles. Digital sampling technology is sure to get frighteningly amazing in the coming decades. However, it's unlikely that acoustic instruments will ever become obsolete.

Chapter 15
Writing Contemporary Jazz

Jazz is a unique kind of composition that, both follows the "rules" of classical music and ignores them. Jazz really has its own theoretical system that is generally more informal, but no less complicated, than classical music. There are many styles of "jazz" composition dating back to the first decade of the twentieth century. This chapter focuses on modern jazz, which begins around 1945. Like other chapters in this book, the information presented here is merely an overview of select, key points.

The Almighty ii-V-I

Since melodic lines are often improvised over a set of chords, jazz composers often focus on writing clever chord progressions. This is not to say that jazz composers are uninterested in composing beautiful melodies. There are scores of striking melody writers. The pianists Bill Evans, John Lewis, and Thelonius Monk are three such examples. However, jazz composers do tend to be preoccupied with harmonic possibilities. This is because they often look for harmonic designs that lend themselves well to improvisation.

One harmonic model that's constantly used in the music of The Great American Songbook and bebop tradition is the ii-V-I chord progression. Generally speaking, this progression comes in two forms: major ii-V-I's and minor ii-V-i's.

ii-V-I chord changes come in many different "flavors." The exact chords played are determined only in part by the written chord symbols. Ultimately, chordal players make decisions on the fly about what harmonic extensions to use and what to leave out. Overall, the best accompanists understand the gentle balance between taste and excessiveness when voicing chords.

Don't take the Roman numerals indicated above too literally though. In jazz, you will virtually *never* hear a chordal player voice ii-V-I chords without the addition of harmonic extensions. In fact, harmonic extensions are a nearly constant feature in modern jazz. Like all styles of music, chordal inversions are also used to create smooth voice leading. In other words, the order in which notes appear in a chord varies. This usually depends on the chordal instrument being played. The most common chordal instruments in jazz are the piano, organ, other keyboards (such as the Fender Rhodes), the vibraphone, and the guitar (acoustic and electric). Moreover, in ensemble situations, chordal instruments often omit the roots of chords, leaving them to be played by the bass player.

One thing's for sure: You will find the major ii-V-I progression employed in hundreds (perhaps thousands) of songs. A few random examples include: "Have You Met Miss Jones," "How High the Moon," "I'll Remember April," "Joy Spring," "Misty," "Scrapple from the Apple," and many, many more. The song "Tune Up," by Miles Davis, contains virtually all ii-V-I chords. You will also find ii-V cadences used habitually by jazzers as "turnarounds."

A turnaround typically occurs in the last measure of the form. It is used as a connecting harmonic sequence that bridges the gap between the end of one chorus and the beginning of a new chorus. (For information on forms, see Chapter 11.) When using turnarounds, the ii chord is usually played during the first half of the measure and the V chord is played during the second half of the measure. The ii-V chords may also be played on beats three and four, respectively. Turnarounds are used when a tune begins on a I or i chord.

Variations on ii-V-I (and i) Chord Progressions

Figure 15-1 shows a basic ii-V-I chord progression. As mentioned earlier, jazz musicians would not play this progression so literally. In Figure 15-2 you will see how a jazz pianist might interpret this progression. Then, in Figure 15-3, you will see the progression laid out for a pianist and a bass player. Notice how the bassist plays roots on downbeats (with the chords).

FIGURE 15-1: Basic ii-V-I chord progression

TRACK 49

FIGURE 15-2: Jazz ii-V-I chord progression

How these chords would typically
be labeled on a lead sheet.

FIGURE 15-3: Jazz ii-V-I chord progression with upright bass

TRACK 51

Right hand is free to solo or play a melody line!

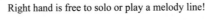

piano

upright bass

In the first measure, passing tones connect chord tones (roots).

FIGURE 15-4: Jazz ii-V-I played on a guitar

TRACK 52

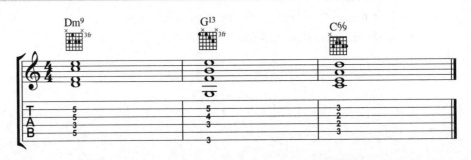

Lastly, a jazz guitarist might voice a major ii-V-I chord progression as seen in Figure 15-4.

There are many other ways to vary this progression while still retaining the underlying ii-V-I movement. For example, Figure 15-5 shows how to implement a flat five on the ii chord, a flat nine on the V chord, and a major seven/nine on the I chord.

FIGURE 15-5: Using a flat five, flat nine, and major seven/nine

TRACK 53

Figure 15-6 shows yet another option using a chromatic movement in the top voice. Notice the use of a flat thirteen in the V chord.

You can also use a sharp nine on the V chord as shown in Figure 15-7. In this example, the chromatic movement in the upper voice has still been maintained.

FIGURE 15-6: Chromatic movement in the upper voice

TRACK 54

FIGURE 15-7: Using a sharp nine on the V chord

TRACK 55

Lastly, minor keyed ii-V-i's are found in dozens of songs. You'll see this progression employed in the opening bars to "What Is This Thing Called Love," "Beautiful Love," and "Old Folks" to name a few. Minor ii-V-i's will usually include a flat five on the ii chord and a flat nine on the V chord. You may also see a major nine interval added to the ii chord and a flat thirteen added to the V chord. The chief difference between major ii-V-I varieties and minor ii-V-i varieties is the minor i chord itself. See Figure 15-8 for two examples of minor ii-V-i's.

FIGURE 15-8: Minor ii-V-i Chord Possibilities

TRACK 56

This leads to a critical point: In jazz, you do not restrict the use of ii-V-I or ii-V-i progressions to the home key. Jazz constantly shifts through keys without warning. However, the home key is almost always the final destination after a stream of smooth, albeit temporary, modulations. Figure 15-9 shows you a chord progression that uses major ii-V-I's to build a longer harmonic form. In tunes that use ii-V-I's, the I chord is sometimes thwarted in place of back-to-back ii -V's. You will see this occur between measures eight and nine in Figure 15-9. To make this figure more fun, a solo line has been written to complement the chord changes. In this case, the solo instrument is a guitar.

FIGURE 15-9A: Multiple ii-V-I chord progressions with guitar solo

TRACK 57

FIGURE 15-9B: Multiple ii-V-I chord progressions with guitar solo

In this figure, the left hand of the piano (bass clef) plays a "walking" bass line.

Tri-Tone Substitution

As implied earlier, chordal players love to reharmonize chord changes from what they see in fake books or on lead sheets, etc. In fact, this is an important skill that defines, in part, one's jazz artistry. One stock way to vary ii-V-I's or ii-V-i's is to use *tri-tone substitution*. This substitution centers on the V or dominant chord in the chord progression. To use this technique you simply swap out the written V chord—with all of its harmonic extensions—and instead play a V chord (again, with various extensions) located a tri-tone above or below the original chord. This works because the *third* and *seventh* of any dominant chord is enharmonically identical to the *seventh* and *third* of the dominant chord located a tri-tone away. Sound confusing? It really isn't. However, it's is best understood through example:

In the key of C major, the V^7 chord is a G^7. The interval located a tri-tone away from G is a D♭. So, swap out the G^7 from your ii-V-I chord progression, and instead, use a D♭^{7} chord. As mentioned above, these two chords are interchangeable because the B (third) and F (seventh) of the G⁷ chord are enharmonically the same as the C♭ (seventh) and F (third) of the D♭⁷ chord. Remember too that thirds and sevenths define most chord types. (In the case of diminished and augmented chords, thirds and fifths become salient elements.)

Figure 15-10 shows a tri-tone substitution along with chordal extensions. In this case, the tri-tone substitution is voiced as a thirteenth chord. Observe how the tri-tone substitution makes the bass line move chromatically. If you haven't guessed this by now, jazz and chromaticism go hand in hand.

FIGURE 15-10: Tri-tone substitution

TRACK 58

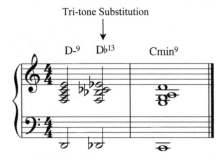

Using Modes with ii-V-I (or i) Chords

First developed by the ancient Greeks, modes are an important musical element used to create melodies and improvise. Modes can be built on all seven pitches in the major scale. For example, the C major scale is also known as the Ionian mode since it's built on the first scale degree. Similarly, if you build a mode on the sixth scale degree in C major you will get an Aeolian mode or an A natural minor scale. Figure 15-11 shows all seven modes as derived from naturals or white keys on the piano presented in ascending order. Bear in mind that, at least as far as this book is concerned, the terms "mode" and "scale" are interchangeable.

As illustrated in Figure 15-11, the intervals in the Dorian mode are: whole, half, whole, whole, whole, half, whole. In C major, this becomes: D to E (whole), E to F (half), F to G (whole), G to A, (whole) A to B (whole), B to C (half), and C to D (whole).

The minor third and the major sixth intervals of the Dorian mode largely define this scale. All in all, the Dorian mode is really just a natural minor scale with a raised (major) sixth. In fact, the Dorian mode uses the same notes as the natural minor scale located a perfect fourth below or a perfect fifth above the mode's root. For example, the notes in an A minor scale (A, B, C, D, E, F, G) match those of a D Dorian mode (D, E, F, G, A, B, C). The only difference is the starting pitches.

FACT

The Dorian scale is typically used to play over minor chords that do not contain alterations (e.g., a flat five). For example, if you have a major ii-V-I chord progression, you will likely want to use the Dorian mode on the ii chord.

Lydian Dominant Scale

The Lydian dominant scale is the *fourth* mode of the melodic minor scale. In other words, it starts on the fourth scale degree of the melodic minor. Often, musicians look at the Lydian dominant as a hybrid of two scales. Specifically, it's seen as a synthesis of the Lydian mode, which is a major scale with a raised fourth, and the Mixolydian mode, which is a major scale with a flatted seventh; see Figure 15-11.

The Mixolydian mode is also similar to the bebop dominant scale. In fact, the only difference between these scales is the addition of a leading tone in the latter. This creates chromatic movement at the top end of the scale. See Figures 15-12 and Figure 15-13 for the bebop dominant scale and the Lydian dominant scale, respectively.

Bebop Dominant Scale Versus Lydian Dominant

On its own, the bebop dominant scale may be used over any V^7 or dominant chord. However, the fourth scale degree can be problematic given the fact that the dominant chord contains a major third. If not handled properly, the perfect fourth of the scale can clash in a disagreeable manner with

FIGURE 15-11: The seven basic modes

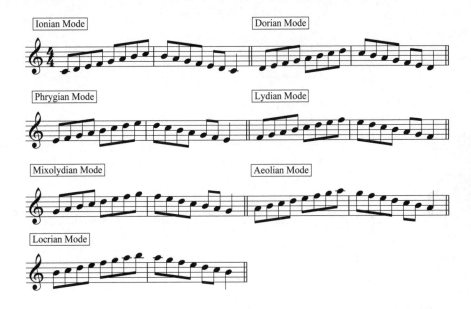

FIGURE 15-12: The bebop dominant scale

This specific bebop dominant scale would be used over a C^7 chord.

the third of the V^7 chord. (This is especially true if your melody hangs on the fourth scale degree.) Therefore, composers and soloists either use this interval cautiously or they avoid it altogether. The other option is to use the Lydian dominant scale, which allows you do construct hip, modern sounding lines. Two examples of Lydian Dominant jazz lines are shown in Figures 15-14.

FIGURE 15-13: The Lydian dominant scale

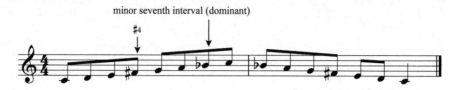

FIGURE 15-14: Lydian dominant jazz lines

TRACK 59

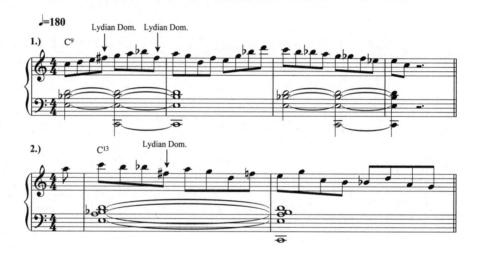

In summary, sensible scalar options for a straightforward major ii-V-I chord progression becomes the Dorian, Lydian, Dominant, and Lydian modes, respectively; see Figure 15-15. This assumes you wish to sound "contemporary."

FIGURE 15-15: Combining ii-V-I chords with modes

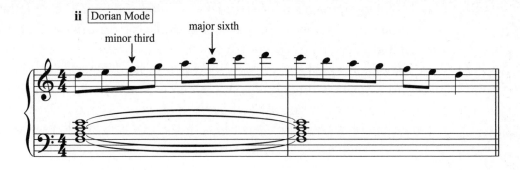

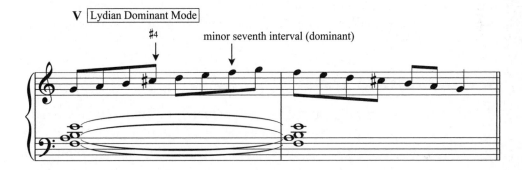

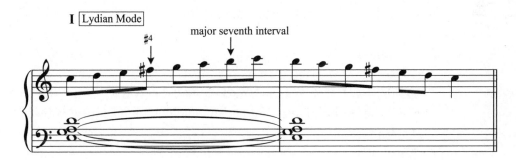

These chords are presented here without roots.

The Melodic Minor Scale

When ii-V-I or ii-V-i chord progressions are altered in some fashion, you will need to think about other scale choices. Often, the melodic minor may be used to navigate over certain altered chords. First of all, note that, in jazz, the melodic minor is used while ascending *and* descending. Let's look at some examples:

- ii^7 ($\flat$5) chords pairs up nicely with the melodic minor scale found a minor third *above* the root. So if you have a Dmin7$^{(\flat 5)}$ chord, the notes F, G, A$\flat$, B$\flat$, C, D, and E (F melodic minor) may be used to build solos or melodies.
- Another use is the melodic minor over a V chord that contains either a flat nine or a sharp nine. In both cases, the melodic minor scale located one half step *above* the root of the chord should be used. For instance, you may use the notes G$\sharp$, A$\sharp$, B, C$\sharp$, D$\sharp$, E$\sharp$, and F double sharp (enharmonically a G natural) in conjunction with a G$^{7(\flat 9)}$ chord.
- Lastly, the melodic minor scale is the perfect choice when using minor-major seventh chords (see Chapter 6). For example, if you see a Gmin(maj^7) you would use an F melodic minor scale to solo or build a melody.

The Diminished Scale

One additional scale you should definitely be familiar with is the diminished scale. Also called an octatonic scale, the diminished scale may be used with altered dominant chords when you have a flat nine and a natural thirteen. They may also be used over plain vii° (or vii°^{7}) chords. There are three points to remember when using a diminished scale:

1. The diminished scale moves in a whole-step-to-half-step manner or a half-step-to-whole-step manner only.
2. Because of the half-whole or whole-half intervallic model, there are really only three different diminished scales found in the twelve-note western system.
3. Choosing the correct diminished scale can be confusing. To make sure you implement the right one, try this tip: play a diminished seventh chord located one whole step *above* the written vii°^{7} chord (e.g., if the written chord is a F dim^7, you would play a G dim^7). The combination of the notes found in *both* chords comprises the correct scale. In other words, if the written chord were F dim7, you would reference it with a G dim7. The combined notes become: F, G, A$\flat$, B$\flat$, B, D$\flat$, D, E, and F. This is the correct diminished scale for an F dim^7 (although the D$\flat$ is spelled as a C$\sharp$ in the scale.)

If the chord is an altered dominant, like G$^{7(\flat 9)}$, this method becomes a little more complex but no less effective. Here's how it's done: Take the seventh of the written chord and build a diminished seventh chord using the seventh as the root. In this example, the seventh of a G^7 chord is an F. Given this, you would build a diminished chord on F. This becomes Fdim^7. From here, follow the instructions as detailed above. In other words, reference this

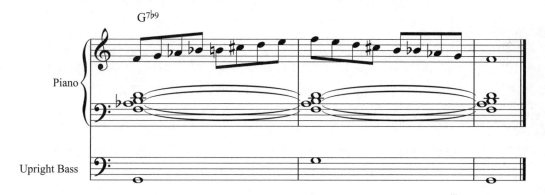

chord (Fdim^7) with the diminished seventh chord found a whole step higher (Gdim^7). When you do this, the notes for the correct diminished scale are revealed (see Figure 15-16).

In summary, when working with scales, whether as a soloist or a melody writer, you should avoid excessive "runs" up and down the keyboard or guitar, etc. This tends to sound non-musical and mechanical. Instead, you should use modes, together with arpeggios, chromatics, and other ornaments, to create lyrical phrases. See Chapter 8 for information on chromatics and review Figures 8-8, 15-9, 15-17, and 15-18 for examples of jazz lines that employ chromatic passing tones on weak beats.

Jazz Blues in Major Keys

Blues in major keys are common in jazz. Select examples include "C Jam Blues," "Jumping with Symphony Sid," "Blue Monk," "Now is the Time,"

"Freddie Freeloader," "Billie's Bounce," "Blue Train," and many, many more. In general, jazz blues contains many of the same elements found in traditional blues. For instance, the twelve-bar form is always maintained and use of blue notes and blues scales are common features. However, jazz blues typically contains chordal substitutions, especially during solos. Unlike traditional blues, jazz blues does not limit itself to I, IV, and V chords (major keys) or i, iv, and V chords (minor keys). Instead, chordal players, bass players, and soloists alike incorporate a variety of chordal substitutions (always with harmonic extensions) into the blues form.

There are dozens of jazz composers who have made indelible contributions to twentieth century music. Key innovators include Jelly Roll Morton, Fats Waller, Duke Ellington, Billy Strayhorn, Tadd Dameron, Dizzy Gillespie, Dave Brubeck, Bud Powell, John Coltrane, Thelonious Monk, George Russell, Charlie Mingus, Gerry Mulligan, Benny Golson, Oliver Nelson, Horace Silver, Bill Evans, Ornette Coleman, Wayne Shorter, Carla Bley, Herbie Hancock, and Chick Corea.

For example, one variety in major blues uses the following harmonic progression: I (four measures), IV (two measures), I (two beats), ii (two beats), iii (two beats), V/iii (two beats), ii (one measure), V (one measure), I (two beats), V/ii, (two beats), ii (two beats), and V (two beats). At this point, the form has cycled around once (twelve measures). This exact chord progression, with harmonic extensions added, is shown to in Figure 15-17.

Other variations exist too. For instance, you may play a ii/IV and a V/IV in measure five just before you switch to a IV chord. This creates a ii-V-I pattern with the IV chord temporarily assuming the role as a "I" chord. You may also add a #iv° chord on the sixth measure of the form just before returning to your home base (I chord). You may also swap out the I chord on measure eleven and use a iii chord instead. This would create a iii-vi-ii-V "turnaround," which is very common.

FIGURE 15-17A: Percy's Bounce

TRACK 60

Percy's Bounce

E. Starr

FIGURE 15-17B: Percy's Bounce

TRACK 60

FIGURE 15-17C: Percy's Bounce

TRACK 60

FIGURE 15-17D: Percy's Bounce

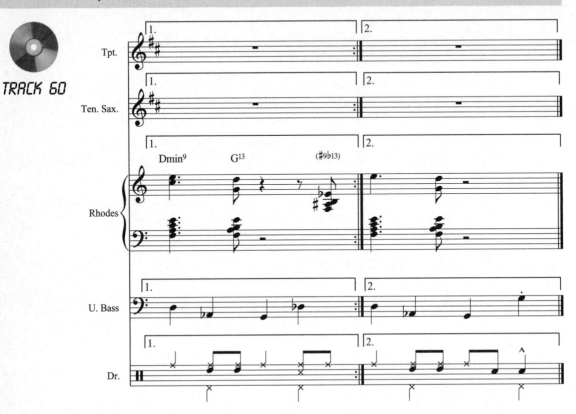

TRACK 60

In *all* of the chords described on page 208, denoted by Roman numerals, you will find various harmonic extensions added at will by jazz musicians. Moreover, in almost all styles of blues, chords such as I, IV, and V are almost always turned into dominant sevenths as the "basic" chordal quality. Other chordal variations and substitutions exist too and you should keep an ear out for these when you listen to jazz artists play major blues.

Jazz Blues in Minor Keys

Jazz blues in minor keys are also popular. Songs like "Birk's Works," "Mr. P.C.," "Five Spot After Dark" and "Footprints" are all minor jazz blues. Like its major counterpart, minor jazz blues also features many chordal variations. For one, the i and iv chords are almost always turned into minor nine chords and you may also use a variety of minor ii-V-i's to add sophistication and complexity to the form. This is seen in Figure 15-18, where the chord progression is denoted as: i (one measure), ii (two beats), V (two beats), i (one measure), ii/iv (two beats), ii/V (two beats), iv (two measures), i (two measures), iii (two beats), VI (two beats), ii (two beats), V (two beats), I (one measure + two beats), and V (two beats). This chord progression is shown in Figure 15-18. As you've come to expect by now, harmonic extensions are added to all of these chords.

If you're brand new to minor blues, you might try a simpler harmonic design first. One version is as follows: i (four measures), iv (two measures), i (two measures), V (one measure), iv (one measure), i (one measure), V (one measure). When playing this progression, be sure to turn the i and iv chords into minor 9th voicings and you may want to add a minor seventh, sharp nine, and flat thirteen (also called flat six) onto the V chord to make this voicing sound more dramatic.

FIGURE 15-18A: Blues for Franny

TRACK 61

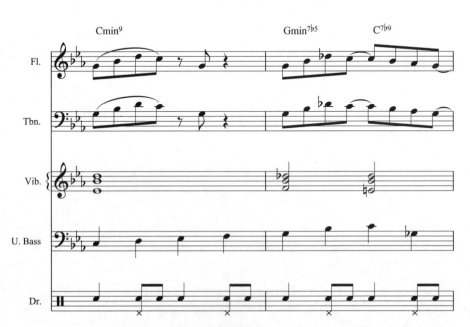

FIGURE 15-18B: Blues for Franny

TRACK 61

FIGURE 15-18C: Blues for Franny

TRACK 61

In this figure, the upright bass plays a "walking" bass line.

Chapter 16

Writing for Strings

This chapter provides information about violin, viola, cello, and double bass. These instruments comprise what is usually referred to as the string family. Technically, the string family is much more diverse, including such instruments as the harp, piano, guitar, mandolin, clavier, zither, dulcimer, lyre, and many others. To be more specific, this chapter details the four instruments that make up the modern *violin* family.

The Violin

The violin is an extremely adaptable instrument that is used not only as a staple in symphonic and chamber music but also in pop milieus, south Indian classical, folk music (from various continents), jazz, and country and western, especially bluegrass. A pick-up may be attached to electrify the violin, and select artists, such as the jazz-fusion violinist Jean Luc Ponty, use solid-bodied electronic violins.

The traditional wooden, hollow-bodied violin is made from seventy different parts and constructing these instruments requires great talent, skill, and knowledge. The most revered violin luthiers in history all hailed from Cremona, Italy. The first, Andrea Amati (exact birth date unknown), is often credited with building the earliest modern violins during the 1500s.

FACT

Andrea Amati's grandson, Nicolo (1596-1684) became the finest luthier in the family line, and his craftsmanship greatly influenced Andrea Guarneri (1623–1698) and Antonio Stradivari (c. 1644–1737). Guarneri's grandson, Giuseppe (better known as 'del Gesù') became the preeminent luthier of his family. All three of these celebrated families produced violas and cellos as well.

The violin is the smallest and highest pitched instrument of the violin family. Like the viola, cello, and double bass, it contains four strings. Violin strings are tuned in two pairs of perfect fifths (G, D, A, E). As illustrated in Figure 16-1, the pitch range of the violin is vast. The lowest note is G3—the G below middle C—ascending all the way up to around C8. The highest notes are produced by natural and artificial harmonics, which will be discussed later in the chapter. Figure 16-1 shows the open strings and the range of the violin.

Sometimes violinists use alternate tunings (e.g., the violin solo in *Dance Macabre* by Camille Saint-Saëns). Alternate tunings are called *scordatura* and this term can be applied to any instrument in the violin family. As a general rule, you should avoid alternate tunings in your compositions. If you *do*

FIGURE 16-1: Open strings and range of the violin in standard tuning

use them, make sure you have a justifiable reason. Furthermore, do not ask the violinist to return to standard tuning during the piece, as retuning during a performance can be tricky.

To hold the violin, the violinist places his jaw on the instrument's chin rest on his left side. He then pinches the violin between the jaw and the underside of the *lower bout* (section of the body that is rounded and curves outward). The left hand is then placed under the neck so that the fingers can traverse the fingerboard. The right hand holds the bow.

To play the violin, the violinist moves the left hand along the fingerboard in a series of positions, often using vibrato. Vibrato is produced by depressing a string on the fingerboard then rapidly "pulsing" or shaking the finger. Vibrato creates greater intensity and expression in the music through slight fluctuations in pitch. Like all instruments in the violin family, the violin may play single lines or double stops (two or more notes played simultaneously).

The violinist's fingers are labeled one through four. The index finger is finger one and the pinky is finger four. Each position transplants the fingers up the fingerboard diatonically. For example, in first position on the G-string, the first note is "A." The finger that plays this note is finger one. Figure 16-2 shows the fingering in first position for all four strings. Technically, there are some fifteen positions. Use of positions also applies to the viola, cello, and double bass.

The undisputed "queen bee" of the string family, the violin is regularly featured in symphonic and chamber music of all kinds from the baroque era onward. Hundreds of violin sonatas alone populate the violin repertoire.

FIGURE 16-2: Fingering in first position on the violin

The Viola

The viola is the slightly larger cousin to the violin and its pitch range places it in the middle register of the violin family (above cello but below the violin). Traditionally, its darker, mellower tone has been used for interior harmonies or as an "inner voice." However, the viola has occasionally stolen the spotlight from its popular cousins, the violin and cello (e.g., the viola solo in the third movement of Johannes Brahms' *Quartet for Strings No. 3 in Bb Major, Op. 67*).

Since the middle of the 1700s, the viola has gradually taken on a greater role in music; one that is beyond mere utility. Much of this has to do with British violist Lionel Tertis, who rose to prominence as a viola specialist during the first quarter of the twentieth century.

FIGURE 16-3: The alto clef

F G A B C D E F G

The viola is notated using a C-clef called the *alto clef.* In this clef, the middle line represents middle C. Figure 16-3 shows the lines and spaces of the alto clef.

The standard tuning for a viola is in two pairs of perfect fifths. The lowest note, C3 is one octave below middle C. For a professional, the highest note on the instrument is around C7 with harmonics; this is three octaves above middle C. Figure 16-4 shows the open strings and range for the viola in standard tuning.

FIGURE 16-4: Open strings and range of the viola in standard tuning

Sometimes violinists play viola and vice versa. This is possible because the violin and viola share many of the same qualities. However, violas contain thicker strings. Similarly, the viola bow is thicker and heavier and it uses more horsehair. Moreover, when moving from the violin to the longer, wider-bodied viola, compensations must be made with regard to holding positions and bow strokes.

In the 1530s, the modern viola became a regular member of the violin family. However, the term "viola" remained generic with varied meanings (both broad and explicit) throughout the eighteenth century. The standard size of a modern viola is about sixteen inches long. However, experimentation with the shape of the instrument's body continues to this day.

Increasingly, composers are writing feature material for the viola. But in comparison to the violin, concertos for viola are still small in number. Perhaps you can add to the emerging canon of featured viola music!

The Cello

The cello or violoncello is larger than the viola but smaller than the double bass. It is played while sitting, with the cello placed between the performer's legs. The cello's forerunner is the bass violin, an instrument first used in 1607 by Claudio Monteverdi *(L'Orfeo)* and Caterina Assandra *(Motetti Op.2)*. Like other violin instruments, a variety of models were made during its early production. Numerous models contained five strings (J.S. Bach wrote for these instruments) and experiments were made with smaller cellos strung over the shoulder *(Viola da spalla)*. However, the design that laid the foundation for modern cello making was Stradivari's Model B and some of these cellos are still in use today.

The cello is written in F-clef or bass clef and its four strings are tuned in two pairs of perfect fifths. It has a range from C2 (two octaves below middle C) to around A7 using harmonics. The open strings and the range of the cello in standard tuning are shown in Figure 16-5.

Sometimes a small attenuator called a *wolf eliminator* is needed to improve the tone of individual notes called *wolfs*. Typically, the note "F" on the G or C strings sounds warbled or it creates an ugly growling tone when bowed. A weighted device clipped to the offending string (between the bridge and the tailpiece) can usually eliminate this. Other instruments in

FIGURE 16-5: Open strings and range of the cello in standard tuning

Open Strings   Professional Range (does not include harmonics)

C   G   D   A

the violin family may also require wolf eliminators, but the cello is the most susceptible.

In symphonic settings, the cello becomes a low-range internal voice. It may double the *roots* of chords (e.g., a C in a C major chord) or it may play perfect fifths. In string quartet settings, it often assumes the role of the bass instrument (see double bass). However, cello implementation is by no means confined to these basic uses. For example, the cello may move in imitative and non-imitative counterpoint with the other three members of the violin family. The cello also enjoys a plethora of solo passages in orchestral and chamber music repertoire. Plus, hundreds of concertos and solo works have been written for the instrument.

The Double Bass

The double bass is the largest instrument in the violin family and it has been in use since the early 1500s. Double bass design, tuning, and stringing has undergone many changes over the centuries. The modern double bass sounds an octave lower than the cello and it is the lowest pitched string instrument in the orchestra, sharing the same register with the tuba and timpani. In general, the bass is used to add "bottom" or low frequencies to music. Harmonically, the bass often plays the roots of chords. Moreover, it is used to propel the rhythm and keep time.

FACT

All instruments in the violin family can be played with a mute and, more and more, composers are taking advantage of this effect. To request a mute, you would write *con sordino* or *con sord.* in your music. Made from various materials, the mute is placed at the bridge. This decreases the instrument's vibrations resulting in a softer, muffled tone.

More than any other instrument in the violin family, the double bass enjoys wide use in dozens of styles and sub-styles including jazz, country and western, rock-n-roll, and occasionally, contemporary pop. In the orchestra, the double bass adds strength and power to the music. It is especially good at creating ominous or menacing moods; you will often hear the bass used to this end in soundtrack music.

However, the bass is much more than just an effect or an accompaniment instrument. The average listener may be surprised to know that over two hundred concertos have been written for the bass. It also has been featured in numerous symphonic passages. Examples include Gustav Mahler's Symphony No. 1 in D Major, Igor Stravinsky's ballet *Pulcinella,* and Benjamin Britten's opera *A Midsummer Night's Dream.*

The double bass is written in F or bass clef. In the modern era, the double bass is tuned in pairs of perfect fourths. The range of the instrument is E1—or C1 if a string extension is used—to around G5 with the use of harmonics. The open strings and range of the double bass in standard tuning are shown in Figure 16-6.

FIGURE 16-6: Open strings and range of the double bass in standard tuning

Open Strings   Professional Range (does not include harmonics)

The bottom note represents a low C extension found on many professional model basses.

Notes on the double bass sound one octave *lower* than written.

There are two types of bowing techniques used by double bassists. They are known as the French style and the German style, respectively. Two virtuosos in bass history are largely responsible for the supremacy of these styles. Domenico Dragonetti was a proponent of the German bowing style during the early nineteenth century. Another Italian, Giovanni Bottesini, showed the effectiveness of the French style in the 1850s and beyond. Today, both techniques are widely used.

The French grip is similar to violin and viola bowing (i.e., the hand is placed *over* the bow). As such, the bows themselves resemble large violin bows. The German design allows the bassist to clasp the bow in the web of the hand with the thumb overtop and the fingertips resting on the frog. Using this grip, the thumb and pinky finger act as a fulcrum. German style is commonly referred to as an *underhand* bowing.

General Bowing Techniques

All instruments of the violin family are played one of two ways: by plucking the strings (pizzicato) or through contact with a bow (arco). Bowing is the most common way to play stringed instruments in symphonic and chamber music settings.

The bow uses fine horsehair. When the bow is drawn across the strings, friction produces a tone. This wouldn't be possible without rosin. Rosin is a hard, sticky substance made of tree sap. When applied to the bow, the bow hairs grip the strings.

The two important parts of the bow are the *frog* and the *tip.* The bow hairs are suspended between these points, and the frog is where the string player holds the bow. The most basic bow strokes are down and up bows. In the modern era, the universal rule is that strong beats are played as down bows while weak beats are played as up bows. In 4/4, this means that beats one and three are down bows while beats two and four are up bows. The symbols for up and down bows are shown in Figure 16-7. A down bow begins at the frog and moves to the tip. An up bow is just the opposite.

FIGURE 16-7: Up and down bows

Unless you're writing music for children or amatuers, you do not need to indicate down and up bows in your music.

⊓ = down bow

V = up bow

Bowing techniques used by modern string players include:

- **au talon:** bowing at the frog. This produces louder and thicker tones
- **punta d'arco:** bowing at the tip. This produces thinner, delicate tones.
- **col legno:** hitting the strings with the stick or wood of the bow; a percussive effect.
- **sul ponticello or sul pont:** bowing close to the bridge of the violin. This produces a coarse, nasal tone.
- **sul tasto:** bowing over the fingerboard of the violin. This produces a light, airy tone.
- **détaché:** to bow each note separately. Nothing is indicated in the music except the notes themselves.
- **legato:** attached, slurred notes. When a slur is written, the notes will be grouped together as one connected phrase.
- **tenuto:** play each note for its full value. Alternating full-length bows are usually used.
- **portato:** the pulsing of legato (slurred) notes with a single up or down bow.
- **staccato:** short, detached notes (usually with alternating bowing).
- **spiccato:** the bow bounces on the strings using distinct, controlled bow strokes. This produces very short notes. Often, composers use the term *sautillé* synonymously.
- **marcato:** long, accented, detached notes. Each stressed note is attacked separately without slurring.
- **martelé:** "hammering" the strings. Each bow stroke is strong and accented but short (similar to marcato but with staccato notes).
- **jeté:** the bow strikes the strings then rebounds several times in rapid succession. Often used for fast, delicate, staccato arpeggios. The term ricochet *(ric.)* may be used as a synonym.
- **tremolo:** "rolled" notes using fast up and down bows.
- **sul G, sul D, etc.:** This tells the string player to use only a specific string such as the G-string or the D-string, etc.

Figure 16-8 shows some of these techniques are they are notated in music. Legato strings are common in virtually all styles of music and are written using slur markings; see Figure 16-8.

FIGURE 16-8: Détaché, legato, tenuto, portato, staccato, spiccato, marcato, martelé, and tremolo bow strokes as seen in notation

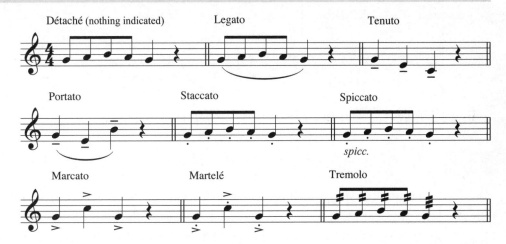

As a composer, you will want to be aware of bowing techniques since each one produces distinct timbral and textural variances. You will probably find that you use détaché, legato markings (slurs), and staccato markings (dots) the most. However, if you are aware of other bowing techniques, you can bring greater color, texture, and diversity to your compositions.

Pizzicato Techniques

If nothing is specified in the music, string players will automatically play *arco*. Therefore, if pizzicato is desired, the composer must write *pizz.* underneath the staff. If the composer wants to return to bowing, he must also write *arco*. Back and forth pizz. to arco passages are not uncommon. This is illustrated in Figure 16-9. Again, this passage is scored for a string quartet.

FIGURE 16-9: Arco and pizzicato markings

TRACK 62

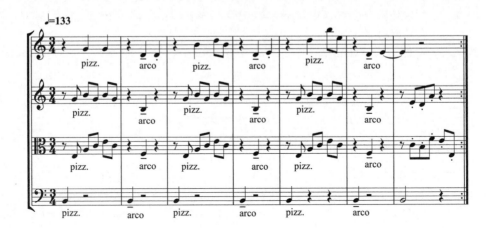

On violin, viola, and cello, the forefinger of the right hand generally plays pizzicato notes. On double bass, the forefinger and middle fingers are used when playing jazz and other popular musical forms; pizzicato is also employed almost exclusively in these styles. Occasionally, a multiple motion "slap-snap" technique is used on bass too. To do this, the bassist uses the entire palm of the hand and/or the thumb to strike the strings. For the snap motion, the bassist literally grabs the string with the fingertips then releases it. This produces a loud, percussive snap as the string slaps against the fingerboard.

In classical music this is called snap or "Bartok" pizzicato (derived from composer Bela Bartók who was the first to use this technique). The symbol for this is shown in Figure 16-10.

Another form of pizzicato resembles the strumming of a guitar. Here, the string players brush their forefingers and sometimes thumb across the strings. It's used when pizzicato chords appear in the music and some indication is made to strum rather than pluck. If you write more than two note chords, string players will assume you mean to strum from the lowest note to the highest note in your chord. You will hear this technique used in the penultimate movement of Nikolai Rimsky-Korsakov's *Capriccio Espagnol.*

Left-handed pizzicato is yet another style of pizzicato. This technique can be deceiving because the string player often integrates the bow at the same time. To execute a left-handed pizzicato, the string player will dig into the string with the pad of the finger then release it. In essence, this technique uses an inverse flicking motion. Electric guitarists use this technique often and refer to it as a *pull-off*. Niccolò Paganini's twenty-fourth caprice from his collection *Twenty-Four Capricci, Op. 1* was the first to employ this technique. When notated, a plus sign (+) appears in the music as shown in Figure 16-11.

Moreover, a pizzicato may be paired up with a glissando or a slur. A glissando or *gliss.* means to slide into another pitch (usually many steps away). Also, a rare style of pizzicato requires the string player to use the nail of the finger to pluck the string. This technique simulates the sound of a plectrum or guitar pick. To indicate this in your music, you would write *nail pizz.* under the notes. However, you should use restraint when writing this effect since it's painful to play. Lastly, if you write *secco* next to a pizzicato marking, the string player will deaden the note immediately after plucking.

FIGURE 16-10: A snap pizzicato symbol

An accent is implied in this pizzicato marking.

FIGURE 16-11: Left-handed pizzicato

Using Harmonics

Harmonics are effects that produce extremely high-pitched notes. The timbre or tone color of a harmonic is different from other notes due to the way the note is produced. Composer and violinist Jean-Joseph de Mondonville first used *natural harmonics* in violin sonatas in the 1730s. A natural harmonic is produced on an open string by lightly touching the string at a point, or node, that changes how the string vibrates. When the violinist plays a natural harmonic, the fundamental pitch does not sound. Instead, a much higher overtone is heard. They are easiest to play on a violin as you move up or down the fingerboard breaking the string length into thirds. The first position is closer to the pegbox, the second is near the middle of the fingerboard, and the third is near the highest point on the fingerboard (close to the F-holes).

Another kind of harmonic is created when the string is depressed (stopped) and another finger touches a node along the fingerboard. This is called an *artificial* or *false harmonic*. Both types of harmonics can be bowed or plucked. When they are bowed they add a high shimmer to the music that adds a unique brightness (even shrill) quality to a composition. They have been used with great success by nineteenth and twentieth century composers. One famous use of artificial harmonics is found in the finale of Peter Ilyich Tchaikovsky's Violin Concerto in D major, Op. 35. Figure 16-12 shows how to notate harmonics for violin. Use the same notation for viola, cello, and double bass. Be sure to see Chapter 19 for more information on composing for strings.

FIGURE 16-12: Natural and artificial harmonics

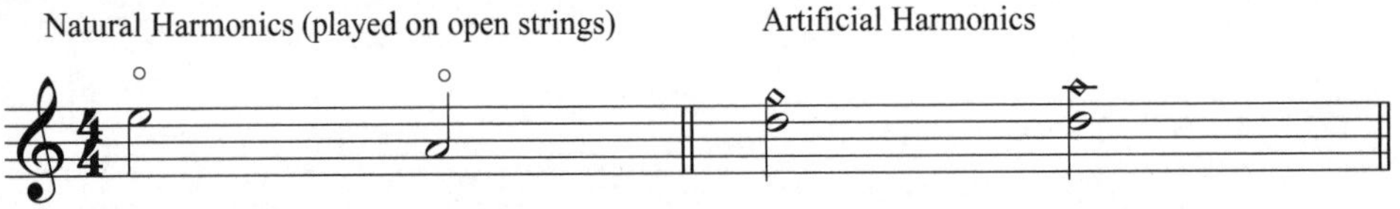

To play artificial harmonics, the pinky finger lightly touches the stopped string a perfect fourth or a perfect fifth above the main note. When you touch a perfect fouth above the main note, the note that sounds is two octaves above the main (stopped) note: in this case D. When you touch a perfect fifth above the main note, the harmonic produced is one octave above the touched note: in this case A.

Chapter 17

Writing for Wind Instruments

This chapter presents fundamental information about writing for woodwinds and brasswinds. The material presented here really only scratches the surface; much more could be written about any one of these instruments. In order to expand your knowledge further, study scores, method books, and orchestration books. Also, bear in mind that instrument ranges on wind instruments may vary depending on the instrumentalist and the make and model of the instrument being played. To be safe, you should generally avoid notes in the extremely low or extremely high registers of all wind instruments.

The Clarinet Family

The clarinet is a large family of transposing instruments. The B♭, A and E♭ soprano clarinets, and the B♭ bass clarinet are the four most common instruments used today. However, many more clarinet varieties exist. Of these four clarinets, the soprano B♭ is the most widely used. It is employed in concert bands, orchestras, chamber ensembles, Klezmer bands, and jazz. In jazz, it's used primarily in Dixieland and swing genres. The bass clarinet is also used in these contexts although it's less common in jazz and rare in Klezmer.

All clarinets are cylindrical in shape and contain the following main parts:

- Mouthpiece (includes a single vibrating reed)
- Barrel
- Upper joint (also called a left hand joint)
- Lower joint (also called a right hand joint, and with the upper joint comprises the instrument's body)
- Bell (made of silver-plated brass and upturned on the alto clarinet, basset-horn, bass clarinet and other lower pitched clarinets)

Professional model clarinets—like oboes and English horns—are usually made from African Blackwood. Student models are made of plastic.

The keywork design of the clarinet is called the "Boehm system." This system is erroneously attributed to the German inventor Theobald Boehm who designed a fingering system for the flute. The clarinet's fingering design was developed by the Frenchman H.E. Klosé and Auguste Buffet jeune. These innovators based their design on the pioneering work of Boehm.

Clarinet Range

The pitch range of the clarinet is divided into four registers. From low to high these registers are:

- Chalumeau
- Throat (also called intermediate or break)
- Clarinet (also called clarion or clarino)
- Extreme

The chalumeau range produces dark, woody low notes. The throat is problematic because, from around G to B♭, there is a technically difficult "break" between registers. Student clarinetists have a difficult time creating pitches in this zone or above it. Even professionals prefer to avoid the area around F4 to A4 since these are weaker tones.

The mouth and fingers are used to play *all* wind instruments. In each case, the musician blows into the instrument while the fingers depress keys (woodwinds) or valves (brasswinds). On some wind instruments, pitch changes require the player to open and close (cover and uncover) small holes in the body of the instrument. For example, the recorder and penny whistle use this system of finger holes exclusively; the western concert flute uses a hybrid of keys with tone holes.

The clarinet range is the most expressive, natural, and resonant. As a composer, you should focus on this range (from A4 to B5). The extreme range produces squeaky and/or shrill notes that should only be used for effect or other special purposes. The soprano B♭ clarinet range is illustrated in Figure 17-1. The B♭ bass clarinet sounds exactly one octave lower than its soprano counterpart.

FIGURE 17-1: Written range of a soprano B♭ clarinet

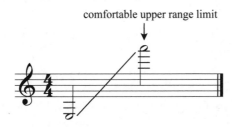

comfortable upper range limit

B♭ Transposition

Notes produced by B♭ pitched instruments are written a whole step higher than concert pitch. For example, middle C (C4) on the piano—a concert pitched instrument—appears on the first ledger line below the staff in the G-clef. This same note transposed for a B♭ instrument becomes a D natural. These rules also apply to key signatures. For instance, if a piano part is written in C major, it will be written in D major on B♭ pitched instruments.

In reverse, if you want a B♭ instrument to read a middle C, the concert pitch would become a B♭. Similarly, if you want to write a part in C major for a B♭ instrument, concert pitched instruments would be notated in B♭ major. This is illustrated in Figure 17-2.

FIGURE 17-2: Transposition from concert pitch to B♭

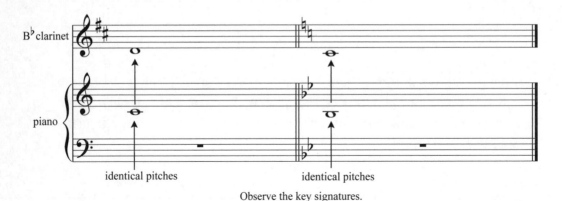

Observe the key signatures.

This transposition information correlates to B-flat instruments such as the B-flat clarinet, B-flat trumpet, and the soprano saxophone. However, the bass clarinet, tenor saxophone, and B-flat baritone horn sound an octave plus a major second below concert pitch.

The Saxophone Family

Invented around 1840 by Adolphe Sax, the saxophone or sax has become one of the most popular instruments in music. The saxophone is similar to the clarinet, and often, clarinetists play saxophone and vice versa. In fact, according to the Hornbostel-Sachs musical instrument classification system, the saxophone *is* a type of clarinet.

This conical instrument was originally intended for symphony orchestras and military bands. However, the saxophone has become a staple in jazz music. It's also been widely used in blues, rock-n-roll, pop genres, and chamber settings (e.g., saxophone quartet).

There are many saxophone varieties. However, the most common types, from highest to lowest pitch are: soprano, alto, tenor, and baritone (sometimes called a bari). All of these saxophones are transposing instruments. The soprano and tenor saxophones are pitched to B♭ while the alto and baritone saxophones are pitched to E♭. Transposition from concert pitch to E♭ is shown in Figure 17-3. This means that notes in concert pitch must be transposed up a *major sixth* to be played correctly by some E♭ instruments.

FIGURE 17-3: Transposition from concert pitch to E♭

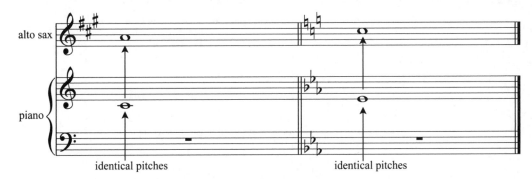

Observe the key signatures.

This transposition information correlates to E-flat instruments such as alto saxophone. Other E-flat instruments, such as the baritone saxophone and the E-flat bass clarinet, sound an octave plus a major sixth below concert pitch.

Clef Substitution

Since baritone and alto saxophones are pitched to E♭, they may use *clef substitution* to read bass clef parts that are written in concert pitch. Here's how it's works: The saxophonist will read the bass clef concert pitched part in treble clef, and add three sharps to the key signature. For example, if the music is written in C major, the saxophonist will read it as if it's A major. If the music is written in a flat key, the saxophonist must take away three flats. If there are only two flats (e.g., B♭ major) the saxophonist will take away both flats then add one sharp and read the music in G major. If there is only one flat, the saxophonist will take away one flat and add two sharps thus reading the music in D major. Because of clef substitution, in a pinch, alto and baritone saxophones can read music written for trombone, bassoon, tuba, and double bass.

Saxophone Ranges and Effects

Figures 17-4 through 17-7 show the comfortable pitch range for each of the four major saxophone types. Higher pitches may be rendered through the use of overtones in the altissimo register. However, proficiency in this ultra-high register depends on the level of the player.

FIGURE 17-4: Written range for the soprano saxophone

FIGURE 17-5: Written range for the alto saxophone

A high F-sharp key is needed to play this note.

Sounds a major sixth lower than written.

FIGURE 17-6: Written range for the tenor saxophone

A high F-sharp key is needed to play this note.

Sounds a major ninth lower than written.

FIGURE 17-7: Written range for the baritone saxophone

A high F-sharp key is needed to play this note.

Some instruments can play a low A.

Sounds a major thirteenth lower than written.

Many effects are employed on the saxophone. Some of these include growling, multiphonics, and slap tonguing. Growling creates a coarse tone on the saxophone. In order to produce this effect, the saxophonist must sing gutturally while blowing into the horn. Multiphonics allows the saxophonist to create two different pitches at once. Although these pitches usually warble and clash, the effect is quite stunning. Lastly, slap tonguing creates a percussive sound or "pop" on the saxophone. This occurs when the reed slaps against the mouthpiece as the tongue drives downward and a tight suction around the lips is released.

ALERT!

Controlling the flow of air through *any* wind instrument is a major concern. Like all wind instrumentalists, saxophonists use a technique called "overblowing" to jump to upper registers. This simply means forcing more air through the horn. Unintentional and uncontrolled overblowing often results in shrill squeaking noises.

The Flute and Piccolo

The western concert flute and its cousin, the piccolo, are staples in orchestras, wind ensembles, and marching bands. The flute is also used in chamber music and it is not uncommon in jazz, Latin music, and even modern rock (e.g., the Jethro Tull band).

While the concert flute is a member of the woodwind family, it is not made of wood, but rather, sterling silver, or on student models, silver-plated alloys. Both the flute and the piccolo are pitched to C, and they use the same fingerings. However, the piccolo sounds one octave higher than the flute. Moreover, its notes appear on the staff one octave lower than concert pitch. The range of the flute is notated in Figure 17-8 and the range of the piccolo is notated in Figure 17-9.

The western concert flute has three main parts:

FIGURE 17-8: Range of the western concert flute   **FIGURE 17-9:** Written range of the piccolo

May be played with a B footjoint.

Octave shifts are made by changing the blowing angle and by using less air as you jump to higher registers.

Sounds an octave higher than written.

- The headjoint
- The body
- The footjoint

The flutist blows into an opening on the lip plate of the headjoint, called the embouchure hole. Unlike other woodwind instruments, the concert flute and piccolo are held perpendicular to the flutist's body and "side-blown." As such, they are classified as *transverse* instruments. Unless an effect is used to transform the tone, the sound created by the concert flute is smooth and silky and it's especially good for performing trills and mimicking birdsong. A versatile instrument, the flute may also be used to create suspense or woeful laments. Moreover, its sister, the piccolo, has the ability to soar and soliloquize above any other instrument in the orchestra.

Double Reed Instruments

The oboe, English horn, and bassoon are used almost exclusively in orchestras, chamber ensembles, and concert bands. Unfortunately, they have not had significant crossover into popular milieus (unless they appear in an orchestra that plays pop music).

It's very difficult to even make a sound on a double reed instrument, and beginners must practice hard to develop their embouchure, or mouth position. However, for students who work diligently, the payoff is great because double reed instruments all have hauntingly beautiful tone qualities and their contribution to the orchestra is immeasurable.

The oboe and the English horn (often called a *cor anglais)* are very similar instruments. In fact, the English horn is nothing more than a tenor oboe pitched in F. The oboe itself is pitched in C. In orchestral settings, the oboe is often used to invoke majesty, sophistication, and elegance. The oboe may also be used to convey darker emotions, but as the composer Hector Berlioz warned, it cannot convey anger or threat very well.

FACT

Double reeds are made from Arundo donax cane that is carefully folded then bound together with wire. Some instrumentalists purchase premade reeds. However, most professionals use a variety of tools to make their own reeds.

Breathing and Range on the Oboe and English Horn

When writing for any wind instrument, you must remember that musicians must have regularly spaced rests so that they may breathe. However, oboists and English horn players have a greater ability to play longer lines without a break since they exhale less air per note. Why? Their embouchure is so tight that only a small amount of air is released when they play. The result is that longer, uninterrupted phrases may be created.

When compared to other woodwind instruments, the range for the oboe and English horn is somewhat limited. The range for the oboe is notated in Figure 17-10 and the range for the English horn is illustrated in Figure 17-11.

The Bassoon

Like the oboe, the bassoon is conical. Two versions of the instrument, both pitched to C, are in use today. The first is the German or "Heckel" system. The second is the French or "Buffet" system. The difference between them lies in the keywork and the bore specifications (i.e., the instrument's hole). The former is more common among today's bassoonists.

The bassoon's range is larger than you might expect. For example, the modern Heckel-style bassoon spans some five octaves. In the right hands, the Buffet-style can reach even higher notes. Despite its vast compass, composers traditionally view the bassoon as a baritone registered instrument. As such, the bassoon typically plays in octave ranges below the oboe and cor anglais in orchestral contexts. The range of the bassoon is illustrated in Figure 17-12.

FIGURE 17-10: Range of the oboe

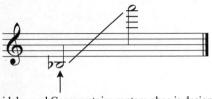

The widely used Conservatoire-system oboe is designed to play this low B-flat. The much less common Viennese oboe usually does not contain a low B-flat key.

FIGURE 17-11: Written range of the English horn

Sounds a perfect fifth lower than the written notes.

FIGURE 17-12: Range of the bassoon

Absolute top note. It's best not to write above E5.

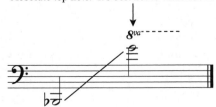

The bassoon has often been used to evoke humorous or silly emotions in music. However, this instrument is capable of producing a whole assortment of emotions. For example, the fluttertongue technique used on many wind instruments (including flutes, trumpets, and trombones) is particularly alarming and menacing on a bassoon. More and more, composers are expanding the role of the bassoon as a solo instrument, a member of the double reed family, and as a color within the orchestra.

The Trumpet

In the brass section, the trumpet is located at the top of the pitch spectrum. Because of this, composers tend to write parts that soar above the orchestra. This often means sudden blasts of energy designed to add excitement and power to the music. Despite this use, the modern trumpet is extremely versatile and has the ability to invoke a plethora of moods and emotions. For this reason, the trumpet has been used in a wide range of musical settings outside of the orchestra. This includes brass choirs, marching bands, big bands, jazz combos, funk groups, and rock bands. The trumpet is also featured in several ethnic styles of music (e.g., Klezmer, Polka, and Afro-Cuban).

There are many varieties of trumpets—pitched in an assortment of keys—including period instruments that are still used today (e.g., natural or valve-less trumpets). There is also a bass trumpet typically played by trombone players. However, the three most common instruments are the B♭ trumpet used by both classical and non-classical musicians, the C trumpet used by orchestral trumpeters, and the piccolo trumpet, used by classical trumpeters primarily for baroque repertoire. Scores by Igor Stravinsky and Maurice Ravel also call for Petite Trompette in D, which in performance, is effectively a piccolo trumpet. Additionally, many of John Adams' works employ the piccolo trumpet.

The B♭ flugelhorn is also popular among jazz artists, and the B♭ cornet is a mainstay in Dixieland and British Brass Band music. Moreover, the cornet appears in scores by Igor Stravinsky, Hector Berlioz, Claude Debussy, and César Franck. These instruments are all end-blown horns made out of brass with shiny, flared bells. One factor that distinguishes cornets, flugelhorns, and trumpets is the shapes of their bore. Trumpets have cylindrical bores while the flugelhorn and cornet have conical (cone-shaped) bores.

Piston Valves versus Rotary Valves

With the exception of the four-valve piccolo, most trumpets feature three piston valves. Rotary valve trumpets in C and B♭ also exist but these are less common among non-classical musicians. Select orchestral players in the United States maintain an interest in rotary valve horns expressly for their use in romantic period Germanic music (Beethoven, Brahms,

Bruckner, Wagner, Mahler, etc). European classical players outside of England and France use rotary horns exclusively (e.g., The Vienna and Berlin Philharmonics). Both types of horns require regular lubricating with valve oil so that the valves don't stick during performance.

Trumpet Mutes

Trumpeters are known for their extensive use of mutes. These mutes not only reduce the volume of the instrument, they significantly change the timbre. Mutes are usually inserted into the bell of the trumpet, although a few are clipped to the bell. In notation, you must write *con sord* to tell a trumpeter to use a mute and *senza sord* to indicate when to remove the mute. If you do not specify which mute to use, it's assumed you mean a straight mute. The five standard trumpet mutes are:

- Straight mute. This is the most common type of mute in classical music; it creates a nasal tone.
- Cup mute. This mute is similar to a straight mute but more subdued.
- Harmon mute (wah-wah mute). This mute creates a thin, buzzing tone. When the left hand is used to choke then release the airflow, a "wah-wah" effect is created. The Harmon mute is typically used by modern jazz musicians (e.g., Miles Davis). It may be used with or without its stem; when the stem is in place, the air is channeled more directly through the mute and the result is that the horn is less muffled.
- Plunger mute. This is simply a rubber cup from a sink plunger. It's held in the left hand and often used to mimic the human voice.
- Bucket mute (velvetone mute). This mute takes away the brightness (high frequencies) of the trumpet, and instead, gives it a more velvety tone.

Trumpet Range

Range on the trumpet is especially tricky to determine since the ability to hit extremely high notes on the instrument depends largely on the player. However, some general approximations have been made in Figures 17-13 and 17-14 for the B♭, C, and B♭ piccolo trumpets. Many trumpeters assert that

FIGURE 17-13: Written range of the B♭ and C trumpets

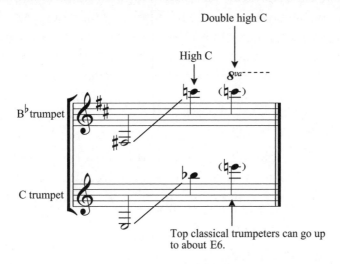

Note: Very few trumpeters can hit double high C's.
Those who can, specialize in high note playing.

FIGURE 17-14: Written range of the B♭ piccolo trumpet

Depending on the leadpipe, the piccolo trumpet
may be pitched to either A or B-flat.

the piccolo trumpet does not allow one to play any higher than they do on regular sized trumpets. Rather, the piccolo trumpet is used to bring greater precision and articulation to parts written in upper registers.

The French Horn

Usually referred to simply as the "horn," the French horn is a unique member of the brass family. In the orchestra, it typically bridges the timbral and dynamic gap between the softer woodwinds and the vociferous trumpets, trombones, and tubas. Horns are often used for long tones in the middle register of the orchestral pitch spectrum. Frequently these long tones will sweep into the music in a portentous or solemn manner. Other times, solo horns are used to create gentle or rapturous melodies. When several horns are played in a section, the instrument brings great strength and stability to harmonies.

If unraveled, the French horn's tubing would be longer than any other brass instrument in the orchestra, with the probable exception of the bass and contrabass tubas. Like other brass instruments, the horn contains a flared bell, mouthpiece, and valves. Modern horns are conical-bored and they have three rotary valves, which were added to the instrument around 1827.

The Role of the Right Hand

Whereas trumpeters and tubists manipulate the valves using their right hands, horn players use their left hands to depress the rotary valves. A horn player's right hand is placed in the bell to control the pitch and timbre of the instrument. The right hand may also be used to create a number of effects on the horn. The most common effects are:

- Stopped horn. Thrusting the hand deep within the bell creates a stopped or *gestopft* horn. The result is a muted buzzing sound. In notation, a "+" symbol means stopped and an "o" means open. However, if you wish to write long passages for stopped horn, you should write the words "stopped" and "open."
- Open-stopped horn. An open-stopped horn begins with an open, full-bodied tone followed by a sudden stop. This creates a sharp decrease in dynamics and may be used for sudden timbral contrasts.
- Handhorn. To play a handhorn, the hornist manipulates the right hand inside the bell so that additional notes may be added to the harmonic series. The harmonic series refers to the playable notes or pitch frequencies within a given register.

- Hand glissando. To create a hand glissando, the hornist moves the hand gradually from an open to closed position. This bends the pitch and a glissando is formed. Hand glissandos are not common. The most famous use is in Benjamin Britten's *Serenade for Tenor, Horn and Strings*.

Notation, Range, and Note Splitting

Today, the French horn is usually scored in G-clef although an older style of notation uses the bass clef. Moreover, in previous centuries, horns were not necessarily pitched to F, which is the current standard. These clef and key discrepancies occasionally leave contemporary musicians transposing on the spot or wondering what octave to play in. "Old notation" can be problematic for modern hornists.

Due to the long coiled tubes and the funnel-like mouthpiece, the French horn has an enormous pitch range. However, the range of the French horn varies depending on the player's level of expertise. This is further complicated by the fact that hornists tend to have range specialties. In other words, some players focus on material in the "high horn range" while others concentrate on material in the "low horn range." See Figure 17-15 for the approximate range of the horn.

FIGURE 17-15: Range of the horn in F

Sounds a perfect fifth lower than written

In general, the horn is seen as an extremely difficult instrument due to the fact that the instrument's harmonics are located so close to one another. Because of this, the hornist must implement subtle lip pressure so that pitch changes can be made without "splitting" notes. When a note "splits," the tone becomes distorted and ugly.

The Trombone

There are many instruments in the trombone family. However, the most common are the tenor trombone and the bass trombone. The trombone is a featured member of symphony orchestras, concert bands, and chamber ensembles (e.g., brass choirs and brass quintets). Like the trumpet and saxophone, the trombone is also a mainstay in popular genres including jazz (all eras), big band, and Latin music.

On all wind instruments, tonguing is an essential technical skill used to play rhythms (e.g., triplets) and expression marks (e.g., staccato). On each instrument, syllables are "tongued" or enunciated; this purposely interrupts and structures the airflow. Single, double, and triple tonguing patterns are employed so that a multitude of rhythms and articulations may be created.

The trombone's long telescopic slide allows the trombonist to change pitch without the use of valves. As the slide is pulled out, the pitch gets lower; as the slide is pulled in the pitch ascends. However, with the exception of the slide, the trombone is very similar to its brass siblings. Like the trumpet, it has a cylindrical bore. And like all brasses, the buzzing of the lips on a mouthpiece generates the sound. This sound travels through a network of pipes—some of them "S" shaped—until it's released at the bell.

There are seven positions on the trombone and each one produces a distinct harmonic series. This refers to the notes a trombonist creates without changing the length of the tubing (i.e., moving the slide). With the exception of the tuba, the trombone uses more air than any other wind instrument. Therefore, more breaths are necessary and composers must allot for this in their music.

There are usually three trombones in an orchestra: two tenors and a bass. Typically, music is scored in bass clef for both types of trombones. However, classical trombonists must also be able to read parts in tenor and alto clef.

The tenor trombone and the bass trombone also have the same compass. However, lower notes on the bass trombone are more clearly defined. In other words, the bass trombone can play notes in the trigger and pedal ranges with greater accuracy; see Figure 17-16. Although the tenor and bass trombones are both pitched to B♭, they read music in concert pitch. The trombone also uses the five mutes outlined earlier in this chapter; see Trumpet Mutes.

FIGURE 17-16: Range of the trombone

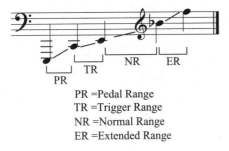

PR = Pedal Range
TR = Trigger Range
NR = Normal Range
ER = Extended Range

Unlike the trumpet or any other brass instrument, the slide trombone can create beautiful, arcing glissandos with ease. This effect has sometimes caused the trombone to be looked upon with mirth since these glissandos can sound comical and even cartoonish.

On the other hand, the trombone has the ability to bring solemnity and power to an arrangement, and symphonic composers have long exploited its dynamic muscle. Moreover, jazz musicians have proven the subtle, lyrical qualities of the instrument (e.g., swing trombonist Tommy Dorsey). Lastly, in contemporary music, composers have successfully used the trombone to explore multiphonics and microtonality.

The Tuba

The tuba is the largest and lowest pitched member of the brass family. It is used in symphonic and concert band repertoire and in brass choirs and brass quintets. Tubas are also used in so-called "oom-pah" bands where a "two-beat" feel is employed (e.g., Dixieland and polka music). Lastly, the sousaphone—a tuba worn around the shoulder—is a staple in military and civilian marching bands. Tubas come in four main sizes: tenor (euphonium), bass tuba, contrabass tuba, and Wagner tuba. (The Wagner tuba is usually played by French hornists.) Tubas are pitched in five different keys: BB♭, CC, E♭, EE♭, or F. The double letters refer to very low octave ranges. In concert bands, where no strings are present, tuba parts tend to be more active and many tubas are used. The standard tuba used in this context is usually a BB♭ model.

In string orchestras, there is typically only one tuba player and parts tend to be more functional than exciting. However, it was the orchestral tradition that first embraced the tuba. Specifically, it was Hector Berlioz's *Symphonie Fantastique* (1830) that introduced the tuba to concertgoers. What's more, composers such as Richard Strauss, Jean Sibelius, Dmitri Shostakovich, Sergei Prokofiev, Igor Stravinsky, George Gershwin, and others used the tuba as a significant voice in the orchestra and not merely as a utility "low note" player. In symphony orchestras, the CC pitched tuba is the most prevalent, except in Germany, Austria, and Russia where they favor the BB♭.

Like its brass brethren, the tuba is an intricate network of tubing with a flared bell and a mouthpiece. (In this case, a very large bell and mouthpiece.) It has a conical bore and either piston valves, rotary valves, or both. Piston valves are more common in the United States and England. Depending on the player's level of proficiency, three to six valves may be used; students typically use a three-valve system while professionals use at least four.

With the exception of British brass band music, tuba parts are written in bass clef and in concert pitch. Because composers typically do not specify the type of tuba to be used, tubists must be able to interpret the music and transpose if necessary. One exception to this is the F Wagner tuba, which is notated accordingly. Overall, tubists must choose the horn type that best matches the demands of the composition and/or the musical setting; this is one reason why orchestral tubists in the United States typically use the concert pitched CC tuba. Figure 17-17 shows the range for CC bass and contrabass tubas; note that the range is the same.

FIGURE 17-17: Range for CC bass and contrabass tubas

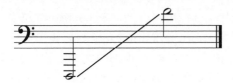

The Significance of Embouchure

When it comes to playing any wind instrument, the embouchure becomes the single most important technical detail. Poor embouchure means poor intonation, poor tone, and limited facility in general. Embouchure refers to:

- The position of the lips on the mouthpiece (brass)
- The position of the mouth around the mouthpiece (single reed instruments)
- The position of the mouth around a folded, exposed reed (double reed instruments)
- The position of the lower lip against an embouchure hole (flute and piccolo)

E-QUESTION

As a composer, why should I worry about embouchure?
You do not have to specifically concern yourself with embouchure. However, it's so fundamental to playing wind instruments that you should be aware of the role it plays in sound production. Good composers are knowledgeable about the instruments they write for. Further, you will develop deeper relationships with musicians if you understand the technical demands they face.

For brass, lip coverage on the mouthpiece is a critical factor. On single reed instruments, proper synchronization of the teeth, lips, and oral cavity itself become principal concerns. On the flute, the direction of the airflow is paramount, and on double reeds, a tight seal around the reed is required to even utter a sound.

Embouchure varies greatly from instrument family to instrument family. Many subtle factors influence the development and maintenance of embouchure. In addition to the aforementioned, facial muscles, the jaw, and the instrumentalist's posture affect the sound quality that is produced.

Chapter 18
Writing for Drums and Percussion

Aside from the human voice, percussion comprises the oldest instrument family in history. Because of this, music of all kinds, styles, and eras use percussion instruments. This chapter teaches you about the most common instruments found in a symphony orchestra and in popular music. Overall, drums and percussion encompass more than just rhythm. Depending on the instrument, they can be used to for melody, harmony, counterpoint, and texture too.

The Percussion Family

A percussion instrument is any instrument that is hit or struck. The percussion family is extremely broad and it continues to expand as technology produces new instrument variations. By definition, percussion includes orchestral instruments such as the snare drum, bass drum, woodblock, triangle, tambourine, cymbals, and pitched instruments such as the timpani, xylophone, marimba, glockenspiel, vibraphone, and tubular bells. It also incorporates a slew of ethnic instruments from around the globe such as bongos, congas, timbales, maracas, claves, castanets, bodhrans, bones, doumbeks, djembes, surdos, repiniques, cuicas, tablas, and scores of others. Moreover, electric (digital) drums are an increasingly popular member of the percussion family.

ALERT!

Don't forget about small percussion when you compose. There are literally dozens of instruments to choose from and you're only limited by your imagination. For example, a tambourine will add a Latin, Spanish, or gypsy flair to your music. Woodblocks can sound like galloping horses or tap dancers, and rain sticks simulate a downpour. To make your music really sparkle, try using a triangle to keep the beat.

Lastly, the percussion family also includes any *found object* that is struck. Found objects are non-instruments used for percussive effect in contemporary music. Examples include brake drums from automobiles, coffee cans, pots, pans, cups, wine glasses, rocks, logs, PVC pipes, boxes, and just about anything else a performer can dream up. The sky is really the limit.

The Snare Drum

The snare drum is the flagship of the percussion family. Marked by a sharp, snappy tone, the snare drum (or side drum with snares) was first associated with military music. Its antecedent, the tabor, initially appeared in fife and drum corps in medieval Europe as early as the 1300s. The Swiss army had a particularly strong impact on the art of snare drumming, especially the development of snare drum *rudiments*. Rudiments are a collection of rhythms, patterns, and stickings. Initially, rudiments were designed by and for military snare drummers. Today, drummers of varied backgrounds and disciplines use rudiments to build technique and stick control. Rudiments are to snare drumming as scales are to definite pitched instruments.

Snare drums are always double headed. In the modern era, heads are all made of Mylar (plastic) though calfskin was popular throughout the 1950s. Modern snare drums have varied shell depths and circumferences. For orchestral or chamber group uses, snare drums are usually 6" × 14" (depth × diameter). Marching drums are often twice the depth, or 12." They can be made of metal or contain several wooden plies.

What separates a snare drum from its cousin, the tom-tom, is its use of metal or gut wires, which attach to the bottom head of the drum and give it a distinctive sound. These wires are collectively called the *strainer*. The lever used to tighten the strainer against the head, or oppositely, release the wires from the head is called a *throw-off.*

The snare drum has a myriad of uses in orchestral music. Whenever a composer wants to represent war, an approaching army, or a parade, etc. the snare drum is implemented. It is also used to play sudden rim shot accents and explosive rolls, which add excitement and intensity to any composition. More contemporary uses of the snare drum focus on nuance and color. This is achieved by releasing the throw-off to a down position or by playing with wire brushes instead of wooden sticks. Sometimes felt mallets, fingers, and hands are also used strike the snare drum.

Figure 18-1 shows you neutral clef. This clef is used to represent the snare drum in notation (as well as any other indefinite pitched instrument).

FIGURE 18-1: Neutral clef

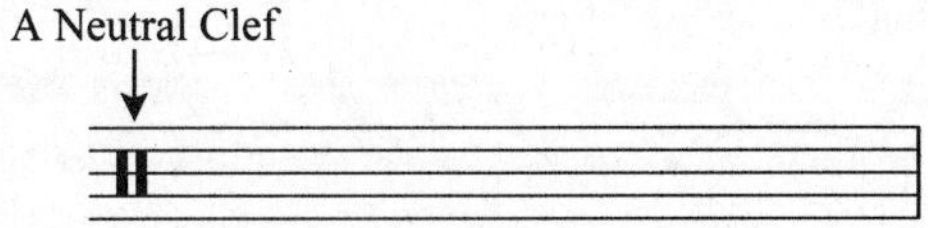

A Neutral Clef

FIGURE 18-2: Snare drum rudiments

TRACK 63

1. Single Stroke Roll (As sixteenth notes and thirty-second notes.)

R L R L R L R L R L R L R L R L

OR...

R L R L R L R L R L R L R L R L R L R L R L R L R L R L R L R L R L R L

2. Double Stroke Roll (Long Roll) (As a whole note and thirty-second notes)

RRLLetc...   R R L L R R L L R R L L R R L L R R L L R R L L R R L L R R L L

3. Single Paradiddle (As sixteenth notes)   > = Accent (play louder)

R L R R L R L L R L R R L R L L

4. Flam (As quarter notes)

Grace Note

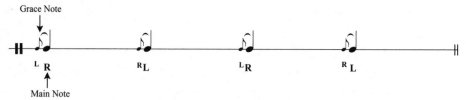

ᴸR   ᴿL   ᴸR   ᴿL

Main Note

5. Three Stroke Ruff (As quarter notes)

Grace Notes

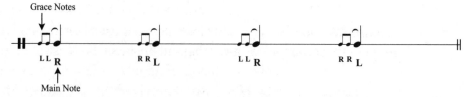

ᴸᴸR   ᴿᴿL   ᴸᴸR   ᴿᴿL

Main Note

6. Buzz Roll (Multiple Bounce)

(Often written with a "Z")   (Pulsing the Roll Using Sixteenth Notes)

R L R L R L R L R L R L R L R L

Figure 18-2 shows the six most important rudiments. All six of these rudiments serve as the foundation for other, more elaborate, rudiments. Use these rudiments and others (see *www.pas.org*) as the basis for snare drum parts in your work.

The Bass Drum

The bass drum is the largest drum in the percussion section. A typical concert bass drum measures 36 inches in diameter. The concert bass drum is played with a weighted felt mallet in the right hand. Percussionists may also roll on the drum using dual mallets with both hands. Sometimes a crash cymbal is mounted on top of the bass drum, with the tapered edges facing upward. The percussionist then holds a crash cymbal in his left hand, hovers over the mounted cymbal and bass drum, and plays both instruments at once. This type of instrumental multitasking is common in percussion sections.

FACT

Like the snare drum, the concert bass drum is double-headed. This allows for a complex blend of overtones to sound when the bass drum is struck. The drum is either suspended on a ring-shaped apparatus or it sits atop of a foldable metal stand.

In classical music, the bass drum was used infrequently prior to the work of eighteenth century opera composer Christoph Willibald Gluck. Franz Liszt was the first composer to write bass drum rolls. From the nineteenth century onward, the concert bass drum has enjoyed great use in orchestral music. It's also commonly used in percussion ensemble music as well as mixed ensemble chamber works that incorporate percussion.

In addition to its role as a timekeeper, the bass drum is used for vociferous accents or to create a dark, ominous mood. For example, the bass drum can accurately simulate the rumble and crackle of thunder. Although it has an indefinite pitch, the concert bass drum produces a myriad of low and sub-low frequencies that add great depth to the texture of any ensemble.

Figure 18-3 shows some examples of bass drum part writing. Here, you will see a typical bass drum part for a march and a waltz. You will also see an example of a roll followed by two measures of syncopated, accented notes. In this figure, vertical accents are used. This tells the percussionist to play with extra force.

FIGURE 18-3: Concert bass drum examples

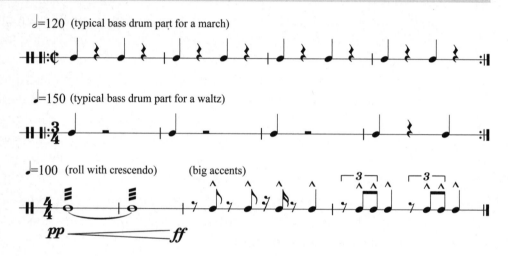

Cymbals, Crotales, and Gongs

A cymbal is a round, concave plate with a protruding bell made from alloys of brass, tin, or other metals. Cymbals are either held as a pair or suspended on a stand. If the cymbals are handheld, straps (usually leather) are knotted through a hole in the cymbal's bell. Percussionists pinch the straps with the thumb and forefinger, then crash them together slightly askew so that the sound doesn't choke. When the cymbal is suspended, it's usually struck with a soft mallet(s). Dramatic rolls or "swells" are common in symphonic and chamber group settings.

Cymbals come in a variety of sizes from very small (6" and 8" splashes) to crashes and rides ranging from 20" to 24." The mallet, stick, or brush used to strike the cymbal determines the sound(s) produced. The cymbal's thickness also plays a significant role in tone production.

Small, tuned metal plates called *crotales* are cousins to the cymbal. These thick plates are arranged like the bars on a glockenspiel (keyboard style) and notated in G-clef. Another cousin to the cymbal is the tam-tam or gong. These definite and indefinite pitched metal plates were first invented in Indonesia. Large tam-tams are particularly thunderous. In fact, no other symphonic instrument can create such an ear-splitting blast.

In western music, the French romantic era composer Hector Berlioz first featured cymbals in his work. By the late nineteenth century, cymbals were a mainstay in the orchestra. They are used to bring zeal to marches, intensity to crescendos, and gusto to thematic climaxes.

Mallet Instruments

There are five mallet instruments used by western percussionists. All of these instruments contain metal, wooden, or plastic bars arranged like a piano keyboard. This means that they contain two rows of notes: a front row of naturals and a back row of sharps and flats. The five types of mallet instruments used in symphonic, chamber, and/or marching band music are:

- Orchestra bells (also called a glockenspiel, bell lyre, or "glock")
- Xylophone
- Vibraphone (also called a vibraharp or vibes)
- Marimba
- Tubular bells (also called chimes)

FIGURE 18-4: Mallet instrument ranges

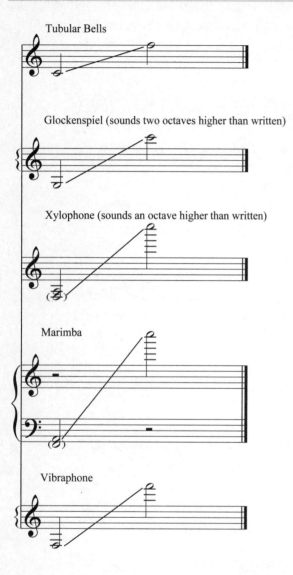

Mallet instruments have their roots in ancient Africa and Asia. In Europe, the xylophone was first used in the early 1500s; the glockenspiel was first introduced in the late 1760s; tubular bells were developed in 1886 for Sir Arthur Sullivan's cantata *The Golden Legend;* manufacturers Leedy and Deagan built their first marimbas and vibraphones in the second decade of twentieth century and design innovations made them popular in the 1930s.

There is a considerable difference between each of these instruments. This is due to the size of the bars, the material used to make the bars, and the mallets used to play them. Orchestra bells, for example, are high-pitched metallic bars played with hard plastic or brass mallets. This creates a transparent, sharp tone. The wooden and kelon (plastic) xylophone also has a pointed sound, given its middle to high octave range and the hard mallets used to strike the instrument.

All xylophones contain two sets of resonators. These long tubes (situated under the bars) help to carry the sound of the instrument out into the concert hall. The marimba and vibraphone also have resonators. However, both of these instruments create a mellower, darker tone. Additionally, marimbas and vibraphones are played using two or four mallets—depending on the piece—and the mallet tips are woven from soft yarn.

FIGURE 18-5A: Eight bar mallet example

TRACK 64

FIGURE 18-5B: Eight bar mallet example

TRACK 64

This example is based on an Amin$^{9\#11}$ chord.

Despite their similarities, marimbas and vibraphones also have great contrasts. For one, marimbas are made of rosewood while vibes are made of aluminum. Vibraphones also contain a dampening system (complete with pedal) to control the instrument's sustain. Moreover, vibes have a motor and pulley system, which spins round discs mounted inside the resonator tubes. When the motor is turned on, the discs rotate creating a pulsating vibrato effect.

Marimbas have a lower octave range, and in terms of size, this instrument is the granddaddy of the mallet family. Tubular bells are also an imposing instrument. They are made of long tubes of metal suspended on a stand and played using wooden or plastic hammers. Tubular bells have virtually one role in music: to simulate the peal of church bells.

Mallet players are used to playing fast, complex lines up and down each of these keyboard instruments. When writing for orchestra bells, however, be careful not to write too many high-speed rhythms, as this will create a discordant wash of sound (unless you purposely want that effect). Bell music is particularly effective when simple parts are written in octaves. When using only two mallets at fast tempos, you should also avoid writing large octave leaps. If you *do* want to write mallet music that spans many octaves, compose for four-mallet marimba or vibraphone. Figure 18-4 shows the standard octave ranges of each of the instruments discussed. Some exceptions may occur, depending on the instrument and model.

Figure 18-5 features the glockenspiel, the xylophone, the marimba, and the vibes in a sample composition. In this short example, the xylophone takes the helm as the melody instrument (soloist) supported by punctuations from the "glock." The smooth-toned vibes and marimba assume the role of harmony.

Timpani

Timpani are indispensable members of the symphony orchestra. They also have wide appeal and application in chamber ensembles. Additionally, many twentieth century composers have written solo works for this instrument and there are even a handful of timpani concertos.

Also called kettledrums, timpani are shaped like large kettles with a membrane or batter head. Like other contemporary drums, the head is plastic, although it used to be fashioned from goat or calfskin. On professional models, the kettle or bowl is made of copper and well-maintained drums always have a beautiful golden sheen. Timpanists use soft to semi-hard felt mallets to play these drums and they always strike the head near the rim. When a roll is written, the modern timpanist also always uses single strokes (see Figure 18-2 for the notation and sticking of a single stroke roll).

Timpani contain an elaborate tuning mechanism. Older models often used hand cranks and a chain drive. However, most current models use a tension rod tuning system complete with a foot pedal. When the pedal is depressed the drum raises in pitch as the tuning mechanism pulls the head taut.

There are five standard timpani sizes in use today. They are: 32", 29", 26", 23", and 20." A standard set of timpani contains only the bottom four drums (minus the 20" kettle). This is sufficient for *most* orchestral music. Often amateur ensembles, such as elementary and middle school bands, use only the middle two sizes (29" and 26"). This is okay since these types of ensembles play simplified arrangements with limited tuning range. The highest drum—called a *piccolo* timpani—is needed only for select twentieth century works (such as Leonard Bernstein's *Overture to Candide)* and other postmodern repertoire.

Timpani are popular with composers because they serve two roles. They add rhythmical punch to music, and they contribute to the composition's harmonic content. In the baroque and classical eras, this usually meant tuning the drums to perfect fourths or perfect fifths. When tuned in this fashion, the drums are used to emphasize I and V chords (authentic cadences). During these eras, the timpani also typically played in tandem with the trumpet section.

Beethoven was one of the first composers to expand the role of timpani beyond perfect fourth and fifth intervals and predictable rhythmical punctuations. His symphonies featured more varied tuning intervals and even brief solos (e.g., the second movement of Symphony No. 9). Modern repertoire requires the timpanist to make numerous pitch changes on the fly and with great precision. Because of this, timpanists must have excellent relative pitch. (Professional timpanists often use an "A" tuning fork as their point of reference.)

Figure 18-6 shows the pitch range for a standard set of four timpani.

FIGURE 18-6: Pitch range for a standard set of four timpani

Timpani is always written in bass clef.

With detuning, the top and bottom drums may be able to play a whole step lower or higher, respectively.

The Drum Set

The drum set is the most widely played percussion instrument. In fact, the drum set has become the shining star of the percussion family, spawning dozens of celebrity musicians such as Gene Krupa, Buddy Rich, Ringo Starr, Ginger Baker, John Bonham, and Neil Peart, among many others.

The drum set is a collection of instruments that allows one person to play several instruments at the same time. Jazz drummers in the first quarter of the twentieth century first developed this instrument, as did percussionists working in vaudeville theatres and pit orchestras. By the dawn of the swing era (c. 1935), the drum set became a featured instrument in big bands.

FACT

The drum set or *trap set* emerged around 1900. The manufacturing of bass drum pedals by Ludwig Co. in 1909 ultimately allowed the drum set to flourish. In its early period, the drum set consisted of a bass drum, a snare drum, Chinese tom-toms, and Turkish cymbal(s). Many drummers also attached dragon's mouths (woodblocks), cowbells, and whistles onto their kits.

Flamboyant showmen such as Chick Webb, Gene Krupa, and Buddy Rich brought the drum set to the forefront in popular music. Today, most western musical idioms feature this instrument. In addition to popular music forms, the drum set is also employed in ethnic and world genres, religious musical styles, and even contemporary classical.

Notating Drum Set Music

As you might guess, in drum set notation, the lines and spaces of the staff symbolize drums and cymbals. Due to the fact that the drum set contains indefinite pitches, the clef you use for the drum set is neutral like other indefinite pitched percussion instruments. Figure 18-7 shows a legend of drums and cymbals as they appear on the staff.

FIGURE 18-7: Drum set legend

DRUM SET LEGEND

BD = Bass Drum
2nd BD= Second Bass Drum
(double pedal or double kick)
SN = Snare Drum
T1= High Tom-tom or Rack Tom 1
T2 = Middle Tom-tom or Rack Tom 2
FT = Floor Tom-tom
HH = Hi-Hat (closed)
O = Open Hi-Hat

+ = Closed Hi-Hat (used only when open HH patterns are present)
⋈ = Half Open Hi-Hat
HH Ft.= Hi-hat Foot
Ride = Ride Cymbal
CR= Crash Cymbal
RS= Rim Shot
CS = Cross Stick
CB = Cowbell
WB = Woodblock

Keep in mind that drum set notation is not 100 percent standardized, although most composers and authors use the system shown in Figure 18-7, give or take some minor variations. One common notational variance is the indication of a ride cymbal on the space above the top line (where the hi-hat is also written).

X-shaped note heads are also used to indicate cymbals (including the hi-hat) while traditional circles are used to indicate drums. Other auxiliary percussion instruments, such as cowbells or woodblocks, are spelled out with triangle shaped note heads. Rim shot notation can vary. A diamond-shaped note head is shown in Figure 18-7. Cross-sticks (a type of rim shot) are usually written with an "x" on the snare drum line.

A rim shot is created when the drummer strikes the head and the rim of the drum at the same time. A cross stick is created by placing the stick on top of the batter head in a perpendicular fashion. Then, using a snap of the wrist, the drummer strikes the rim of the drum with the shaft of the stick. This creates a clicking sound not unlike a clave.

In most cases, drums and cymbals contain note stems that point upward while the bass drum and hi-hat foot typically point downward. Exceptions to this may occur when the feet are highly integrated with the hands for fills and solos.

If you to write for drum set you must understand popular music forms. This means that you should have an understanding of jazz, rock, and Latin styles. In rock, hip-hop, rap, rock-blues, and modern country and western, drum set beats are almost always written in 4/4. Moreover, they revolve around a "kick-snare-kick-snare" model; kick is slang for bass drum. This drum pattern is shown in Figure 18-8.

A swing beat—used primarily in jazz and country swing—has a triplet feel. Instead of emphasizing the bass drum and snare, swing emphasizes the ride cymbal and the hi-hat foot. This is shown in Figure 18-9.

Lastly, one of the most common Latin styles is the bossa nova from Brazil. This style emphasizes a 3+2 cross stick pattern on the snare drum and a soft but punchy ostinato in the bass drum. This beat is shown in Figure 18-10.

Use these three beats as the basis for drum set parts in your music. However, bear in mind that these grooves are just the tip of the iceberg.

FIGURE 18-8: Basic rock beat

TRACK 65

FIGURE 18-9: Basic swing beat

TRACK 66

How it is played...   How it is often written...   Another common shorthand...

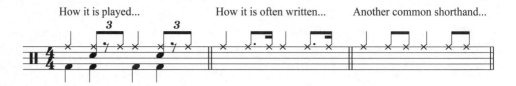

FIGURE 18-10: Basic bossa nova beat

TRACK 67

clave: (1)   (2)   (3)   (1)   (2)

A 3+2 clave pattern is used here. This pattern is often featured in Latin music.

Thousands of variations exist. Moreover, if you plan to write extensively for drum set, you will need to familiarize yourself with a wide variety of sub-styles. For many more drum set grooves, see *The Everything® Drums Book* and *The Everything® Rock Drums Book*.

Chapter 19
The Orchestra

The word "orchestra" is really a pat term used to describe a wide variety of large ensembles. For example, in the 1930s swing orchestras (also called big bands) became popular. And in the East, the word has been used to describe numerous large ensembles from different countries. This includes the Japanese gagaku orchestra, the Indonesian gamelan orchestra, and the Chinese drum and gong orchestra. This chapter focuses on the Western European orchestral tradition. As such, you will learn about its history and its uses from its inception to the modern day.

The Birth of the Orchestra

It's hard to say exactly when the first orchestra was formed. Indeed, definitions of what officially constitutes an orchestra can vary. Arguably, the first known orchestra was Monteverdi's pit ensemble for *L'Orfeo* in 1607. However, it was the French model that spurred the development of the orchestra, as we know it.

In 1673, French court composer Jean-Baptiste Lully gathered a large group of musicians to mount his opera *Alceste* in the city of Versailles. Lully's unique ensemble caught on when foreign dignitaries visited the French court and returned home (primarily to Germany) determined to create the same kind of musical display in their own courts. What made Lully's ensemble "orchestral" was the variety of instruments he employed. His orchestra was predominantly strings, augmented with wind instruments that supported the strings. By 1675, he added timpani drums. He also doubled instruments, especially the violins.

The *concerto grosso* was a key form that developed in the middle baroque period. Spearheaded by Arcangelo Corelli, and culminating in the works of Antonio Vivaldi, the concerto grosso emphasized thematic, textural, and instrumental contrasts between a full orchestra called a *ripieno* and a small consort called a *concertino*. This form was used extensively by both Handel and Bach, and reinvigorated in the twentieth century by composers Igor Stravinsky, Ernest Bloch and Bohuslav Martinu.

In the 1680s and '90s, the orchestra became popular among many composers of the middle baroque period. However, orchestras from this era were much smaller than the modern orchestra, consisting primarily of stringed instruments of the violin family. This included the violin, viola, violoncello, and the now obscure bass viola da gamba.

Additionally, recorders, flutes, oboes, and bassoons were often added to the ensemble as well as two (French) horns. Sometimes, timpani drums were also employed. Lastly, a basso continuo group was used to render the harmonic structure of the piece and the bass notes of the composition. Of these instruments, the recorder has fallen out of favor as a regular member of the orchestra as well as the viola da gamba, and continuo instruments such as the harpsichord, theorbo, organ, and lute.

Basso continuo is unique in western classical music for two reasons. Firstly, baroque composers rarely specified what instruments should be used to perform this role. Secondly, using figured bass, which is defined in Chapter 2, the continuo group would improvise the harmonic structure of a piece. With the demise of the continuo group in secular music (around 1775) music became almost totally predetermined by the composer with regard to instrumentation and notation.

Before Conductors

In the Middle Ages, music theorist Guido de Arezzo developed the *Guidonian Hand*. Its use of finger signs and spatial movement anticipated the conducting tradition but it was ultimately a tool used to teach *solfege* (do, re, mi, etc.) and sight singing. In other words, the Guidonian Hand was not used to mark time or lead musicians who were reading notated parts. With the arrival of the orchestra, the conductor was soon to follow. However, its development was remarkably slower than you might expect.

Baroque orchestras did not feature a conductor, per se. Famously, Lully led his musicians by tapping a staff on the floor. However, this practice proved fatal when during a performance he struck his toe, gangrene set in, and he died shortly thereafter.

In this era, the concertmaster (first violinist) usually set tempos, made decisions about bowing, expression, and ornamentation, and effectively guided the ensemble.

The Brandenburg Concertos

In the late baroque period, the orchestra took on greater significance. Increasingly, it was seen as a powerful and effective collection of instruments capable of communicating artistic ideas without the aid of the human voice. One of the finest examples of this is J.S. Bach's Brandenburg Concertos.

FIGURE 19-1: Instrumentation for Brandenburg Concerto No. 4 in G Major

It's difficult to say exactly when Bach composed these six all-instrumental works. However, they were gifted to Margrave Christian Ludwig of Brandenburg-Schwedt in 1721 in hopes of obtaining financial support. A bigger fan of George Frideric Handel, the margrave offered no largesse and instead shelved Bach's work. When the manuscripts were discovered in the nineteenth century, they were immediately championed as priceless works of the period.

The orchestration for the Brandenburg Concertos varies from piece to piece. Figure 19-1 shows the instrumentation for the Brandenburg Concerto No. 4 in G major, which is a concerto grosso. Here, a single violin and two flutes (flauto) play the *concertino* and the other six instrument groups play the *ripieno*.

You will notice the instrument "violone" in the score. This is also called a bass viol. Today, this part would be played by a modern four-string double bass, and a harpsichord usually plays the continuo part. In Bach's day, however, parts were somewhat interchangeable as long as the register and pitches were maintained. For example, the two flute parts indicated in Figure 19-1 could be replaced with two recorders and the continuo part could have been played on a theorbo (though likely Bach played it himself on the harpsichord).

The Classical Orchestra

In the classical period, most orchestras featured primary and secondary violins, violas, cellos, and contrabasses: a paradigm that continues to this day. Additionally, two oboes, two French horns, a bassoon, and a continuo instrument (usually an organ or harpsichord) were used during the first half of the period. In this sub-period, the cellos, basses, and continuo usually played the same line. However, the keyboard player often added an improvised harmony part (chords) as well.

From around 1790 to 1815—the so-called high classical period—woodwind instruments (reeds and flute) gradually took on equal partnership in the orchestra, and specialists began to appear. For example, in earlier periods, oboists often doubled on the flute. However, in the high classical period, musicians started focusing on one instrument only. Soon, virtuosos appeared, and as you might imagine, composers began featuring soloists more in their work.

Additionally, in the high classical period, composers began writing independent lines in the lower registers in place of the usual continuo parts. As such, the cello and double bass no longer mirrored one another. Moreover, the bassoon also took on a greater autonomy. Another key development was the use of the pianoforte in place of the harpsichord (see piano history in Chapter 12).

The Mannheim School

During the classical era, the symphonist was effectively born and the Mannheim School greatly influenced its development from the high classical period onward. Founded by Johann Stamitz, this composer/musician collective (active in the court of Mannheim from around 1740 to 1778) is known for many innovations that are still used today. Some of these include:

- The Mannheim crescendo (whole orchestra swell)
- The Mannheim roller (extended crescendo with ascending melody and ostinato bass line)
- The Mannheim sigh (placing more emphasis on and elongating the first note in a pair of slurred notes)
- The Mannheim rocket (rising arpeggios from low to high at a swift pace)
- Mannheim birds (imitating bird song to brighten solo passages)
- The grand pause (The orchestra suddenly stops playing only to resume with great verve; this creates suspense and forward momentum in the music.)

Haydn, Mozart, and Beethoven

Three symphonists ultimately dominate the classical era: Franz Joseph Haydn, Wolfgang Mozart, and Ludwig Van Beethoven. Beethoven, however, is seen as transitional figure whose work embodies both "classical" and "romantic" elements depending on the period in his life.

All three of these composers have extensive catalogs of all-instrumental chamber work, sonatas, and concerti. However, they also viewed the symphony as a powerful method of artistic expression as evidenced by their prodigious output. Mozart wrote forty-one symphonies and his friend and mentor "Papa" Haydn wrote a whopping 104. By comparison, Beethoven was less prolific, penning only nine symphonies. However, each Beethoven symphony is regarded as a major work of the period. Moreover, from an historical perspective, his ninth "choral" symphony is arguably the most significant work of the nineteenth century.

FIGURE 19-2: Instrumentation to Symphony No. 40 in G Minor, K. 550

Allegro Molto By W.A. Mozart

Flauto
Oboi
Clarinetti in B♭
Fagotti
Corno 1 in B♭
Corno 2 in G
Violino I
Violino II
Viola
Violoncello e Contrabasso

Figure 19-2 shows the instrumentation to Mozart's Symphony No. 40 in G Minor, K. 550, his penultimate symphonic offering. This is one of Mozart's most famous symphonies, due in large part to the unforgettable theme of the first movement. It's also one of two symphonies he wrote in a minor key. Interestingly, trumpets and timpani are omitted from his score. In 1788, when this piece was composed, these instruments were still optional, though this musical philosophy was rapidly changing. The first, second, and fourth movements are written in sonata form.

Sonata Form

Sonata form is the most widely used form in symphonic and chamber music from the classical period to the twentieth century. It is commonly used in the first movement of a three or four movement composition. Because of this, sonata form is often termed "sonata-allegro" form. This appellation is used because the classical symphony usually begins with a fast (allegro) movement. However, this label is misleading because composers often use sonata form for multiple movements in a single work.

At first blush, sonata form may be viewed strictly as another formal model. However, deeper examination reveals, as theorist D. F. Tovey asserted, that sonata form encourages a certain manner of expression that is both dramatic and dynamic. Indeed, there is an explicit "psychology" built into "sonata style" compositions. Perhaps this mindset is best exemplified by the neat and tidy symmetry inherent in the structural underpinning of the form.

FACT

The classical concerto (a multimovement work for orchestra and soloist) usually follows sonata form during at least the first movement. However, in Mozart piano concertos, this strict model becomes quite freewheeling and elastic. In fact, Mozart stretches the parameters and rules of sonata form so much; his concerti are often analyzed as free form *fantasias*.

Sonata form ultimately reduces to an earlier model called rounded binary (see Chapter 11). This means that sonata form breaks down to an A, B, A¹ formula. However, in sonata form, A is represented by the *exposition*, B is represented by the *development*, and A¹ is represented by the *recapitulation*. The only element in sonata form that belies rounded binary is the optional *coda* used by composers to extend the tonic harmony and intensify the movement's conclusion.

Exposition (A)

The exposition introduces primary thematic material called the *first subject group* presented in the home key. After the first subject group is stated, the music undergoes a *transition* and a formal key change. In major keyed symphonies and chamber works, the tonic key usually modulates to the dominant key. In minor keyed symphonies and chamber works, the tonic key usually modulates to the minor dominant or relative major key. After the modulation, *secondary thematic material*, called the second subject group, is presented. The exposition then concludes with a diminutive *codetta* or *closing theme* in the key of the second subject group.

Development (B)

The development expands the material first introduced in the exposition. This section is the least predictable. Usually, there may be many sub-sections of the development and a great deal of harmonic exploration is employed. This includes multiple key shifts, the fragmentation of themes, and playful motivic sequencing. There may even be the introduction of new thematic material.

The composition is at its most unstable during the development if only because it's constantly in a state of harmonic flux. However, for these same reasons, the development is also exciting and emotionally intense. Toward the end of the development, a *retransition* prepares the music for a restoration of the tonic key, and with it, the return of the first subject group. Often, a protracted dominant seventh chord signals the end of the development.

Recapitulation (A1)

The recapitulation reinstates the main thematic material in the tonic or home key. Like the exposition, the opening material (first subject group) is presented. This is then followed by a transition, and the reiteration of the second subject group. However, the transition does *not* include a modulation, and therefore, the second subject group is also presented in the home key. This is then followed by the codetta, also in the tonic key. After the recap, the piece may simply end or move into a *coda* (see above).

Romantic Era Orchestra

In the nineteenth century, the orchestra not only grew in size and instrument variety, it expanded beyond aristocratic circles and court performances, and became a public institution. As such, independent orchestras arose as bona fide arts organizations in major cities throughout Europe. In the mid to late nineteenth century, orchestras were also formed in the New World. These included The New York Philharmonic, The Boston Symphony Orchestra, The Chicago Symphony Orchestra, and The Montreal Symphony Orchestra. Given this proliferation, the profession of "orchestral musician" was legitimized with regular wages, and later on, the support of music unions.

In 1859 Russia, The Russian Music Society (an organization that was part music school part performing arts ensemble) promoted the symphonies of Beethoven and eventually homegrown composers Pyotr Tchaikovsky and Nikolai Rimsky-Korsakov. Conductor Mily Balakirev premiered many new works of the period. A member of the Russian *Mighty Handful*, Balakirev vigorously supported the nationalistic music of Russia.

Then, as now, there were two categories of orchestras: concert orchestras (with a preplanned season and/or concert series) and theatre orchestras designed for opera and other vocal styles. It was during the Romantic Period that these distinctions first materialized gradually over time.

Instruments and Orchestral Techniques

In the romantic period, many new instruments were brought into the orchestra. Some of these innovations were short lived, but they paved the way for additional developments. For example, the serpentone, bombardon, ophicleide and cimbasso were all used to add depth and power to the brass section during the first quarter of the nineteenth century. After 1830, however, tuba varieties supplanted these more primitive aerophones. However, the concept of using low register brass instruments was retained. Instrument technology also produced brass instruments with valves as well as better keywork on woodwinds. For example, adding valves onto the French horn allowed for one instrument to be played in different keys. All of this increased the musical possibilities of these instruments. Richard Wagner's

FIGURE 19-3: Instrumentation for Brahms's Symphony No. 2 in D, Op. 73

experimentation with unorthodox instruments (such as the Wagner tuba) also had a lasting effect of the size and color possibilities of the orchestra.

Wagner's use of *leitmotifs*—reappearing themes that symbolize a person, place, idea, object, mental state, or mystical force—also had a lasting effect on Richard Strauss, Gustav Mahler, and Anton Bruckner. Moreover, the leitmotif paved the way for greater emphasis on programmatic expression. This was especially true as the leitmotif cross-pollinated with the one movement *symphonic poem*. Largely credited to Franz Liszt, the symphonic poem (also called tone poem) is a descriptive, programmatic orchestral work that recounts the story of Greek myth, prose, history, and other imaginative subjects; symphonic poems are not generally written in sonata form.

Figure 19-3 shows the instrumentation for one romantic period symphony. In this case, you will see Johannes Brahms's Symphony No. 2 in D, Op. 73. While highly venerated, Brahms's music is structurally conservative for the period, at least in comparison to his rivals Liszt and Wagner. Like his mentor Robert Schumann, Brahms's legacy is rooted in the traditions of the classical form, though you will see that his position in history encouraged him to use a considerably larger orchestral palette than Mozart of Haydn.

Since you may not know German, here's a list of the instruments you may not recognize: Flöten (flute), oboen (oboe), klarinetten (clarinet), fagotti (bassoon), hörner (French horn), trompeten (trumpet), posaunen (trombone), pauken (timpani), and bratsche (viola).

FACT

In the Romantic period, baton conductors first appeared on a rostrum in front of the orchestra. As music directors, they made major decisions about how music should be interpreted and performed. The conducting profession became widespread by the mid nineteenth century. In 1843, Hector Berlioz wrote in the first textbook dedicated to orchestration, that musicians act as "intelligent machines" and the conductor plays them like "an immense piano."

Igor Stravinsky: The Height of Modernism

When Igor Stravinsky appeared on the scene in 1910, music was undergoing major changes. Tonality was being challenged and the orchestra was recast as an instrument for musical revolution (if only for a brief time). With the exception of the Second Viennese School, no one epitomized this shift away from romanticism to eyebrow raising modernism more than the Russian-born Stravinsky. In fact, the premier of his ballet *The Rite of Spring* (1913) caused a riot in Paris.

Writing for Sergei Diaghilev's dance company, Ballets Russes, the young Stravinsky brought a fresh approach to harmony. For example, in *Petrushka,* he experimented with polytonality (simultaneous use of multiple keys). This is illustrated in the second section of the ballet where the first and second clarinets play an ascending line together. In this passage, the first clarinet plays a C major arpeggio and the second clarinet plays an F♯ major arpeggio a tri-tone lower. This harmonic movement has since been dubbed "the Petrushka chord."

Figures 19-4 and 19-5 show examples of the orchestra at the height of modernism. Here, you will see the instrumentation to Part IV of Stravinsky's ballet *Petrushka.* Additional instruments are used in the original 1911 score

FIGURE 19-4: Woodwind instrumentation for *Petrushka*

Part IV   By Igor Stravinsky

The Nursemaids Dance with the Coachmen and Stable Boys

Fl. I. II.

Fl. III.

Fl. IV.

Ob. I. II.

Ob. III.

Ob. IV.

Cl. I. II.

Cl. III.

Cl. IV.

Fag. I. II.

Fag. III.

Fag. IV.

Depending on the part (tableau) of the ballet,
other instruments are used as well; see text.

depending on the section or passage. (The ballet is structured into four parts called *tableaux*.) These supplementary instruments, which are not shown in Figures 19-4 and 19-5, include: bass clarinet, contrabassoon, cymbals, two snare drums (one played offstage), two tambourines (one played offstage), triangle, tam-tam, glockenspiel, xylophone, piano, and celesta.

Decades later, in 1947, Stravinsky reworked the ballet for a smaller, more manageable orchestra. Both versions are used today. You may be confused about some of the instruments indicated in Figure 19-5. They are translated as such: Cor. (French horn), Pist. (cornet), Gr. Cassa (bass drum), and Arpe (harp).

The Contemporary Orchestra

The twentieth century orchestra saw both great innovation and great trials for the orchestra. In the first half of the century, composers inflated the already sizable romantic era orchestra (as you saw in the *Petrushka* figures). Saxophones, cornets, flugelhorns, and the Wagner Tuba were some of the instruments added. However, in the twentieth century most orchestras fell back on "the classics" and therefore older styles and formats prevailed. In the long run, this had deleterious effects since the orchestra gradually became seen as a

FIGURE 19-5: Brass, percussion, and strings instrumentation for *Petrushka*

Part IV   By Igor Stravinsky

The Nursemaids Dance with the Coachmen and Stable Boys

Depending on the part (tableau) of the ballet other instruments are used as well; see text.

musical dinosaur. In fact, by the end of the twentieth century, lay audiences generally viewed the orchestra as stodgy, conservative, and old-fashioned.

Despite this, the twentieth century did bestow some instrumental innovations. For example, the modernist and postmodernist movements resulted in the inclusion of ethnic percussion instruments, found instruments, and other gizmos and gadgets into the percussion section. With the exception of timpanists, percussionists had long played a subservient role in the orchestra. However, the twentieth century saw the advent of the percussion concerto, and in general, composers such as Béla Bartók, Sergei Prokofiev, George Gershwin, Leonard Bernstein, and Iannis Xenakis, among many others, began to feature percussionists in their orchestrations.

Another twentieth century innovation was the occasional implementation of electronics, multimedia, and popular instruments in orchestral settings. Experimentations with the Theremin, tape loops, synthesizers (Minimoog), electric guitars/basses, the drum set, and various digital instruments gave the orchestra a contemporary edge.

Additionally, "pops" concerts became fashionable beginning in 1895 with the founding of The Boston Pops. Today, pops concerts feature the orchestra playing easy listening "classics," popular music arrangements, and collaborations with trendy singers and other celebrities. Examples of "pops concert" singers include the smooth-toned crooners Josh Grobin, Sarah Brightman, and k.d. lang. While orchestral purists have long argued that pops concerts are tacky, these events help to keep otherwise struggling orchestras in the black. Many classical music fans, and scholars alike, fear that the orchestra may be in decline. However, it's doubtful that it will ever cease from being an internationally recognized musical institution.

Appendix A
Essential Composers

The following is a partial list of essential composers. This catalog only includes western composers of major significance; for information on jazz composers see Chapter 15.

Composer names appear on this list in loose chronological order from the Middle Ages to the twenty-first century. After each name, one or two compositions have been recommended. However, keep in mind that many of these composers have extensive catalogs. An asterisk (*) appears next to composers of extra special significance.

Hildegard of Bingen—*Ordo Virtutum*

Léonin—*Magnus Liber*

Pérotin—*Viderunt omnes* and *Sederunt principes*

Philippe de Vitry—*Roman de Fauvel*

*Guillaume de Machaut—*Messe de Nostre Dame*

*Guillaume Dufay—*Ecclesie militantis* and *Missa Sancti Jacobi*

Johannes Ockeghem—*Missa pro defunctis*

Josquin des Prez—*Motet: De profundis clamavi ad te*

William Byrd—*Cantiones, quae ab argumento sacrae vocantur*

Giovanni Gabrieli—*In Ecclesiis*

Giovanni Pierluigi da Palestrina—*Missa sine nomine*

*Claudio Monteverdi—*L'Orfeo*

Johann Pachelbel—*Canon in D major*

Arcangelo Corelli—*Concerto grosso in G minor, op.6 no. 8 (Christmas Concerto)*

Alessandro Scarlatti—*Il Pompeo*

Johann Joseph Fux—*Overture in D minor*

François Couperin—*Les Goûts réunis*

*Antonio Vivaldi—*The Four Seasons*

Georg Philipp Telemann—*Viola Concerto in G major*

Jean-Baptiste Lully—*Miserere*

Jean-Philippe Rameau—*L'enrôlement d'Arlequin*

*Johann Sebastian Bach—*Brandenburg Concertos* and *The Art of Fugue*

Domenico Scarlatti—*Sonata in G minor, Allegro* and *Sonata in A major, Andante*

*George Frideric Handel—*Messiah* and *Giulio Caesare*

Giovanni Battista Pergolesi—*La serva padrona*

Christoph Willibald Gluck—*Orfeo ed Euridice*

Carl Philipp Emanuel Bach—*Die Israeliten in der Wüste*

*Franz Josef Haydn—*Symphony No.104* and *The Creation, Opus 33*

Johann Christian Bach—*Symphony Op. 3 No.6 in G major*

Luigi Boccherini—*Cello Concerto No. 9*

Antonio Salieri—*La fiera di Venezia*

Muzio Clementi—*Op. 25, Six Sonatas For Piano*

*Wolfgang Amadeus Mozart—*Symphony No. 40 in G minor, K. 550* and *Don Giovanni*

Luigi Cherubini—*Les deux journées*

*Ludwig Van Beethoven—*Symphony No. 5 in C minor, Op. 67* and *Symphony No. 9 in D minor, Op. 125 "Choral"*

Johann Nepomuk Hummel—*Piano Concerto No. 2*

Niccolò Paganini—*Twenty-four Caprices, for Solo Violin, Op.1*

Louis Spohr—*Symphony No. 9 in B minor, Op. 143 "The Seasons"*

Carl Maria von Weber—*Der Freischütz*

Gioachino Rossini—*The Barber of Seville (Il barbiere di Siviglia)*

Gaetano Donizetti—*Fausta*

*Hector Berlioz—*Symphonie Fantastique* and *Harold en Italie*

Mikhail Glinka—*A Life for the Tsar*

*Franz Schubert—*The Erlking* and *Symphony #8*

Fanny Mendelssohn—*Das Jahr*

Felix Mendelssohn—*A Midsummer Night's Dream* and *Symphony No. 4 The "Italian" Symphony*

*Frédéric Chopin—*Préludes* (Op. 28) and *Études* (Op. 10 and Op. 25)

*Robert Schumann—*Frauenliebe und –leben* and *Symphony No. 3 "Rhenish"*

*Franz Liszt—*Hungarian Rhapsodies*

*Giuseppe Verdi—*Rigoletto* and *La Traviata*

*Richard Wagner—*Der Ring des Nibelungen* and *Tristan und Isolde*

Charles Gounod—*Roméo et Juliette*

Jacques Offenbach—*Les Brigands*

Clara Schumann—*Six Soirées Musicales*

César Franck—*Symphony in D Minor*

*Anton Bruckner—*Symphony No. 5 in B♭ Major*

Johann Strauss II "The Waltz King" —*The Blue Danube*

Alexander Borodin—*Prince Igor*

*Johannes Brahms—*Symphony No. 1* and *Variations on a Theme by Joseph Haydn*

Camille Saint-Saëns—*The Carnival of the Animals*

Georges Bizet—*Carmen*

Modest Mussorgsky—*Boris Godunov* and *Pictures at an Exhibition*

*Pyotr Ilyich Tchaikovsky—*The Nutcracker* and *1812 Overture*

Antonín Dvořák—*Symphony No. 9, in E Minor "From the New World"* (Op. 95)

Edvard Grieg—*Piano Concerto in A minor, Op. 16*

Nikolai Rimsky-Korsakov—*The Flight of the Bumblebee* and *Scheherazade*

Edward Elgar—*Pomp and Circumstance Marches*

*Giacomo Puccini—*La Bohème* and *Turandot*

*Gustav Mahler—*Symphony No. 5* and *Das Lied von der Erde*

*Claude Debussy—*Clair de Lune* and *Pelléas et Mélisande*

*Richard Strauss—*Also Sprach Zarathustra* and *Don Quixote*

Jean Sibelius—*Finlandia*

Erik Satie—*The Gymnopédies*

Amy Beach—*Concerto for Piano in C♭ Minor* and *Symphony in E minor "Gaelic"*

Ralph Vaughan Williams—*Symphony No. 3 "Pastoral"*

Alexander Scriabin—*Piano Sonata No. 2 in G♭ minor*

*Sergei Rachmaninoff—*Symphony No. 2 in E minor, Op. 27* and *Piano Concerto No. 2, Op. 18*

*Arnold Schoenberg—*Pierrot Lunaire* and *Five Pieces for Orchestra*

*Maurice Ravel—*Daphnis et Chloé* and *Boléro*

Ottorino Respighi—*The Pines of Rome*

Leos Janacek—*The Makropulos Affair*

Frederick Delius—*On Hearing the First Cuckoo in Spring*

Charles Ives—*The Unanswered Question* and *Symphony No.4*

Gustav Holst—*The Planets*

*Béla Bartók—*Piano Concerto No. 3* and *Music or Strings, Percussion and Celesta*

Zoltán Kodály—*Háry János*

*Igor Stravinsky—*The Rite of Spring* and *The Firebird Suite*

Edgard Varèse—*Ionisation*

Anton Webern—*Passacaglia, for orchestra, -opus 1*

Alban Berg—*Wozzeck*

Sergei Prokofiev—*Lieutenant Kijé* and *Peter and the Wolf*

Darius Milhaud—*Le Boeuf sur le toit*, op. 58

Paul Hindemith—*Mathis der Maler*

Carl Orff—*Carmina Burana*

*George Gershwin—*Rhapsody in Blue* and *Porgy and Bess*

Francis Poulenc—*Stabat Mater*

*Aaron Copland—*Fanfare for the Common Man* and *Appalachian Spring*

Dmitri Shostakovich—*Symphony No. 7 in C major, Op. 60 "Leningrad"*

Elliott Carter—*Variations for Orchestra* and *String Quartet No.1*

Olivier Messiaen—*Quartet for the End of Time* and *Four Rhythmic Studies*

Samuel Barber—*Adagio for Strings*

Alan Hovhaness—*Symphony No. 2, Mysterious Mountain*

*John Cage—*4'33''* and *Sonatas and Interludes*

Benjamin Britten—*Peter Grimes*

*Leonard Bernstein—*West Side Story* and *Candide*

Iannis Xenakis—*Metastasis*

György Ligeti—*Atmosphères*

Luciano Berio—*Un re in ascolto* and *Sinfonia*

Pierre Boulez—*Le marteau sans maître* and *Pli Selon Pli*

Morton Feldman—*Three Ghostlike Songs and Interlude (Voice, Trombone, Viola, Piano)*, and *Coptic Light*

George Crumb—*Ancient Voices of Children*

Terry Riley—*In C*

*Steve Reich—*Piano Phase* and *Music for 1 8 Musicians*

*Philip Glass—*Einstein on the Beach* and *Satyagraha*

John Corigliano—*The Red Violin* (soundtrack) and *A Dylan Thomas Trilogy*

Toru Takemitsu—*A Flock Descends into the Pentagonal Garden*

Ellen Taaffe Zwilich—*Three Movements for Orchestra (Symphony No. 1)* and *Symbolon*

Joan Tower—*Concerto for Orchestra*

John Adams—*Nixon in China*

Appendix B

Resource Guide

The resources offer additional information on a whole host of topics related to
instruments, voice, composition, arranging, orchestration, theory, and more.
This guide is by no means exhaustive.
Therefore, use these web links and book
recommendations as a catalyst for your
own research. Keep in mind that, over
time, some of these links may become
inactive.

Websites

Instruments/Voice

✎www.pianosociety.com

✎www.piano.com

✎www.violinonline.com

✎www.vsa.to (The Violin Society of America)

✎www.americanviolasociety.org (American Viola Society)

✎www.cello.org (Internet Cello Society)

✎www.isbworldoffice.com (International Society of Bassists)

✎www.trumpetguild.org (International Trumpet Guild)

✎www.ita-web.org (International Trombone Association)

✎www.hornsociety.org (International Horn Society)

✎www.iteaonline.org (International Tuba Euphonium Association)

✎www.clarinet.org (International Clarinet Association)

✎www.nfaonline.org (National Flute Association)

✎www.flute.com

✎www.saxophone.org

✎www.idrs.org (International Double Reed Society)

✎www.guitar.com

✎www.pas.org (Percussive Arts Society)

✎www.operainternational.org

✎www.allaboutopera.com

✎www.operastuff.com

✎www.classicalsinger.com

*✎www.soundjunction.org

*✎www.philharmonia.co.uk/thesoundexchange

*✎www.expertvillage.com

*Includes videos of expert musicians showing how to play their instruments plus additional insights into music and composition.

General

✎www.oxfordmusiconline.com (The online authority on music theory, history, and more; includes Grove Music Online)

✎www.wikipedia.org

✎www.amazon.com

✎www.youtube.com

✎www.chordwheel.com

✎www.allaboutjazz.com

✎www.allmusic.com (All Music Guide)

✎www.afm.org (American Federation of Musicians)

✎www.gramophone.co.uk (classical music magazine)

✎www.andante.com (classical music magazine)

✎www.downbeat.com (jazz magazine)

✍www.jazziz.com (jazz magazine)

✍www.rollingstone.com (rock magazine)

Books

Adler, Samuel. *The Study of Orchestration.* Third Edition. New York: W.W. Norton, 2002.

Bach, J.S. *371 Harmonized Chorales and 69 Chorale Melodies with Figured Bass.* Albert Riemenschneider, ed. New York: G. Schirmer, Inc., 1986.

Berlioz, Hector, and Richard Strauss. *Treatise on Instrumentation.* Mineola, NY: Dover Publications, 1991.

Black, Dave, and Tom Gerou. *Essential Dictionary of Orchestration.* Van Nuys, CA: Alfred Publishing Company, 1998.

Blatter, Alfred. *Instrumentation and Orchestration.* Second Edition. Schirmer, 1997.

Boyd, Malcolm. *Bach: Chorale Harmonization and Instrumental Counterpoint.* London: Kahn & Averill Publishers, 2000.

Brindle, Reginald Smith. *Musical Composition.* Oxford: Oxford University Press, 2007.

Davis, Richard. *Complete Guide to Film Scoring.* Boston: Berklee Press, 2000.

Forsyth, Cecil. *Orchestration.* Mineola, NY: Dover Publications, 1982.

Fux, John J. *The Study of Counterpoint.* Revised Edition. New York: W.W. Norton, 1965.

Leonard, Hal. *The Real Book: Sixth Edition.* Milwaukee: Hal Leonard Corporation, 2004.

Levine, Mark. *The Jazz Theory Book.* Petaluma, CA: Sher Music, 1995.

Pease, Ted. *Jazz Composition: Theory and Practice.* Boston: Berklee Press, 2003.

Piston, Walter. *Harmony: Fifth Edition.* Revised by Mark DeVoto. New York: W. W. Norton, 1987.

Rameau, Jean-Philippe. *Treatise on Harmony.* Mineola, NY: Dover Publications, 1971.

Rimsky-Korsakov, Nikolay. *Principles of Orchestration.* Mineola, NY: Dover Publications, 1964.

Russo, William, Jeffrey Ainis, and David Stevenson. *Composing Music: A New Approach.* Chicago: University Of Chicago Press, 1988.

Schoenberg, Arnold. *Fundamentals of Musical Composition.* London: Faber and Faber, 1999.

Schonbrun, Marc. *The Everything® Reading Music Book: A Step-by-Step Introduction to Understanding Music Notation and Theory.* Avon, MA: Adams Media, Inc., 2005.

Index

YOU SHOULD CAREFULLY READ THE FOLLOWING TERMS AND CONDITIONS BEFORE USING THIS SOFTWARE PRODUCT. INSTALLING AND USING THIS PRODUCT INDICATES YOUR ACCEPTANCE OF THESE CONDITIONS. IF YOU DO NOT AGREE WITH THESE TERMS AND CONDITIONS, DO NOT INSTALL THE SOFTWARE AND RETURN THIS PACKAGE PROMPTLY FOR A FULL REFUND.

1. Grant of License

This software package is protected under United States copyright law and international treaty. You are hereby entitled to one copy of the enclosed software and are allowed by law to make one backup copy or to copy the contents of the disks onto a single hard disk and keep the originals as your backup or archival copy. United States copyright law prohibits you from making a copy of this software for use on any computer other than your own computer. United States copyright law also prohibits you from copying any written material included in this software package without first obtaining the permission of F+W Media, Inc.

2. Restrictions

You, the end-user, are hereby prohibited from the following:

may not rent or lease the Software or make copies to rent or lease for profit or for any other purpose.
You may not disassemble or reverse compile for the purposes of reverse engineering the Software.
You may not modify or adapt the Software or documentation in whole or in part, including, but not limited to, translating or creating derivative works.

3. Transfer

You may transfer the Software to another person, provided that (a) you transfer all of the Software and documentation to the same transferee; (b) you do not retain any copies; and (c) the transferee is informed of and agrees to the terms and conditions of this Agreement.

4. Termination

This Agreement and your license to use the Software can be terminated without notice if you fail to comply with any of the provisions set forth in this Agreement. Upon termination of this Agreement, you promise to destroy all copies of the software including backup or archival copies as well as any documentation associated with the Software. All disclaimers of warranties and limitation of liability set forth in this Agreement shall survive any termination of this Agreement.

5. Limited Warranty

F+W Media, Inc. warrants that the Software will perform according to the manual and other written materials accompanying the Software for a period of 30 days from the date of receipt. F+W Media, Inc. does not accept responsibility for any malfunctioning computer hardware or any incompatibilities with existing or new computer hardware technology.

6. Customer Remedies

F+W Media, Inc.'s entire liability and your exclusive remedy shall be, at the option of F+W Media, Inc., either refund of your purchase price or repair and/or replacement of Software that does not meet this Limited Warranty. Proof of purchase shall be required. This Limited Warranty will be voided if Software failure was caused by abuse, neglect, accident or misapplication. All replacement Software will be warranted based on the remainder of the warranty or the full 30 days, whichever is shorter and will be subject to the terms of the Agreement.

7. No Other Warranties

F+W MEDIA, INC., TO THE FULLEST EXTENT OF THE LAW, DISCLAIMS ALL OTHER WARRANTIES, OTHER THAN THE LIMITED WARRANTY IN PARAGRAPH 5, EITHER EXPRESS OR IMPLIED, ASSOCIATED WITH ITS SOFTWARE, INCLUDING BUT NOT LIMITED TO IMPLIED WARRANTIES OF MERCHANTABILITY AND FITNESS FOR A PARTICULAR PURPOSE, WITH REGARD TO THE SOFTWARE AND ITS ACCOMPANYING WRITTEN MATERIALS. THIS LIMITED WARRANTY GIVES YOU SPECIFIC LEGAL RIGHTS. DEPENDING UPON WHERE THIS SOFTWARE WAS PURCHASED, YOU MAY HAVE OTHER RIGHTS.

8. Limitations on Remedies

TO THE MAXIMUM EXTENT PERMITTED BY LAW, F+W MEDIA, INC. SHALL NOT BE HELD LIABLE FOR ANY DAMAGES WHATSOEVER, INCLUDING WITHOUT LIMITATION, ANY LOSS FROM PERSONAL INJURY, LOSS OF BUSINESS PROFITS, BUSINESS INTERRUPTION, BUSINESS INFORMATION OR ANY OTHER PECUNIARY LOSS ARISING OUT OF THE USE OF THIS SOFTWARE.

This applies even if F+W Media, Inc. has been advised of the possibility of such damages. F+W Media, Inc.'s entire liability under any provision of this agreement shall be limited to the amount actually paid by you for the Software. Because some states may not allow for this type of limitation of liability, the above limitation may not apply to you.
THE WARRANTY AND REMEDIES SET FORTH ABOVE ARE EXCLUSIVE AND IN LIEU OF ALL OTHERS, ORAL OR WRITTEN, EXPRESS OR IMPLIED. No F+W Media, Inc. dealer, distributor, agent, or employee is authorized to make any modification or addition to the warranty.

9. General

This Agreement shall be governed by the laws of the United States of America and the Commonwealth of Massachusetts. If you have any questions concerning this Agreement, contact F+W Media, Inc., via Adams Media at 508-427-7100. Or write to us at: Adams Media, a division of F+W Media, Inc., 57 Littlefield Street, Avon, MA 02322.